Blessed Basil Moreau taught his religious family the perennial Christian proclamation: "Our only hope is in the Cross." As educators in the faith, the Congregation of Holy Cross strives to live this charism and bring the whole world to Christ. These reflections in this wonderful book help to carry on this great ministry.

Daniel R. Jenky, C.S.C.
Bishop,
Diocese of Peoria, Illinois

True to the Holy Cross tradition, these reflections speak to both our minds and our hearts, inspiring in the reader the profound faith in God and the passionate zeal for serving him that has characterized the Congregation of Holy Cross and its works since the times of Fr. Moreau and Fr. Sorin.

John Jenkins, C.S.C.
President,
The University of Notre Dame

This extraordinary book of reflections by Holy Cross religious of all ages provides a linkage and a continuum of spiritual insights from the time of Blessed Basil Moreau to those who follow in his footsteps in Holy Cross today. It is a book of spiritual jewels that will inspire all who use it.

E. William Beauchamp, C.S.C.
President,
The University of Portland

This book integrates the spiritual insights of the founders of the Congregation of Holy Cross with those of its current members. The result is a delightful series of daily meditations reflecting on God's presence in the midst of our daily activities.

Mark Cregan, C.S.C.
President,
Stonehill College

These simple yet honest reflections stir the heart and move the soul to a deeper realization of God's presence in our lives.

Thomas J. O'Hara, C.S.C.
President,
King's College

This book of reflections will introduce the reader to the rich history and spiritual traditions of Holy Cross. Holy Cross religious, and those who know Holy Cross well, will deepen their own appreciation for the charisma of the Congregation of Holy Cross in the world.

David T. Tyson, C.S.C.
Provincial Superior,
Indiana Province of the Conregation of Holy Cross

I thank the members of the Congregation of Holy Cross for sharing their spiritual tradition with all of us. May these daily reflections inspire all who read them to have their hearts changed not to become better for themselves but better for our world.

Kathy Andrews
CEO,
Andrews McMeel Publishing

Those who marvel at the colorful and diverse members of Congregation of Holy Cross will be delighted at this glimpse at the spirit and ethos of the community. Whether written by the founders, the elder statesmen, or the youngest members, these reflections of both priests and brothers reveal the heart and character of the congregation in ways as vibrant and varied as the men themselves.

Mary Jo Tully
Chancellor,
Archdiocese of Portland, Oregon

This marvelous book could be described as the autobiography of a living heritage. The many people who offer insightful reflections from their life experience in Holy Cross provide a glimpse into grace at work. This book celebrates holiness and hope, and it invites readers to find both in everyday life. *The Cross, Our Only Hope* will be a valuable resource for all who follow Jesus.

Joel Giallanza, C.S.C.
Vicar for Religious,
Diocese of Austin, Texas

The Cross, Our Only Hope is a wonderfully inspiring collection of reflections that flow from the life experiences of Holy Cross religious from every age and in every pastoral setting. What unites them is a deep love of Christ and his Church.

Edward A. Malloy, C.S.C.
President Emeritus,
The University of Notre Dame

The experiences of the individuals offering their personal interpretations of the instructions of our founders is a grace-filled legacy of a community that continues to respond to the needs of the Church all over the world. These daily reflections are indeed a gift to the Congregation of Holy Cross and to the many people it serves.

Donald Stabrowski, C.S.C.
Provost,
The University of Portland

With this book we walk in the company of those Holy Cross religious who have been the soul of our beloved university as well as those other places where they have held up the Cross for nearly two centuries.

Lawrence S. Cunningham
John A. O'Brien Professor of Theology,
The University of Notre Dame

ANDREW GAWRYCH, C.S.C., graduated from the University of Notre Dame with a Bachelor of Arts degree in Government and International Relations in 2002. He received a Master of Divinity degree from the University of Notre Dame in 2007 and took final vows in the Congregation of Holy Cross in August of that year.

After graduating in 2004 from Seattle University with Bachelor of Arts degrees in Philosophy, History, and English, **KEVIN GROVE, C.S.C.**, joined the Congregation of Holy Cross. He is currently pursuing a Master of Divinity degree at the University of Notre Dame.

THE CROSS,
OUR ONLY HOPE

Daily Reflections
in the Holy Cross
Tradition

Edited by
ANDREW GAWRYCH, C.S.C.,
and KEVIN GROVE, C.S.C.

With a Foreword by Hugh Cleary, C.S.C.

ave maria press AMP notre dame, indiana

Founded in 1865, Ave Maria Press is a ministry of the United States Province of Holy Cross.

www.avemariapress.com

ISBN-10 1-59471-162-3   ISBN-13 978-1-59471-162-6

Cover and text design by John Carson.

Printed and bound in the United States of America.

FOREWORD

by Hugh Cleary, C.S.C.,
Superior General of the Congregation of Holy Cross

THE CONGREGATION OF Holy Cross rejoices in the beatification of our founder, Fr. Basil Moreau, C.S.C. His Holiness, Benedict XVI, promulgated the beatification decree on September 15, 2007, the Patronal Feast of the Congregation, Our Lady of Sorrows. Fr. Moreau's beatification is a confirmation of his vision, his mission, and his unique role as model and intercessor in our lives and those of our collaborators.

This exciting moment in our history offers the grace-filled opportunity to encounter Fr. Moreau with a fresh perspective. As a person of faith bringing God's love to a secular and sometimes cynical age, his is a life worth imitating.

Fr. Moreau formed the Congregation of Holy Cross in the aftermath of the French Revolution, exhorting his religious to conform themselves to Christ by trusting in Divine Providence, by finding hope in the Cross of self-emptying, by standing by others as the Mother of Sorrows stood by her Son, and by working together zealously as educators in the faith. These core virtues comprise the mainstay of the Holy Cross tradition.

The editors of this wonderful volume of daily reflections have compiled the images of the Holy Cross tradition as expressed through our founder, his earliest collaborators, and the *Holy Cross Constitutions* that constitute our rule of life. Holy Cross patronal saints and feast days are also highlighted. Using all these resources, the editors asked today's Holy Cross religious to reflect for us on these specific, significant themes, sharing with us their everyday experiences of religious life and ministry.

Their stories of hope, the stories of the beautiful reflections of this book, ground us not in power, pleasure, or wealth, but in the simple yet all-meaningful truth of God's self-forgetting, self-emptying love. They have given us inspiring reflections of their trusting dependence upon God, their single-hearted intimacy with God, and their willing surrender to God. Their wisdom will surely help us to pray and grow closer to Christ.

Holy Cross religious have been consecrated, set apart, not to condemn this age but to love and transform it. We have a long, illustrious tradition of working closely in our mission with lay collaborators and friends who find the Holy Cross tradition and charism particularly vital for them. We encounter Christ living within us and among us. We pray that his mission and ministry will truly be our own.

These reflections will accompany us each day through a year of grace. They will help us to be people of faith in a secular age. They have hope to bring to us. Happy are we who live in their promise.

INTRODUCTION

by Andrew Gawrych, C.S.C.,
and Kevin Grove, C.S.C.

IT IS BOLD to claim that the Cross of Christ is our hope. It is even bolder to believe and live the Cross as our only hope. Yet we in the Congregation of Holy Cross, a Roman Catholic religious order of priests and brothers, profess this truth as the center of our spiritual tradition. Our motto is: *Ave Crux, Spes Unica*—Hail the Cross, Our Only Hope. And for more than one hundred fifty years, our priests and brothers have worked to bring the hope of the Cross to schools, universities, parishes, and other ministries on five continents of the globe. Now, through this book of daily reflections, we seek to share our tradition so that others might grow closer to God through reflection and prayer with us.

The congregation offers the world not only our hope in crosses, but also our trust in Divine Providence, our familial spirit and unity, our eucharistic fellowship and worship, our belief that education is both of the mind and the heart, and our apostolic zeal to make God known, loved, and served. These are the hallmarks of the Holy Cross tradition and the subjects of the reflections in this book. Each daily reflection begins with a quotation from the spiritual tradition of Holy Cross: the writings of Fr. Jacques Dujarie, Fr. Basil Moreau, Fr. Edward Sorin, or the *Holy Cross Constitutions*. These spiritual insights are followed by reflections written by a priest, brother, or seminarian in the congregation, who explains the meaning of this tradition through our life and ministry today.

Given that the Holy Cross tradition, even as it is presently lived, is rooted in the congregation's founding, we present this brief introduction to our history and spirituality so that readers might reap the most fruit from these reflections.

To begin, Holy Cross is named for a place. The name of the order is *Congregatio a Sancta Cruce* (hence the initials C.S.C.), literally the "Congregation of Holy Cross." We are named for a small French town called Sainte-Croix on the outskirts of Le Mans in northwestern France. This little known fact is important to the identity of the congregation and our tradition. For while we serve the Cross of Christ, our mission developed out of Sainte-Croix—a town with real people and problems, one that needed both teachers and preachers. This rooting in a local community has shaped the mission of Holy Cross such that we seek to foster deep commitments to the mission of the Church in whatever place we might be and with whomever we might serve. The reflections in this book capture this "rootedness" of the Holy Cross tradition, presenting the greatest principles of our spiritual heritage in the most concrete examples of our daily lives.

The time in which Holy Cross was founded shaped us as well. In the last decade of the eighteenth century, the French Revolution brought upheaval to all of French society, including the Church. Church property was seized, priests were arrested and executed, and religious communities were expelled from France. The departure of many religious from France also meant a sharp decline in the number of teachers. Children in the countryside of northwestern France received little or no education in matters of faith.

In response to this need, a priest named Jacques Dujarie began to gather young men to instruct the youth. Fr. Dujarie himself had been but a seminarian during the height of the French Revolution. He had to live in hiding for a time, even working as a lemonade salesman, and was ordained in secret. Nonetheless, he persevered. After the revolution, he began with four young men, sending them out to the countryside under the direction of local pastors. These young men, numbering 105 at their peak, became the Brothers of St. Joseph, and later, along with Fr. Moreau's Auxiliary Priests, the first men of Holy Cross. Despite receiving little formation, the brothers nevertheless began educating the children of the French countryside in the faith that had gone untaught for a generation. Fr. Dujarie, however, grew in age, and his health declined. He agreed, with approval from the bishop, to turn over the leadership of the Brothers of St. Joseph to a young and energetic priest of the Diocese of Le Mans named Basil Moreau.

Basil Moreau was born in 1799 in the village of Laigné-en-Belin. His father was a wine merchant who also tended a small plot of land. Not from a wealthy background, when Basil Moreau entered St. Vincent's Seminary in 1816, his father walked him to the school. Basil Moreau was of an extraordinarily bright mind, and after ordination in 1821 he studied with the Sulpicians in Paris. He returned to Le Mans as a professor, first of philosophy and then dogmatic theology and scripture at the seminary. By 1835, Fr. Moreau had also organized a group of young and energetic priests to travel around the diocese preaching parish missions. These preachers were known as "Auxiliary Priests." Fr. Moreau received control of the Brothers of St. Joseph in 1835 and by 1837 had merged the Brothers of St. Joseph with the Auxiliary Priests. Holy Cross was born. The priests were called the Salvatorists of Holy Cross and the brothers were the Josephites. The laywomen whom Fr. Moreau invited to join in this mission became the Marianites of Holy Cross. Together, his vision was that they would comprise but one holy family—modeled on Christ the Savior, Joseph, and Mary. Fr. Moreau gave to each group a special patron: the Sacred Heart of Jesus to the priests, St. Joseph to the brothers, and Our Lady of Sorrows to the Marianites. Eventually, Our Lady of Sorrows was designated as the patroness of the entire congregation. These devotions continue to be celebrated feasts of the Holy Cross year, and are highlighted in the readings and reflections in this book.

Within a few short years of founding Holy Cross, Fr. Moreau sent his priests, brothers, and sisters out into the world. Gradually they left France for Algeria, the United States, Canada, and the part of India that is now Bangladesh. Fr. Moreau, the superior general, continued to live in France, communicating with his fledgling communities in Holy Cross through circular letters offering both practical advice and spiritual exhortation.

Before the new foundation of Holy Cross was four years old, Fr. Moreau sent seven talented young men, one priest and six brothers, to the United States. They journeyed to the Diocese of Vincennes in southern Indiana and eventually settled in South Bend on the St. Joseph River. Fr. Edward

Sorin, born in 1814 and raised in a noble French family, had attended major seminary at the same school in which then thirty-five-year-old Fr. Moreau was a young professor. Fr. Moreau later invited the young Fr. Sorin to join his Auxiliary Priests. Fr. Sorin accepted and later professed, along with Fr. Moreau, the vows of poverty, chastity, and obedience in the name of Holy Cross. Creative and deliberately immersed in the ideals of his new homeland, Fr. Sorin was a man of action. In South Bend, he and the brothers founded what would become the University of Notre Dame. Moreover, Fr. Sorin oversaw the mission of Holy Cross in the rest of the United States, including foundations in New Orleans and later what would become St. Edward's University in Austin, Texas.

Fr. Moreau and Fr. Sorin, both bright, devoted, and energetic, disagreed about operations within Holy Cross. Ultimately, financial crises and structural problems led Fr. Moreau to resign his position as Superior General of Holy Cross. He lived his last days estranged from his community, residing in a small house with his blood sisters and cared for by the Marianites of Holy Cross. After the resignation of the first man elected to succeed Moreau, Fr. Sorin was elected the new superior general and worked to guide the fledgling congregation out of its financial and organizational crises. Both Moreau and Sorin, visionaries in their own right, shaped Holy Cross in its earliest years. And in spite of conflicts between the two, the effects of which lasted for generations in the congregation, we men of Holy Cross are truly the sons of both. The spiritual writings of these two men reveal a continuity that forms the foundation of the Holy Cross tradition.

In 1986, after the Second Vatican Council called upon religious orders to return to the spirit, aims, and inspirations of their founders, the General Chapter of the Congregation of Holy Cross, the highest governing body of the community, approved a new version of the order's *Constitutions*. In writing the *Constitutions*, which provide a definition of daily life in Holy Cross from prayer to community life, the congregation purposefully reflected on the life of Fr. Moreau and the Holy Cross tradition. Eloquent, even poetic at times, they are at once both a beautiful articulation of and a moving reflection on our religious life in Holy Cross. In fact, much of the language we use today to describe ourselves, our community, and our mission comes from the *Constitutions*: "educators in the faith," "a great band of men," "men with hope to bring." The final of the eight *Constitutions* is a meditation on the Cross of Christ entitled "The Cross, Our Hope." Calling on the community to "learn how even the Cross can be borne as a gift," this constitution makes Holy Cross one of if not the only religious congregation or order whose rule includes a constitution on the Cross.

In many ways, the Holy Cross tradition is a blend of different traditions and spiritualities. Fr. Moreau himself had several different spiritual influences. Although clearly a product of the French School of spirituality that dominated post-revolutionary France, Fr. Moreau also drew on the wisdom of the Jesuits, whose founder influenced his own thinking; the Sulpicians, with whom he taught in the seminary; and the Trappists, with whom he made his annual retreat. Moreover, he never forced his own particular devotions and asceticisms, of which there were many, on the congregation. Certainly, Holy Cross had shared practices and disciplines that marked its communal life, including perpetual eucharistic adoration and its devotions to the Sacred Heart of Jesus, St. Joseph, and Our Lady of Sorrows. Yet these communal practices and prayers purposefully left ample space for each member's unique spiritual life to grow and bear fruit in the common mission. To this day, Holy Cross consists of a rich diversity of personalities, temperaments, and spiritualities—a diversity that shines through in the daily meditations that follow. At the same time, we can identify and name a Holy Cross tradition that gives the congregation its specific and unique character as a religious community:

- The Holy Cross tradition includes the community's trust in Divine Providence. We believe that God's providential hand is always at work in the world and in our lives, including in times of hardship, trial, suffering, and loss.
- The Holy Cross tradition includes the familial spirit and unity that mark not only our own community life, but also our parishes, schools, universities, missions, and other apostolates. We extend our family to all with whom we live, work, and minister, not only giving others a warm and hospitable welcome, but also inviting them to be a part of our lives and mission.
- The Holy Cross tradition includes our eucharistic fellowship and worship around the table of the Lord. We regularly celebrate this greatest of all table fellowships in which we grow especially close as a brotherhood and receive the nourishment of Christ's body and blood for our apostolic service in his name.
- The Holy Cross tradition includes the education of both the mind and the heart. Whether in schools, colleges, universities, parishes, or other settings, we serve as educators in the faith, seeking to cultivate people's minds and hearts

so as to prepare them not only for citizenship on this earth, but, more importantly, for citizenship in heaven.

- The Holy Cross tradition includes our apostolic zeal to make God known, loved, and served. We have a burning desire to spread the good news of Jesus Christ, and our community exists precisely to be sent in response to the call of the Spirit in order to serve the needs of the Church and of the wider world.

- Above all, the Holy Cross tradition includes our confidence in the Cross as our only hope. We believe that the Cross is more than a dead piece of wood that we bear; it is a living thing, a new tree of life that is planted in our lives. As we allow this tree of the Cross to take root and to grow in our lives, it begins to bear fruit, giving us new, abundant life. We thus learn how the Cross can be *borne* as a gift precisely from letting the Cross be *born* in our lives. In this, we have no greater teacher and example, we believe, than Mary, who stood at the foot of her Son's Cross. Her suffering and grief as a Lady of Sorrows teach us a great deal about the Cross and about hope. And in the end, it is this belief in the Cross as our only hope that provides order, meaning, and life to the Holy Cross tradition.

The following daily reflections invite not only those who know us as parishioners, students, alumni, colleagues, and friends, but all those who seek God with sincere hearts to reap these fruits of the Holy Cross tradition. The reflections hold back no part of that tradition and our life as a community, including our religious vows of poverty, chastity, and obedience. Nearly two hundred Holy Cross religious from all over the world have contributed to this book, offering their insights and wisdom from their life and ministry in the congregation. Although the Holy Cross family also includes three congregations of sisters, this book, given our different histories, ministries, and constitutions, focuses on the men's community—the Congregation of Holy Cross.

These reflections are meant to be read as part of personal, familial, or communal prayer and meditation each day. They roughly follow the Church's liturgical year, while giving special attention to Holy Cross feasts and other major celebrations in the Church. As a result, these reflections can enrich the lives not only those who wish to pray with Holy Cross, but also with the wider Church.

Our prayer is that these reflections will transform you as you journey deeper with us into the Holy Cross tradition over the course of the year. We pray that by the end of the year you will be able to live and proclaim together with us that the Cross is our only hope—*Ave Crux, Spes Unica!*

JANUARY

January 1

May we start on this new year with a firm conviction that, having enrolled ourselves and pledged our lives under the glorious standard of the holy Cross, we must, to the last breath, further or check its progress according to how we fight vigorously or cowardly the battle in which we are engaged.

—Edward Sorin

A FEW DAYS after 9/11, I was home with my family in Rhode Island. My niece Amy, a flight attendant on United 175, had been killed when her plane went into the second tower. Things at home were in a frenzy, much of it fueled by incessant media attention. So, two of my brothers and I did what we had often done growing up when we wanted to "escape." We got into my brother's boat and headed off. A few miles out, we turned off the engine and sat bobbing in the waves. From that distance everything on shore looked peaceful. One of us remarked how great it would be just to stay out on the ocean forever, but after an hour or so we knew it was time to go back into the fray.

That event reminds me of what God's call is to each of us regarding our discipleship: We belong in the fray. Jesus used to take essential time away for prayer, but he always came down off the mountain. The first disciples used to go fishing when things got rough, but they always came back ashore to be renewed by Christ's embrace. Fr. Sorin, a man who knew much about having to start over when a fire destroyed his life's work and beloved university, believed that Divine Providence calls us not to be passive observers, keeping pain a safe distance away. We are, rather, to start each year, each day, with new courage and bold footsteps, fully engaging our hearts and minds in the lives of others because that is what Christ has commissioned us to do.

Peter Jarret, C.S.C.

January 2

"Come, follow me." It was the Lord Jesus calling us.
—Holy Cross Constitutions

I FIRST DISCOVERED my vocation to the priesthood when I was a mere sophomore in high school, but it was not until my senior year in college that I decided to act on my calling. During those in-between years, I routinely entered into "confidential" meetings with my parents to see about the feasibility of living my life as a priest. Every time I would become convinced that Jesus was calling me to the priesthood, I would back off, believing it to be too hasty, too different, too frightening.

After countless late night conversations, I finally had enough courage to leave home and visit Moreau Seminary at Notre Dame for the first time. When I was just a few blocks away, I pulled over to the side of the road and called home. Upon answering, I told my dad that I was going to return home because the seminary just wasn't for me. Being a wise father of six, he responded, "They're priests for goodness sake. Please go and hear what they have to say." I went. And now I am a priest in the Congregation of Holy Cross.

So often we are tempted never to leave what is comfortable or what is familiar in our lives. Yet we are challenged to trust that God is always guiding us along the right path. Trust is an absolutely essential part of our spiritual lives because it triumphs over fear, anxiety, and popular opinion. By willingly following the Lord's call in our lives, we most clearly demonstrate our trust for the One who is always true. "Come," he beckons, "follow me."

Peter McCormick, C.S.C.

January 3

Our consecration is a public one, for we are called to stand forth in service and witness. It is desirable therefore that we ordinarily be known and seen as members of the congregation. The symbol of the congregation, the cross and anchors, is worn to identify us as members of Holy Cross.

—Holy Cross Constitutions

HAVING THE CROSS and anchors as our congregational symbol leads to confusion at times. People see us wearing it and ask, "Are you in the Navy?" I am often glad they at least ask because it gives me the opportunity to explain who I am and what the symbol means. Our cross and anchors are an image of our motto: *Ave Crux, Spes Unica*—Hail the Cross, Our Only Hope. The cross stands upright with two anchors laid over it, the anchors being an ancient Christian symbol of hope.

In reflecting on our congregational symbol, I have always been more intrigued by the anchors than the cross. I have wondered frequently why exactly anchors have been a long-standing symbol of hope for Christians. Anchors keep ships secure amid stormy seas. They are immensely heavy and sturdy and yet seem so small in comparison to the objects they hold in place. They have two arms reaching out to grasp the ocean floor to resist the force of the unstable ship. O how much like hope they are! Hope settles us amid the turbulence of our lives. Hope weighs heavily on our hearts and yet seems so insignificant when our worries and cares are larger than life. Hope is our arms grasping for anything that will root us against the forces moving us away from God. As Christians, our hope in the Cross is all of this and the firm comfort that through our faith, this Cross leads to the resurrection.

Gregory Haake, C.S.C.

January 4

Imagine, when kneeling enraptured before the Crib, to see the Blessed Mother offering you the Divine Child to hold in your arms for awhile, as she did to some favorite saints; the marvel would be as it always was to my mind, how such a favor could be borne and not burst instantly the poor human heart.

—Edward Sorin

I CAN TELL that mothers are nervous whenever I hold their children. I'm afraid of dropping them, and they flop around in my arms and on my lap like a loose sack of potatoes. I imagine that's how most of us would accept the Christ Child, awkwardly and hesitantly. It is more responsibility than we desire or merit.

The kid in my arms quickly grows nervous and scowls before beginning to cry, but the Christ Child didn't wail even when he was handled roughly. God entrusted him to us, and we rejected him. Mary continues offering him to us even after we return him limp into her arms. The image rends the heart even more poignantly than our meditations upon the selfless-ness of the Father's original gift.

We usually pray cognizant of ourselves as God's children. We constantly ask that he watch over and guide us. We would be better off imagining ourselves charged with the responsibil-ity of holding the Christ Child and keeping him safe. If we live instead as if God is in our care, then the fundamental dynamic of our lives ceases to be a constant struggle against a parent's authority and becomes one of yearning to protect the gift we love most by devoting ourselves to its every need. It is awkward to switch roles, but the more we learn to embrace the Child rather than simply hold him, the more he trusts us and our hearts beat together as one.

James B. King, C.S.C.

A soldier of the Cross expects to rest only when under the sod. Indeed, a very serious task stands before us to meet the views of Divine Providence.

—Edward Sorin

WE IN HOLY Cross have never been particularly good at waiting around for God to get something done. This is not to say that what we have accomplished and what we continue to endeavor has not been, from beginning to end, from inspiration to completion, primarily God's work. It's just that, seemingly, we like to try to quicken God's hand from time to time.

We have taken our cue from Abraham, who through love of his people and faith in God's goodness, bargained regularly with God. Memorably, as God prepared to destroy Sodom, it was Abraham who got the Lord to hold off in the name of forty, then thirty, then twenty, then ten just people. Moses later would follow suit, changing Yahweh's intent to destroy the stiff-necked Israelites with a last-minute plea bargain. We spend our days and nights like Jacob, wrestling with God's angel, demanding that God bless our work, then limping off—but often with blessings in hand. Perhaps one of our patronesses should be the woman in Luke's Gospel who refuses Jesus' refusal to heal her daughter. Instead, she stands before Jesus and, as Notre Dame professor Frank O'Malley once said about the task of any great teacher, "demands to be engaged."

The life in Holy Cross into which we seek to invite those entrusted to us is one of holy impatience, of restlessness. Passivity—not to say contemplation or gentleness—is not an option for all soldiers of the Cross. We are restless in our pursuit to make God known, loved, and served. All the while, we recall that "unless the Lord build the house, they labor in vain who build" (Ps 127:1).

Timothy Scully, C.S.C.

January 6—Br. André Bessette

Let the doors of our houses, and still more the doors of our hearts, be ever open to the pallid countenances of the poor. Should we even be poorer ourselves than they, still let none be ever turned away from us hungry.

—Edward Sorin

"The door is always open." This is something we say to convey our willingness to assist someone in need. Jesus, the only door through which we may achieve salvation, revealed his Father as the very Being of openness: "Knock, and the door shall be opened to you" (Mt 7:7).

Br. André Bessette, C.S.C., was a man who knew how to open doors. He spent most of his life welcoming the stranger, the lost, the sick, and the suffering. But this remarkable porter didn't just open doors made of wood or metal. He opened his heart to whomever he encountered, and he invited them to open the doors of their hearts as well. Whereas many religious served as teachers, pastors, and laborers, Br. André served faithfully for years in the ministry of porter. He spent his life at the door of a school in Montreal and welcomed others in need. He talked to people and listened to them as they waited to do business or receive guidance from the priests. Soon his reputation spread as a healer and a spiritual guide—so much so that hundreds and then thousands started coming to Montreal to see him.

Whenever anyone asked Br. André for a cure or for an answer, he would get a little angry and say, "It is not I who heals. That comes from God alone. Go, ask St. Joseph to bring your petition to God." Like St. Joseph, Br. André was completely opened to God's will. He believed that, through service to our brothers and sisters in need, we are, indeed, serving God. Through the grace and intercession of Br. André, we pray that we may also open doors for one another.

Bill Wack, C.S.C.

January 7

Not a day could pass without bringing us nearer to the Mother of the Savior. My confidence in her was great before, now it is boundless. May her sweet name be forever on our lips and in our hearts.

—Edward Sorin

IT IS NOT a mistake that my desk is located where it is in my office on the thirteenth floor of the library at the University of Notre Dame. All I have to do is turn around and look out the window, and there Mary is atop the Dome, enshrined in gold as Fr. Sorin always wanted. I say to her often, "This is your place. We call it 'Notre Dame, Our Lady.' We have some very tough decisions to make regarding your place. And, you need to help us, giving us both the vision of where to move and the courage to go that way. We look to you for that help."

Not a day passes that I do not feel the presence of Our Lady because as I look out my window, there she is. I hope that some day I will meet her, and she will say that Notre Dame is a wonderful place, and that she is glad that we asked her for help as it grew from a small log cabin in the woods to a great university, the greatest Catholic university in the world. But we did not build this university for personal glory or for pride. We did it because we were working for Mary and for her glory. And all Christians who dedicate their work to the sweet name of Mary can be assured that the glory of their labors will be the glory of her Son.

Ted Hesburgh, C.S.C.

January 8

When I turn from the Crib to the Tabernacle and the Communion Table, I understand. Bethlehem, indeed, was the beginning of the manifestation of God's love for humanity; the Last Supper in the Upper Room was the crowning of that infinite love of God for me.

—Edward Sorin

SINCE I AM a priest and professor at the University of Notre Dame, the cribs I most often look upon are in the Basilica of the Sacred Heart, at the Grotto, and in Corby Hall—the Holy Cross community residence on campus. The tabernacles and communion tables to which I turn to celebrate the Eucharist are also on campus, usually in some student residence or in the chapel of Malloy Hall where my faculty office is located. There, in the image of the Infant Jesus and in the sacred bread and wine of the Eucharist, I behold with awe the manifestation of God's infinite love. The love I see, even though I see it in these particular places, is without conditions or limitations. It is universal, not only for me, not only for the students, faculty, staff, and friends of the Notre Dame family, but for all those of the human family, especially the poor and powerless.

I believe that God's disclosure of love is always an invitation. For me, it is a call to serve our students in the classroom and residence halls, to teach them so that their minds are informed and their hearts inflamed, and to render this loving service with all my mind and heart. For the worldwide family of Holy Cross, and indeed for all people of good will, God's self-communication in Christ is a call to work lovingly for the welfare of all. It is a call to receive God's love with gratitude and to embody it, without conditions or limitations, in our mutual relations and in our search for truth, beauty, and goodness.

Gene Gorski, C.S.C.

January 9

Once in their life the shepherds and the Magi beheld Him in the Manger; but I, every day, poor sinner, receive Him, not in my arms, but in my own bosom, in my very heart, so that I may say with St. Paul: "I live: no, not I, but Christ lives in me!"

—Edward Sorin

I HAVE OFTEN taken the daily reception of the Eucharist for granted. It becomes quite easily just another routine component of the Mass. More often than not, I get the most meaning from the well-read epistle or gospel, the nicely crafted and well-delivered homily, or the beautifully moving music. And then, on cue I rise and follow the crowd to take nourishment. Regrettably, there are times when all this happens and I am completely unaware of the monumental value of the moment.

But when I am focused, it is then that I am overwhelmed with awe by the gift that Christ is giving to me and that I am receiving. The body and blood of the Lord, once shed for me on Calvary's height, now dwell mysteriously within my very heart, transforming all who receive him and myself into his body—the Church. The concept is so awesome, so divinely generous, that it completely escapes not only my reason but my power truly to believe it. And yet it is real—it was and it will always be.

Perhaps it would have been eminently better for me to have been present with the shepherds and Magi—physically to have witnessed the Savior incarnate in the world. Perhaps in that one spectacular event, I would have believed totally. But even now, Christ lives and breathes and transforms me. It happens each time I receive his body and blood in bread and wine. Ever so slowly, it is not I who live, but Christ who lives in me.

Philip Smith, C.S.C.

January 10

Fidelity to our vows is the basis and the whole foundation of the whole structure of Holy Cross, in which each one of us has become both a living stone and the builder.

—Basil Moreau

FOR MANY YEARS at Moreau Seminary we had a table in the refectory known as "Table #1." It was the table where some of the older brothers regularly sat. The ones I knew best were Br. James Edwin, C.S.C., Br. James Lakofka, C.S.C., and Br. Chet Ziemba, C.S.C. They taught me as much about fidelity as anyone.

They were men of work. I can still see Br. Chet in his overalls, caring for the grounds at Fatima Retreat Center and feeding the squirrels peanuts. I remember Br. James Edwin huddled in his old brown coat, walking to work in the winter at Ave Maria Press. To this day, Br. James Lakofka still visits his little office at the seminary, shipping vials of Lourdes water across the country. They were men of prayer. Every day began with 6:40 a.m. Mass. Br. James Lakofka read, and Br. James Edwin was sacristan and server. His challenge each day was to light the two altar candles with one match. They were men of simplicity. Br. Chet spent his stipend on bird seed and peanuts. Br. James Lakofka would treat the seminarians to ice cream. Br. James Edwin turned his stipend back in to the superior each month. They wanted for nothing. They were men of community, always at Table #1. There was never a compelling reason not to be. They loved it when we joined them there, and they were always interested in what we were doing.

They taught me that fidelity in life, whether to the vows or any other commitment, is really about faithfulness to the little things. These gentle and kind men became saints, I believe. They were truly living stones and builders of Holy Cross.

Patrick M. Neary, C.S.C.

January 11

And opening their treasures, they offered Him gold, incense, and myrrh. What shall we offer, in imitation of the Magi? It is to be wanting in devotion, says a saint, to adore God and present Him no offering; for it is written: "Thou shalt not appear before me with empty hands." Fortunately, by our profession we have given all we had, and we have done it cheerfully.

—Edward Sorin

WHEN JESUS INVITED the young man to take all that he had and give it to the poor, he was not suggesting that the young man live the rest of his life with nothing. Jesus was inviting him to come, follow him, and be part of a community. Our life in the Congregation of Holy Cross is a treasure beyond measure, more than gold, incense, and myrrh. Whatever gifts we have to bring before God, we bring as a community. In every part of the world, there are schools filled with students who want to learn from us, churches filled with the faithful who want to pray with us, sickbeds filled with people who want to feel the healing touch of Jesus through our touch.

None of us who bears the name Christian, however, appears before Christ alone or with empty hands. United together in Christ, we give him our time by giving it to those who need a few moments to bend our ear when we would much rather be doing something else. We give him our hearts by loving those who cross our paths every day. We give him our minds by opening them to thoughts and ideas that will expand our horizons. We together give him our souls by being men and women of faith, believing that if we do what we do in his name, Christ will speak in our name when we come before God for judgment. This is the peace of Christ. What a treasure beyond measure we all receive in return for so little.

Steve Gibson, C.S.C.

January 12

*Far from me be the thought of attributing to myself the
merit of the truly providential works which have just
arisen under my direction. After God, who alone is the
author of all good, it is to the devotedness of my fellow-
priests and to your own that we owe what can be seen
today at Holy Cross which astounds everybody. I have
been but a simple instrument which the Lord will soon
break that He may substitute for it others more worthy.*

—Basil Moreau

RECOGNITION, CONGRATULATION, AFFIRMATION—these are
the moments in life we usually enjoy the most. It is reward-
ing to have our accomplishments, ideas, and suggestions
acknowledged and acclaimed. But there is more here than
just the flash of good feelings we may experience at being
the center of attention. Such recognition provides us with
valuable information about our attitudes or actions that have
been noted by others. These experiences remind us that we are
valued and appreciated, that our lives have meaning and can
make a difference.

There is, however, a danger in getting caught up in others'
praise. Their affirmations can become a narcotic and dull our
sense of God at work in and through us. We can begin to think
of ourselves as self-contained and solely responsible for all the
good that we accomplish. Fr. Moreau knew what it was like to
be praised with superlatives; yet, he still thought of himself as
a simple instrument in the hands of God. It is an intriguing

image because the effectiveness of any instrument is gauged by how well it does what needs to be done. And ideally, it becomes a seamless extension of the one who operates it.

Whatever we achieve in life reflects God's grace at work in us and through us; it also reflects the many ways we benefit from all that others generously share with us. Like Fr. Moreau, we are all challenged to become simple instruments in the hands of God, to become extensions of God's very self in the world.

Joel Giallanza, C.S.C.

January 13

After seeing and adoring the Infant Savior, oh! for His sake, for the sake of our holy Faith, for the sake of our beloved family, we, too, shall return from the stable by a different road.

—Edward Sorin

AFTER THE MAGI reached Bethlehem they had every reason in the world to be overjoyed. They finally had found the newborn Jesus whom they had been seeking and presented him their wonderful gifts. In fact, we might think they were also deeply satisfied and ready to declare: "mission accomplished." But instead, as Matthew's gospel recounts, they were scarcely halfway through their long journey. Having received instructions in a dream to avoid King Herod, they returned home by a different road.

Fr. Sorin plainly saw a significant lesson in this episode from Christ's nativity that applies to us as well. The command that we go back differently than the way we came puts us in the position of the Wise Men, who saw and believed, and who now carry the good news of God's presence among us, in place of gold, incense, and myrrh. But this obligation to take another route also resonates with the great arc of the biblical drama, which begins in an earthly garden and, after taking a surprising path from the tree of knowledge of good and evil to the very wood of the Cross, ends in a heavenly city. The paths we are called to follow are often strange and new, teaching us to trust in the Spirit. They bring us into contact with unfamiliar people who enrich our knowledge of the image of God. These roads often confront us with difficult choices and challenging situations, which become so many opportunities for a new epiphany as we follow the Way, the Truth, and the Life.

Patrick D. Gaffney, C.S.C.

January 14

We pray with the church, we pray in community and we pray in solitude. Prayer is our faith attending to the Lord, and in that faith we meet him individually, yet we also stand in the company of others who know God as their Father.

—Holy Cross Constitutions

I LOVE PRAYING the liturgy of the hours, the daily prayer of the universal Church that marks the day—morning, midday, evening, and night. As a vowed religious, I am committed to praying it daily, and my faithfulness to this obligation has become an important part of my life. The hours force me to stop what I'm doing at different parts of my day and to pray, acknowledging that all of those things that have been keeping me so busy don't mean much unless I am offering them to God for his greater glory. This rhythm of prayer is a hallmark of religious life. We may be tired or distracted, we might be experiencing dryness in our prayer, but we pray anyway. We may be busy or even overwhelmed by the demands of our day, but we pray anyway. Prayer is non-negotiable.

But our prayer lives, whether as priests, religious, or lay men and women in the Church, aren't just about ourselves. We offer our prayers together as a Church, the people of God trying to lead each other closer to heaven. Our prayer will never be perfect, and often it will even be frustrating. But we trust that God will speak to us in the liturgy, in our common prayers, and even in the silence. So we're called to make that extra effort to spend time with the Lord each day, however imperfect it may be. Because whatever imperfect prayer we can offer—as individuals, as a community, and as a Church—God can use it to transform our hearts and our world.

Steve Lacroix, C.S.C.

☩

January 15

Every action of the Word of God is an action for us to imitate. His life is such a clear model of what our own should be that there is not a single one of His acts of which Jesus Christ cannot say: "I have given you an example so that you can do what I have done." We must look at the Divine Model and know that He wants us to follow Him.

—Basil Moreau

THE ANCIENT FATHERS and creeds declared that our divine Lord is also fully human. I used to interpret this dogma as an expression of how Christ is like us—namely, human. I now understand it also as a call for us to be more like Christ—namely, fully human. In St. Paul's understanding, Jesus is not just a man; Jesus is the Man—the new Adam, the prototype for a new humanity.

Consequently Fr. Moreau advises us to imitate the whole life of Christ because he understands that Christ is not only the Savior of sinful humanity, but also the model for authentic humanity. Jesus' relationships reveal the depth and the breadth of his humanity. He easily engages strangers, and he deeply appreciates solitude. He naturally attends to the downtrodden, and he confidently speaks with the powerful. Moreover, Jesus is an exciting and unpredictable person. His own parables compare him to a king and to a thief. He once satisfies Mary's appeal for a miracle, and later bluntly refuses her request for a meeting. He reinterprets tradition and contradicts our notions of fairness. Finally, no human thing is foreign to Jesus. He celebrates and he mourns. He praises and he rebukes. He easily receives adulation and he obediently embraces humiliation. He trusts, yet he fears.

St. Irenaeus once wrote, "The glory of God is a human being fully alive." What do people fully alive look like? They look like Jesus Christ.

Charles McCoy, C.S.C.

January 16

God gives so much more help to the faithful ones, the zealous ones for even the smallest things. Then grace becomes abundant. It gives strength to our courage, and courage strengthened by watchfulness and fervor leads to the greatest virtues.

—Basil Moreau

DURING MY DEACONATE in Holy Cross I once stood overwhelmed in the ruins of my father's home. He and his family had been murdered during the Rwandan genocide. My father had been a catechist and was my only family member who encouraged me to become a priest. Now, pouring out my anger and resentment through my tears, I prayed, "Lord, let me bury my father when I become a priest." I was asking for a miracle because most people had been dumped in mass graves.

After my ordination, I returned to Rwanda to celebrate a Mass of thanksgiving. At the end of Mass, a man approached me and led me and the other survivors in my family to a mass grave where he claimed my father was buried. As we began to unearth the grave, the first remains that we uncovered were my father's, his identification card still intact. I could hardly believe it. As the priest my father always hoped I would be, I then celebrated a funeral Mass for him, giving him the sendoff in the faith that he deserved. My prayers fulfilled, I exclaimed, "Indeed, with God nothing is impossible!"

In my ministry as a priest I meet many who have suffered so much that they doubt God's love for them or even his very existence. There are those who remain faithful to the Lord and find strength and courage in him to weather the storm. Like St. Paul, it is when they are weak that they become strong through the abundance of God's grace. Their bravery and perseverance inspire us to do the same.

James Burasa, C.S.C.

January 17

Without prayer even the most charming solitude is as a land without water, producing only briars and thorns. But a desert watered by prayer grows and flourishes, takes on an air of joy and is adorned with delicious fruits, because it draws down the blessings of heaven on those who dwell there.

—Basil Moreau

THE DESERT IS no place for the faint of heart. The foolhardy dare not enter. We must not romanticize the desert; too many people have lost their minds and lives there. We must not worry about going to the desert; it is not a place to which we can ever go. The desert comes to us—in the barrenness of loss in the face of death, in the blinding sandstorm of an unexpected life-changing event. These deserts are real. These deserts are dangerous because sometimes people do not survive them. Lingering bitterness overwhelms a once promising life. The depth of loss cripples a carefree spirit. A life change is not well negotiated.

And yet, over the centuries, monks and hermits went out to actual deserts. They were not running away; they were running toward something . . . someone. They discerned that the desert is as much a living place as a dying place. It was prayer that made the harsh desert a place of encounter with God. Deserts for us, too, will come and will come only when God knows we are ready to face them, even though we may feel extremely inadequate in the midst of their unforgiving climates. Like the monks and hermits, it is only by cultivating prayer daily that our own deserts might blossom with the fruits of the Spirit. It won't take away the pain but it will see us through to a new life we never could have imagined. Prayer will always draw down the blessings of heaven on all who encounter the deserts of human life. We need only to wait in our lostness and barrenness, and we, too, will be found and renewed in God's life. That's the Cross and its hope.

Jeffrey Cooper, C.S.C.

January 18

*Christ rules His Church now as ever. When our blessed
Lord expired before the eyes of His cruel enemies, they
too, felt confident that all was over with Him and His
doctrine. We all know what happened three days later.*
—Edward Sorin

IN THE MAGNIFICENT chapel at Moreau Seminary, a rather
unique crucifix hangs in the sanctuary. Many young Holy
Cross religious have spent hours praying in that chapel and
pondering that haunting figure of our Lord. His gaunt and
tortured body bears so strikingly the sins of us all. But I have
always been fascinated by the expression on the sculpture's
face. It is not one of pain and torture, but one that is perhaps
best described as somewhere between sorrow and joy. As a
result, this crucifix has reminded me to see, even in the agony
of the Cross, a glimpse of the resurrection. And through my
life and work in Holy Cross, I have been blessed to see similar
glimpses of the resurrection in the crosses of the people to
whom I minister.

The world around us, however, sees the Cross as folly.
More and more we meet a culture in which suffering has no
place. But for people of faith, for those of us who would dare
to claim the name Christian, we know that the daily crosses
of a life fully lived only bring daily hope.

Although this can be difficult to realize in the midst of our
human suffering, we have the unique position of being able
to gaze upon our crucified Lord and to see not only the sins

of all the world, but to look past the pain and suffering and into the empty tomb. For we all know what happened three days later.

Walter E. Jenkins, C.S.C.

January 19

Distance only increases affection, if it is real and sincere. Should I go to the end of the world, my imagination would bring my friends likewise, as daily companions of my every step.

—Edward Sorin

ONE OF THE greatest joys of my life is my large family. When I was younger there was always someone around with whom I could talk or play games. Even now when we are all adults, I know that I can still call them night or day, and they will always be available to talk with me. Holy Cross has been a natural extension of that experience, bringing me into an even larger family that reaches across many time zones and borders. There is great comfort in knowing that wherever I go, I will always have my brothers in community with me.

Every time we move to another assignment, we take the experiences and friendships that we have made, and we continue to remember the people that we have left behind with phone calls, letters, and especially prayers. Because of this, we never lose them as companions on our journeys, and if we cross paths again, we have a joyful family reunion that picks up right where we left off, celebrating our brotherhood around the table of the Lord.

We strive to do the same with all of our brothers and sisters in the Body of Christ, to keep in our hearts all who have traveled on our journeys with us. That way, even if we do travel to the opposite side of the world, we will never lose them because they are part of who we are, and who we hope to be as companions on the road to God in heaven.

Neil F. Wack, C.S.C.

January 20—Basil Moreau

Zeal is the great desire to make God known, loved and served, and thus to bring knowledge of salvation to others.

—Basil Moreau

LOVE IS A powerful force. It moves spouses to give of themselves in marriage. It compels parents to sacrifice for their children. It inspires priests, religious, and lay ministers to labor for the sake of the gospel. And it's what prompted Fr. Moreau to give up all to follow Christ and to encourage others to do the same.

At the heart of zeal is the love that moves, compels, inspires, and prompts. At a parish like St. Joseph in South Bend, Indiana, where I serve as pastor, zeal is the dynamic, spirited love that motivates us to celebrate the sacraments, visit the sick, feed the hungry, welcome the stranger, and educate children and youth. In worship, service, and education our community acts to make God known, loved, and served.

Sometimes, however, we can become lukewarm in living out our faith and lose sight of the love of God that expresses itself in good works. The same zeal that motivated Fr. Moreau and his band of religious invites us to reject spiritual lethargy and to renew our own baptismal commitment to spend our lives in the Lord's service. As disciples of Jesus, we must ask ourselves continually if we are willing to make the sacrifices that the love of the Lord and his mission require. If we find ourselves lacking in this zeal, we must let the powerful force of his love rekindle our own and move us to even greater action. For we are called to be men and women of zeal, for the glory of God and the salvation of souls!

John DeRiso, C.S.C.

January 21

I am convinced that Providence, which has in the past done everything necessary for the development and perfection of its work, will continue to bestow on us most abundant blessings. To ensure this, we must be constantly animated by the spirit of zeal and generosity which so holy an undertaking requires.

—Basil Moreau

WHEN A BOAT carrying Holy Cross religious to a new mission in Bengal sank within sight of the shore, killing all of those aboard, Fr. Moreau didn't waver; he sent more missionaries. When the first Main Building at Notre Dame was burned down by a catastrophic fire in 1849, basically destroying the whole university at the time, Fr. Moreau didn't despair; he continued to trust that God would provide for the mission in America. He never doubted that Divine Providence would provide for whatever his community needed in its work, even when they faced death, bankruptcy, and natural disasters.

As much as Fr. Moreau urges his sons and daughters to trust unwaveringly in Divine Providence, he also insists that we work hard because we have an essential part to play in the workings of Providence. By our zeal and generosity in serving him, we ensure that God will give us what we need. This serves to remind all of us who follow Christ that God's love for the world isn't a thing that we can have or hold; it is an action that happens through us. It is through our hands cooking and serving that God provides food for the hungry. It is through our listening ears and warm smiles that God provides company for the lonely. It is through our courage in standing up to injustice that God provides solidarity for the poor. Ultimately, our own zeal and generosity are the vehicles through which God provides everything we need.

Dan Parrish, C.S.C.

☥

January 22

You must be "all things to all people," like St. Paul—little with the little, great with the great, seeing in all only the

image of God imprinted within them like a sacred seal
which you must preserve at all costs.

—Basil Moreau

FOR CHILDREN, EVERY moment is an opportunity to play: holding a napkin is an opportunity to play peek-a-boo, being fed an opportunity to play "airplane," a long hallway an opportunity to play "chase me." Life—every moment of it, every person in it—is a gift to be wondered at, enjoyed, laughed at, mishandled, cried over, discovered, learned from, and indeed, transformed by play. When we watch children play, it is just a small leap to imagine their extravagant Creator, the One who came up with giraffes and elephants, the North Pole and the Caribbean, gravity and neutrons, purple and orange and cinnamon red.

And then, there are adults. Perhaps in reclaiming the wonder of little children we in fact can become, as St. Paul exhorted, more open to all. Perhaps, in becoming like children, we can become all things to all people, for we shed the veil of expectations of what the world should be and begin to experience it again with the fresh eyes of Christ.

Our tradition reminds us that Christ played by the Maker's side at creation. Perhaps that is why, when Christ took on human eyes, he had so little difficulty seeing all people for who they were in the sight of God: the Samaritan woman as the town evangelist; Matthew the tax collector as the biographer of the Son of God; lepers, the blind, and those who mourn as inheritors of the kingdom of God. As disciples of Christ, in the footsteps of St. Paul, we are called to see all people, great and small, rich and poor, healthy and sick, as little children see them, as God sees them—images of himself, imprinted with his sacred seal.

Lou DelFra, C.S.C.

☩

January 23

If, as St. Paul says, "Knowledge without reverence makes one proud," and thus becomes dangerous, it is likewise true that reverence without knowledge makes a teacher useless and compromises the honor of the mission of the teacher. That is why Daniel, speaking of the reward prepared for those who teach others, does not assume that they are merely "just" and hence reverent, but also "learned and knowledgeable."

—Basil Moreau

KNOWLEDGE IS ONE of the necessary gifts of our ministry in Holy Cross as educators in the faith. And this is not just true for those in the classroom. We spend our lives trying to attain it. We struggle for it. We spend so much effort trying to attain it. Then we look for new and effective ways to pass it on to each other and to our students. But it is always so partial, so maddeningly incomplete, so changing and quickly obsolete.

Fr. Moreau spent his life pursuing knowledge and teaching it to others. But knowledge for him was never isolated from faith. He championed the full use of reason rigorously to pursue knowledge in all disciplines, including the sciences. Yet he always filtered whatever knowledge he gained through his humble life of prayer. We are privileged to have his life of learning and prayer as an example to guide and inspire all who seek knowledge in this way.

Each one of us is unique, with his or her original insights. And from time to time we need to be reminded that we have something distinct and original to say. If, however, what we say is to be knowledge that we would communicate to others, it cannot go unexamined by the convictions of our faith. Likewise, our faith must be informed by the knowledge we discover. Fr. Moreau knew that the two were not opposed to each other. In his example, we can simultaneously and humbly live the quest for both the purest faith and the deepest knowledge.

Claude Pomerleau, C.S.C.

January 24

Some of the most decisive transformations are God's gracious gifts to us not when we conform to his will but when we have gravely failed him. However the benefits of our formation may disintegrate, however we may fall, we need the supportive confrontation and sensitive encouragement of our confreres for us to be rehabilitated. This is the way some of the wisest and strongest men in our community have, by God's grace, been raised up among us.

—Holy Cross Constitutions

EARLY IN MY religious life and priesthood, I found myself drifting away from my brothers in Holy Cross. Something was causing my resolve as a religious and priest to be undermined. I fulfilled the duties of my ministry, but I did so mostly for show. I was decaying inside and the goodness and graces of my formation were slowly vanishing. I was not the person, priest, and religious that I wanted to be, but I was helpless to do anything about my dilemma. I was an alcoholic.

God, however, would not cease loving or pursuing me and would not let me be destroyed totally by my grave failure to conform to his will. My brothers in Holy Cross sensed my dilemma and realized I was struggling with addiction. They confronted me with sensitive, but tough love, getting me into treatment and onto the path of recovery. They showed me what community and commitment to each other really means: we stand by each other no matter how much we may have failed. They were the conduits of God's grace and love for me. To this day they continue to encourage me to grow and use my gifts and talents for the Church and for the community.

We are all challenged to confront and assist those whom God places in our care when they have fallen and need help in finding their way back to him. From our weaknesses and failures we can gain great strength and experience to share with those with whom we walk the journey to him.

Charlie Kohlerman, C.S.C.

January 25

His Eucharistic presence is the pledge of the God who chose to dwell in the midst of his people. It is especially appropriate then for us to pray in the presence of the reserved Eucharist. Each of us needs the nourishment of at least one half-hour of quiet prayer daily.
—Holy Cross Constitutions

IN OUR MAJOR houses, the chapel is the central room; in our rectories, it is sometimes more modest and tucked away. Yet in both, there, in the tabernacle, the living Lord Jesus is at home with us and we seek to become more and more at home with him. What a tremendous blessing it is to have a special room where we can welcome Jesus and invite him to stay with us.

When we are faithful to gathering in the chapel with Jesus at dawn and dusk, we have the graced opportunity to remain focused on him, the center of our lives. Alone, in that profound quiet, time is not measured, and intimacy steadfastly grows into oneness—the unity Jesus wished for when he gave us himself in the Eucharist. That is the rhythm of religious at prayer, a rhythm in which time and presence nurture our relationship with the Lord.

Not every home will be privileged to have a chapel in it, nor will every person have the keys to a neighboring church. Nonetheless Jesus dwells in every Christian home and makes each a domestic church, where he, indeed, is at home with us and we can grow to be more at home with him. Through time spent in prayer and love shared as family where we live, we can come to discover his presence evermore in every heart and in every home. Then, intimacy and union with Jesus will grow in us each day.

Bob Epping, C.S.C.

January 26

When my mind attempts to measure the great responsibility which weighs on me, I can find no peace save in blind trust in the God of mercies, from whom I expect the help which will compensate my weakness.

—Basil Moreau

As DISTRICT SUPERIOR, I am in a position where I have to continue the development of our young Holy Cross community in West Africa, and the needs are enormous. Most of our members are in formation, and there is always the need to recruit more. While keeping our formation programs and vocational recruitment going, we also must maintain our apostolic ministries and develop new ones. Not to mention, we must protect the interests of Holy Cross both locally and internationally while maintaining a good relationship with the Church. All of these challenges demand not only faith, but also trust in God, bearing in mind that the God who gives the mission will give us what we need to accomplish what has been entrusted to us.

I believe I can live up to these responsibilities. When I realize my own inadequacies, however, the challenge of overseeing the welfare of our personnel, as well as the physical and spiritual development of our mission, can be overwhelming. But I also know and believe that God does not give us a load we cannot carry. Fr. Moreau knew this very well. He knew from his own experience as superior general of Holy Cross that we can expect God to compensate for our personal weaknesses when we spend ourselves in his service. So it is with great credibility and honesty that he encourages all of us who bear responsibility to find peace by putting our complete faith and trust in God.

Paul Kofi Mensah, C.S.C.

January 27

The journey begins before our profession and ends only at our resurrection. We would be created anew to the point when we can say, "It is no longer I who live, but Christ who lives in me." It is the Lord who gives us both the desire and the accomplishment. For our part we must submit to the wisdom and the discipline that will purify us of our selfishness and will make us wholehearted in the service of his people.

—Holy Cross Constitutions

PORTLAND'S DOWNTOWN CHAPEL, an inner-city parish focused on outreach to the poor and needy, finds abundant faith in those who have few possessions. Poverty in our community reveals everyone's openness to believe in something more than themselves. I learn from the heroin addict that living in Christ is not an intellectual pursuit, but a sustained desire for honesty. The homeless and jobless teach me that faith begins when I take the risk of letting go of my security, the fake notions of myself, and the masks that identify me.

We must admit our need for God if we are to live in Christ in any setting. We can only acknowledge God if we are willing to honor our own inner poverty. Faith is not an armor of defense, not a claim to tell others how to live, but an assurance that our lives are in relationship with God who loves us. When we offer the Lord our real needs, then we live out of our most genuine selves, bringing gratitude and love to others. This is life in Christ, who heals our mistakes, anoints our pain, and satisfies our real longings.

We find Christ in unsuspecting places. We serve the Master only to the extent to which we reveal our own poverty and become vulnerable to others. Out of love we discover God calling us to accept those different from ourselves and to learn from those who live fearlessly. The abundant love we seek, Christ living in us, unifies all believers and reveals our call to invite others along the way.

Ronald Patrick Raab, C.S.C.

January 28

Let us join to truly religious conduct a love of work and especially of study.

—Basil Moreau

To STUDY IS to put at risk everything we think we already know. It can be both frightening and exhilarating. As a graduate student in theology, I often found myself on a rollercoaster ride that was as much spiritual and emotional as intellectual. Every time I attended a class or read a new book or article, the synthesis of mind and heart on which I had based my faith and all the actions and commitments that had flowed from that faith came under question, even under attack. But risk is essential to the journey of faith. To engage in study is yet one more form of embracing the Cross as our only hope.

When we allow our minds to be shaped and expanded by new or deeper questions and perspectives, we may temporarily lose what we thought was the foundation on which our lives were built. We can come to see how weak that foundation actually was. And that is where the grace of God enters. Just when it might seem that everything is lost, we are permitted to discover anew that God's truth and love are inexhaustible. The Cross leads to the resurrection, for we are touched by the God who is broader and deeper than any understanding we might think we have. We come to know the living God ever more deeply and experience a firmer foundation for our faith. But just as conversion is a lifelong process, so is the cycle of death and resurrection that goes with study. We keep losing it all, only to gain back even more.

John P. Reardon, C.S.C.

January 29

In consecrated obedience we join with our brothers in community and with the whole church in the search for God's will.

—Holy Cross Constitutions

IN WRITING TO Mother Mary of the Seven Dolors, Fr. Moreau advised, "Let us abandon ourselves to Divine Providence. You can be certain that you are where God wants you to be." I wasn't always sure about this. But over the years I have discovered that such assurance can only come in living each day in abandonment to Divine Providence. Consecrated obedience is about conversion, conforming one's life to Christ. For it is God's will that I seek, not my own.

It is in the search for his will with my brothers in community that I am guarded against the deceptions of my own self will. For the community can see and call forth in me gifts and talents I may not have seen in myself. Consecrated obedience is the path inviting me to move beyond self will and to trust that God is speaking through the very human means of a community, calling me beyond myself even though I may not fully understand it at the time. Obedience invites me to set aside my agenda and to allow God's to take center stage.

Whatever our calling in life, we like to believe that we are capable of thinking for ourselves and deciding what is best. Whether lived as consecrated obedience in religious life or as the obedience of faith, obedience remains a choice made in love in order to liberate ourselves from self will. It is through our openness to trusted friends, wise mentors, and confidants that we move beyond self-interest and become attentive to the voice of God speaking in our lives. As we respond to this voice and enter ever more fully into the life to which we have been called, we discover that we are capable of more than we ever thought possible.

Ken Molinaro, C.S.C.

January 30

Holy Cross is not our work, but God's very own. If each member continues to carry out his own particular obedience in a spirit of loyalty and simplicity and with the spirit of union which is inspiring all the members of the association, God will bless our whole Congregation.

—Basil Moreau

OUR LIVES ARE increasingly complex. Sometimes the pushes and pulls of our daily lives can wear us down and leave us drained. So, too, with the work of the mission. The multiplicity of challenges inherent in a parish, school, or any ministry can be daunting, yet Fr. Moreau reminds us all that whatever we do is never the work of one person alone. We in Holy Cross are gathered as a community precisely to do our mission together. And even more than our unity with each other through Holy Cross, we are simply and most importantly doing the work of God, the One through whom all things are possible.

And so the Lord instructs all of us, those within Holy Cross and every member of the Church of God, that we may be inspired by the awareness of God's presence in our work. He helps us to understand and believe the profound truth that we are called simply to do God's will together. Our Lord comforts us in times of struggle and inspires us in our moments of enlightenment so that we may know that our work, no matter how complex or challenging, is truly God's work. If we humbly ask Christ to lead us and to guide us, we will, through grace, be able to follow wisely the path set out for us—both in our own personal lives and in the shared mission with which God has blessed us.

Tom O'Hara, C.S.C.

☩

January 31

Jesus Christ ascended into heaven to teach us the road which leads there. Come and see the route I have taken to arrive in the place of eternal happiness. Walk after me, do not let my footsteps escape from your view.
—Basil Moreau

AS CHAPLAIN TO the medical care facility of the Sisters of the Holy Cross, I am honored to serve nearly two hundred sisters whose average age is eighty-six. They have been teachers, nurses, administrators, and pastoral care ministers, but now they serve through the ministry of prayer for the needs of the Church and the world. Shortly after I arrived, I was called upon to anoint Sr. Rita Estelle, C.S.C., who was over one hundred and was dying. At her bedside a number of her fellow sisters, as well as nieces and staff, gathered in prayer. As I went to pour holy water upon her, she said softly: "I want to follow Jesus now and forever." She then signed herself with the Cross.

Those who knew Sr. Rita Estelle testified that she always lived her life with her eyes fixed intently on Jesus Christ. As a result, she knew to walk after him even in the last days as her earthly life was drawing to a close. For all of us who have patterned our lives on Christ through baptism, we need courage, humility, and trust in order to keep our eyes fixed on him. This faithfulness requires the continual cultivation of good habits in us—of prayer, Eucharist, retreat, and works of mercy. And we can know, too, that we are sustained on this journey by the prayers of the faithful who have gone before us, of the communion of saints. Thus we, like Sr. Rita Estelle, are not alone as we follow the path that Christ has prepared for us into eternal glory.

Jim Bracke, C.S.C.

FEBRUARY

Let us enter into the Sacred Heart of Jesus forever loving and so prolific in good deeds, especially those of us honored to be priests and charged with bringing others into His heart. Let us celebrate the holy mysteries within the heart of Jesus; let us recite our office there; let us hear the confessions of our penitents there; and let us proclaim God's Word there. In a word, let us fulfill all our duties there and He will permeate the work of our ministry with the most abundant blessings.

—Basil Moreau

ABOVE ALL, WE priests are called and privileged to remember the life-giving death of Christ's Paschal Mystery. We bring about this sacred mystery daily for those with whom we celebrate the Eucharist. Out of the Sacred Heart of Jesus pierced for our offenses on the Cross, the water of baptism and the blood of the Eucharist flowed. This was the dawn of our beloved Church and the way in which Christ's salvific grace was given to all humankind in the sacraments until he comes again. Fr. Moreau must have been swept up into this beautiful mystery of the Sacred Heart as he consecrated all of the priests of Holy Cross to its patronage. For contemporary Holy Cross priests, we too live out in our priesthood the blessings that flow from our love for the Sacred Heart of Jesus.

But the grace that flows forth from his Sacred Heart saves and sanctifies all people. As we are drawn into the mystery of this loving heart, we all are called to live as Jesus did and to imitate him in word and action alike. We try to teach as Jesus did, to embrace repentant sinners as Jesus did, to comfort the sick and the afflicted as Jesus did, to welcome immigrants and foreigners in our midst as Jesus did, and to serve the poor and the downtrodden as Jesus did. In a word, we are to enter into the Sacred Heart of Jesus forever.

Richard V. Warner, C.S.C.

February 2

We have all, doubtless, endeavored to present ourselves to God, like the blessed Child, with as much as possible the same pure intention and the same sincere desire to serve Him, and serve Him alone.

—Edward Sorin

IT WAS SIX o'clock in the morning on February 2, 1944, when twelve other novices and I approached the altar at St. Joseph's Novitiate to kneel before the Blessed Sacrament and pronounce vows of poverty, chastity, and obedience in the presence of the community. It was a profound moment of acceptance into Holy Cross. Yet what we didn't realize was that we weren't fully poor, chaste, and obedient at the moment of profession. That would come later when students, parishioners, and the poor called us forth to live those vows.

Our religious vows are meant to free us to love and serve people, to build the kingdom of Jesus' Father, a kingdom of justice, love, and peace. Having made several visits to our missions in East Africa, I found the real meaning of this love and service. The willingness to share and the simplicity of so many poor people touched me greatly. Often there would be a knock at the door with someone bringing a chicken, a few eggs, and some bananas. It was what I might call a reverse mission.

When this life is over and we meet our Creator, God will ask: "When I was thirsty, did you give me drink? When I was a stranger in your land, did you welcome me? Did you care for me in the widow, the unwed mother, the sick, the leper, and the prisoner?" The extent to which we can say yes to these questions is the extent to which we have said yes to our Christian vocations, whatever our state in life. For those who call forth the love and service we Christians profess are the ones who help us to become evermore like Christ.

Renatus Foldenauer, C.S.C.

February 3

Faith, as well as reason and experience, demonstrates conclusively that "in union there is strength." Union gives rise to strength by blending all the parts into the whole, like mortar which holds the stones of a building together and unites them all with the keystone.

—Basil Moreau

FR. MOREAU KNEW the power of both unity and division. Nineteenth-century France was divided socially, politically, and religiously. Crises accompanied successive waves of revolution. In such times, Moreau realized what shared effort and unified hearts could achieve if they all cooperated with Divine Providence.

In our global culture, we are painfully aware of the divisions, needs, and struggles of peoples around the world. There is so much to be done. On one level, we feel called by the gospel to have compassion and to serve the needs of the world. On the other, we know our personal limits. No one of us can do it all.

It is then that I find consolation in unity with Holy Cross, an international community that is part of the universal Catholic Church. I take comfort in the reality that my brothers and sisters are working around the world. I can imagine the thousands of people who will today deepen their faith, grow in knowledge, be fed and clothed, visited and comforted, gathered and mobilized by us, united sons and daughters of Fr. Moreau, united brothers and sisters in Christ.

For all people of faith, reflecting on our union as members of God's family reminds us that our prayers and labors as well as our attempts to form communities are part of something much bigger. Yet the consolation of knowing that we are united in our efforts does not diminish personal responsibility. The modest energy and limited efforts of any one of us when joined with the whole become a powerful force of hope for a world too often in crisis from forces of enmity and division.

David Guffey, C.S.C.

February 4

Let us never forget that by praying for our beloved departed ones we establish for ourselves rights which eternal Justice will respect when "the hand of God shall have touched us also."

—Edward Sorin

FR. JOACHIM BIMAL Rozario, C.S.C., a fellow Holy Cross priest in Bangladesh, died unexpectedly on this day in 2007. We were classmates in seminary. The loss of such a close friend at the young age of fifty was a shock for me. Since I was studying in the United States at the time, I was unable to attend the funeral. Yet, according to our Bengali custom, I observed three days of prayer for his soul and for his bereaved family and abstained from eating meat and fish. If I had been in Bangladesh, I would have joined in the celebration at the end of the third day in which the family prays together and then shares in a meal. Forty days later, just as the Church celebrates the ascension of Jesus forty days after his resurrection, the family and friends gather again to pray for the deceased. His or her good works and example are fondly remembered and shared by all. On both of these occasions, if a priest is available, we also celebrate Mass.

These traditional Bengali customs, as well as our Catholic traditions of praying for the dead, are not the worship of ancestors. They are gestures signifying the bonds that do not end at someone's death, but continue into our eternal life with God. In remembering and following the good examples of those who have died, we keep them alive among us. This holy remembrance helps to prepare each of us for our own entrance into the communion of saints in the heavenly kingdom.

Eugene Anjus, C.S.C.

February 5

How true it is that our life passes like a shadow, and that its moments are like drops of water which fall to the earth and disappear in its depths. Our duty for the present is to seize upon everything which can contribute to realizing God's designs in our regard.

—Basil Moreau

I WAS HOPING that the day would pass swiftly and unnoticed—but no such luck. I was guided into the large meeting room unawares and was suddenly greeted by about sixty-five friends who shouted, "Happy Birthday!" I have seldom been more embarrassed in my life. After everyone had enjoyed themselves and gone home, I had time to reflect. Eighty years. I could hardly believe it, but it was true. Where had all the years gone? What had I accomplished in those years? I could not come up quickly with satisfying answers to either question. I only knew that I had been deeply blessed by the Lord in every way imaginable—good family, good friends, good ministry, good religious community.

Our lives indeed pass like shadows, as Fr. Moreau wrote. But, as another Holy Cross religious once taught me years ago, it is the shadow of the Cross that makes all other shadows bearable. And at least in my case, those shadows—those many years—have not just been bearable, they have been gifts.

And the gift continues. My task, and the task of all of us, regardless of our ages, is to keep seizing upon everything that can contribute to realizing God's beautiful designs in our lives. For our lives are passing away; days, even years, are as drops of water falling to the earth. The larger challenge, then, is how we might best express our thankfulness for all the time we have already been given.

Thomas McNally, C.S.C.

February 6

As disciples of Jesus we stand side by side with all people. Like them we are burdened by the same struggles and beset by the same weaknesses; like them we are made new by the same Lord's love; like them we hope for a world where justice and love prevail.

—Holy Cross Constitutions

God often appears in our lives suddenly, without prior warning or fanfare. I will never forget the first night after being ordained a priest when a young man came to our house to leave all his personal possessions since he was thinking about taking his own life. Sudden appearances of God in our lives, like this one, nourish our hope because they call us again to his side and teach us that it is when we serve one of the least that we are really serving him. To walk side by side with the neediest, whether that need arises from material or spiritual poverty, is the purpose to which we are called to dedicate our lives. The most beautiful moments of our lives occur at those times we least expect and with persons who are often strangers to us.

The invitation to be light in the midst of the crosses and shadows of our times, to be men and women with hope to bring, is central to our Christian vocations. Fortunately, much more than ideals and dreams sustain our faith. Above all, people, and in particular the person of Christ, invite us to follow him in spite of our own weaknesses. They sustain us with his constant love, which is both complete and free. Each day offers a new opportunity for God suddenly to appear at our side and add still others to the long list of persons who, along the road of our lives, have shown us that there is no sorrow that cannot be healed or injustice that cannot be transformed.

José Ahumada, C.S.C.

February 7

As to vocations, pray much, encourage any you may find, and be assured that if we are the Religious we should be, nothing necessary will ever be wanting to us. As our assurance of this, we have the very words of the Gospel.

—Basil Moreau

MY **EARLIEST RECOLLECTION** of being attracted to the religious life dates back to when I was ten years old. I was standing in front of our living room window and trying to melt the ice on the windowpane with my breath. I knew that at 6:30 a.m. the six religious brothers who taught me would walk by wearing their long black habits. Seven years later, I entered religious life.

A year after my ordination to the priesthood, the position of vocation director became available, and I volunteered. I dedicated my ministry to my patron St. Joseph and his apostle Br. André Bessette, C.S.C. God blessed it, and today there are more than thirty Holy Cross priests who entered the community during my tenure. Many spoke of the great examples they had witnessed among the priests and brothers of our congregation and how they wanted to follow them. Yet God had summoned each one separately and they responded generously.

We in Holy Cross continue to pray for and encourage young men to join our family, sharing in our life and mission. At the same time, we pray for all young people who are discerning God's call in their lives. For we know that the Church needs not only priests and religious, but also faithful married couples, families, and single people if it is to sustain its own and be a witness to the greater world. And so praying and encouraging vocations is the work of all of God's people—that God will bless us richly on our journey to the Father.

André Léveillé, C.S.C.

✠

February 8

Our mission sends us across borders of every sort. Often we must make ourselves at home among more than one people or culture, reminding us again that the farther we go in giving the more we stand to receive. Our broader experience allows both the appreciation and the critique of every culture and the disclosure that no culture of this world can be our abiding home.

— Holy Cross Constitutions

IN HIS INCARNATION, Jesus crosses borders of every sort to meet us where we are. He empties himself in order to take on our humanity and give us his life.

Since the moment of the Incarnation, a crossing of borders has been essential to the mission of Jesus' disciples. In the parable of the Good Samaritan, the priest and the Levite remain on their side of the road, but the Samaritan crosses over to meet the wounded man where he is and to care for him. As followers of Jesus, we, too, cross over to meet people where they are, to embrace and understand their realities, their cultures. In the crossing over, there is a dying to self. We imitate the One who crossed over first out of love for us. Paul calls us to have the same attitude as Jesus, who "emptied himself, taking the form of a slave, coming in human likeness" (Phil 2:6–8).

Sometimes the crossing over is a short, but demanding journey into the life of a friend, a spouse, a son or daughter, a parishioner, a neighbor. At other times, the journey is longer and farther, and takes us literally across many borders into a world and a culture that is not our own. Whatever the case, there will be dying to do on our way to the Father, but we are heartened because we know that the farther we go in giving, the more we stand to receive.

Arthur J. Colgan, C.S.C.

February 9

"I have chosen," says the Lord, "and have sanctified this place that my Name may be there forever, and my eyes, and my heart may remain there perpetually." How fervently each of us should wish these words should apply to our own hearts!

—Edward Sorin

WE IN HOLY Cross are used to it. People always seem to want to make us the Congregation of *the* Holy Cross, but we're not. We are the Congregation of Holy Cross. That little definite article might not seem to make much of a difference, yet it reveals an important truth about our community. We are named for the small French town of Sainte-Croix, where Fr. Moreau founded our congregation. Since then, the particularity of places has been an essential part of our ministries. Both Fr. Moreau and Fr. Sorin understood clearly what Holy Cross might accomplish as a community by working together to sanctify particular places. With this understanding of place, Holy Cross religious have done God's work for almost two centuries, from the classrooms of rural France and Algeria to North America, India, Poland, South America, and Africa. The desire of these countless religious was to fulfill the Lord's stirring command to sanctify whatever piece of the world they were sent to serve.

I can vividly remember all of the places I have been blessed to minister in my over four decades in Holy Cross. I remember the halls of the high schools in Indianapolis, Akron, and Chicago. I remember the campus of Holy Cross College at Notre Dame and now I know well the bluff on the Willamette River on which sits the University of Portland. We all have places that are seared forever into our hearts. Our hope must be that our lives and efforts there have helped to sanctify those very grounds for the people who will follow after us.

Donald J. Stabrowski, C.S.C.

February 10

We accept the Lord's call to pledge ourselves publicly and perpetually as members of the Congregation of Holy Cross by the vows of consecrated celibacy, poverty and obedience. Great is the mystery and meaning of these vows. And their point is simple. They are an act of love for the God who first loved us.

—Holy Cross Constitutions

ALL VOWS ARE sacred. Religious cannot love without them, but how do we speak about them? We profess them publicly and often wear them outwardly, but their living is internal. Indeed the vows are more the quiet expression of the confessional than the bold proclamation of the pulpit. This is not because of any offense committed, but because poverty, chastity, and obedience are about God and the individual's experience of contrition and conversion in the depths of being. Who wants to make public such an inward vulnerability?

At twenty-seven, I made to God forever vows of celibacy, poverty, and obedience. I sought to make absolute the identity I had been working toward since college. As St. Columba once said, I felt "wounded by God's love" and believed that I was called. At twenty-seven, this identity, especially as called by God, was what mattered. I would soon be taught by God that the vows were less about strength and security in my religious identity and more about friendship with God.

Why any of us make a commitment and why we continue in it are two different things. Something hopefully changes in us in the living. It strikes me, two decades as a vowed Holy Cross religious, that more than anything else the pursuit of fidelity repositions us to see and love in ourselves what God sees and loves in us; that is, Christ Jesus. The soul wounded by God's love is one that enters Christ's wounds and discovers a wide compassion and care for the stranger.

Daniel J. Issing, C.S.C.

February 11

O Lord, come to my aid, make haste to help me; Lord, give me a burning desire to seek You, to find You, to follow You, at whatever price.

—Jacques Dujarie

TWICE EVERY DAY, in our morning and evening prayer, we begin with the pleas, "Come to my aid," and, "Lord, make haste to help me." And the goal of every baptized Christian is this union with God. But what does this mean for our everyday lives?

As a young brother, I went to work in Africa on fire with the desire to save if not all of Africa, at least the country to which I was sent for Christ. I worked side by side with many other Holy Cross religious driven by the same desire. Sickness, however, brought me back to the United States, and I tried to understand why this had happened, begging, "Come to my aid; Lord, make haste to help me." The answer came to me from an unexpected source—a child with multiple disabilities. He lived in a state medical facility when I started working with him. His needs were enormous. God, in a sense, took Africa from me and gave me a young man to love, saying, "Deal with it."

The great lesson that I have learned is that when we love others at whatever the price, we need look no further—we have encountered God. By striving to love in this way we are participating in God's gratuitous and all-encompassing love for others and ourselves, thus becoming one with him. This can happen in Africa, a state medical facility, a classroom, or a family table. God is always at our side, always helping us, both enkindling in us the desire to seek, find, and follow him, and guiding us to its fulfillment.

Raymond Papenfuss, C.S.C.

February 12

Little as we may have received, we shall all have some-day to account for it. Whoever has received an obedi-ence, however, insignificant it may appear—a common employment—were it only to wash the dishes, or to sweep the floor, has to fulfill it in a religious manner, not indifferently or loosely or carelessly, for in it angels see the will of God.

—Edward Sorin

"You can always tell a Holy Cross school," the Sister of Mercy said. "It's clean inside and out." After years in other schools, she had been teaching alongside me for many aca-demic terms in one of our co-institutional secondary schools. It was late Sunday night and we had just finished cleaning and resetting the high school cafeteria after weekly bingo, finally locking up and shutting off the lights. Consulting her wristwatch, she half-grumbled, "In other places, they'd leave this to 'the staff.'" Then, with an Irish chuckle, she shook her head. "Here, the brothers roll up their sleeves, and somehow we all find ourselves working with you. Well, see you in school tomorrow."

Brothers in a classroom, moms and dads at home, sisters in a medical setting, or priests in a rectory—it's all the same in that everywhere our daily lives are made up of hundreds of discreet tasks. From complex professional or administrative activities to washing dishes and sweeping floors, we perform routine actions so often that we put our minds elsewhere. Before we know it, our commute is ended, our teeth are brushed. But is there a way to labor in a religious manner so that everyday jobs become offerings to God? Fr. Sorin reminds us that the bridge to the Divine is to see the task as worthy, to fulfill it and not just perform it. To do this, we have to approach our daily tasks with full attention, seeking to see and cultivate holiness in them.

Mark Knightly, C.S.C.

February 13

Our calling is to serve the Lord Jesus in mission not as independent individuals but in a brotherhood. Our community life refreshes the faith that makes our work a ministry and not just an employment; it fortifies us by the example and encouragement of our confreres; and it protects us from being overwhelmed or discouraged by our work.

—Holy Cross Constitutions

FRIENDS, COLLEAGUES, AND students sometimes speak about Holy Cross as though it were a monolith. They ask, "What does the community think about that?" or they offer sweeping statements about "the C.S.C.s." Perhaps they take their cues from concelebrated Masses or large gatherings of the brethren for meetings. It is one view of our brotherhood, and indeed, there are times in which we are united and speak with one voice. But the brotherhood to which we are vowed is more often lived in smaller, more modest groupings. In our university residence halls we share ministry with one or two other Holy Cross religious, and our parishes are staffed with two or three. These dual dimensions of community—the strength of numbers as well as the depth of relationships from daily contact with a few—afford us a rich brotherhood that supports our mission.

Whether in Holy Cross or the wider Church, it's deeply satisfying to be part of something much larger than our individual perspectives and efforts to respond to the gospel. At the same time, it's challenging to be mindful of the collective character and will of so many. Similarly, it's gratifying to share struggles and receive encouragement from a close circle of friends and to do the same for them. At the same time, it's challenging to be stretched beyond our own self-protections and preferences by people who know us well enough to confront our faults. The two dimensions of community are anchors for our life and work together as brothers and sisters in Christ.

Mark L. Poorman, C.S.C.

⚛

February 14

Our hope and our need are to live blessed by faithful and loving relationships with friends and companions in mission, relationships reflective of the intimacy and openness of God's love for us.

—Holy Cross Constitutions

MY FRIEND JOSH loves movies, and it was at his encouragement that I watched the movie *Cast Away*. Stranded on a deserted island for several years, the castaway finds a way to get what he needs to survive: clean water, shelter, food, and, interestingly, friendship. In the absence of other people to befriend, he finds a volleyball, onto which he paints a face. He then names it Wilson and speaks to it as if it were a friend, sharing his fears, hopes, and feelings.

As Josh explained to me, *Cast Away* points out that friendship is one of our most basic needs in life. But when our *Holy Cross Constitutions* speak of friendship, they mean something far more significant than a basic need. To be a true friend to another means trying to reflect the love that God has for each one of us. This means listening unselfishly, challenging when needed, celebrating in times of joy, mourning in times of sadness, and loving unconditionally.

This may seem like a lot to expect from a friend, but this kind of intimacy in friendship is especially critical for those of us who profess the religious vow of chastity. Yet how do any of us find friendships like this? The surest way is simple. If I want to have a friend who is generous, accepting, and honest,

I must first be a person of generosity, acceptance, and honesty. Further, if we hope to be people who reflect the love of God in our relationships, we must strive to know the Lord in prayer and in the sacraments. It is then that we can be open to true friendship and companionship, grounded in our friendship with Christ.

Nate Wills, C.S.C.

February 15

A trial is the Lord's choicest grace, a grace reserved for the purification and strengthening of the saints, a grace which is usually heralded by abundant consolations. After the example of the saints, let us thank God for having initiated us into this secret of His providential action on those He loves.

—Basil Moreau

A NUMBER OF years ago, a committee in South Bend, Indiana, was looking into the possibility of opening a Dismas House. The Dismas movement helps establish halfway houses where recently released prisoners can come to live for a time with a small, core community of believers. As part of a feasibility study, the group was investigating the possibility of recruiting some of these core community members from among students at the University of Notre Dame. When the committee asked my opinion about this possibility, I responded that I had a reservation that some students, especially those from what might be termed "sheltered" backgrounds, might be drawn to get involved in such a project from an overly romantic idea of what it would be like to live with former convicts. To this, one of the committee members rejoined, "Well, I think that is the way God gets us involved in a lot of things." And another member, a young, recently married woman, added, "Even love is romantic, until you get into it!"

Fr. Moreau's words about a trial being the Lord's choicest grace might suggest to some that he had a simplistic and romanticized view of suffering. This was not the way, however, he lived his own, saintly life. Fr. Moreau most certainly knew there is nothing romantic about suffering. It is painful and can be very destructive. Human suffering is to be relieved, not celebrated. At the same time, Fr. Moreau knew intimately the Incarnate God, who relieves human suffering by freely entering into the depths of it—and there revealing a love that is bigger.

Don Dilg, C.S.C.

February 16

It seems to me that no prayer can be sooner heeded than one addressed to the conquerors of the world, who laid down their life for their love of the Cross, on behalf of their remote successors enrolled under the same soul-stirring, divine standard.

—Edward Sorin

OUR HOLY PREDECESSORS in the faith, those valiant conquerors of the world, have all in some way laid down their lives for love of the Cross. For some, including some men of Holy Cross, this love has led to the ultimate sacrifice of martyrdom. For others, and most likely for us, love of the Cross demands taking up our own daily crosses and dying to ourselves in the little matters of life.

Fortunately, we are not alone on this path. Countless others have left their footprints on it before us and they can serve as our guides. We have only to seek inspiration from our predecessors, the communion of saints, and, like them, strive to put on Christ. We follow their examples, we ask for their intercession, and we journey with them as companions. It is through praying in their company that we grow into deeper union with God and all those united in his Son's Cross.

Through our fellowship with the saints, God will accompany us with his grace. All of us who seek to live united with the will of our Heavenly Father will never be abandoned. It is when we accept in faith and in action our soul-stirring, divine standard of the Cross that we immediately see its benefits. Like those men and women before us who bore their crosses to the very end, we too can shoulder our crosses in love and without fear. For the Cross is not without hope.

Mario Lachapelle, C.S.C.

I am a priest to be father to the orphan, the consolation of the widow, the support of the poor and the friend of the suffering.

—Jacques Dujarie

OF ALL THE people who have had an impact on my life as a Holy Cross priest, I am convinced that teachers hold the first place. I remember on one occasion asking Frank O'Malley, my English professor at Notre Dame, what he thought was the most significant mark of a good teacher. Without hesitation he replied, "Knowing how to ask questions and tell stories; that was Plato's way and Jesus', too." I have never forgotten that answer. It has given my life direction and focus whether as a teacher at the high school and collegiate levels, or in the pastoral work that I continue to do today, flying to small villages in rural Alaska as a sacramental minister.

Without a doubt, the natural human desire to find life's meaning amidst the issues and circumstances of our age continues to consume our deepest efforts and longings. There are moments in all our lives when our restless hearts incite us to ask such questions as: Why am I here? What is my call and destiny? Does it make any difference?

Fr. Dujarie clearly had discovered the answer to these questions in his own life. It was to live for others, especially those with the greatest need—the orphan, the widow, the poor, and the suffering. And as we ask these same questions about life's meaning today, we can look to the answer that Fr. Dujarie found for guidance and inspiration. The answers we discern matter greatly because they necessarily affect how we reach out to those most in need around us.

LeRoy E. Clementich, C.S.C.

February 18

At the sight of regions so much in want of evangelical laborers and so widely open to their zeal, who would not address our Heavenly Father in the words of the Lord Himself: "Pray to the Lord of the harvest that He send forth laborers into His harvest"?

—Edward Sorin

"FATHER," HE SAID, "remember the retreats you used to give us? They really helped me to pray and find God in my life." I was touched by the young man's memory of those retreats because I had not worked at the Holy Cross parish in Nairobi, Kenya, for over a decade. He continued, "Now I belong to a prayer group we have just formed to pray for the needs of others. They made me the leader, but we don't know how to begin. I was thinking, Father, that you might come and teach us to pray as you did years ago. How can we pray for others if we are not praying for ourselves?"

His experience of God had given his life meaning and hope. Now, in faith and zeal, he wanted to share with others what God had given him. That is how we become laborers in God's harvest; we get a taste of God's love and mercy, and it drives us to satisfy the hunger for God we see all around us. It drives us to labor with Jesus.

As this young man learned, praying for God to send out laborers is not enough. We need to pray that we ourselves may hear God's call to labor with him. We are all called. Whether this call is to join a prayer group, raise a family, or be a priest or religious, we can join Jesus in bringing in the harvest. There is nothing more satisfying than when our hunger for God meets the hunger of another.

Frank Murphy, C.S.C.

February 19

In consecrated poverty we seek to share the lot of the poor and to unite in their cause, trusting in the Lord as provider.

—Holy Cross Constitutions

In the Beatitudes, Jesus teaches, "Blessed are you who are poor, for the Kingdom of God is yours" (Lk 6:20). How can this be? Are poverty and hunger good things? Certainly not. No one aspires to destitution and hunger, and we as a society must do whatever we can to put an end to these scourges to the human family. So why are the poor "blessed"?

The poor and the hungry are blessed because those in great need know that they have to rely on others to survive. In opening themselves up to others, they are really opening themselves up to God, and that humble reliance is itself a beatitude, a blessing. Woe to us if we close ourselves off from others and from God.

Religious men and women profess the vow of poverty in order to teach them to rely more on God and others, thus experiencing the blessedness of which Jesus speaks. All of us—no matter what our vocation or state of life—must learn to trust in the Lord and his promises more perfectly if we are to grow in holiness. We have a lot to learn from the poor and the needy, who have no choice but to trust in others and in God. When we share their lot and unite ourselves to their cause, we learn more than simply their plight. We discover our own need to open ourselves to Christ's loving care. For therein lies the kingdom of God.

Bill Wack, C.S.C.

February 20

At the foot of the cross, we were so much the object of thought of both mother and Son that the Savior looking down on her with love as He was dying spoke to her a last time. He spoke, not of Himself, nor of her, but of us only. He presented us all to Mary in the person of John as He said to her: "Woman, behold your son."

—Basil Moreau

IN TIMES OF physical or emotional suffering a kind of relief can come when we focus on the suffering of another. I encountered this on a day-long Stations of the Cross in Canto

Grande, Peru. Arriving at the fourth station where Jesus meets his Mother, the people carried an image of Mary out to meet our traveling image of Christ crucified. An outbreak of tears throughout the crowd released countless burdens as the people meditated on the power of a Mother's sorrow at the suffering of her Son.

In my own life, the contemplation of Mary's sorrows at the foot of the Cross has many times relieved excruciating physical pain that no medication could alleviate. Fr. Moreau's prayer, in the midst of all his suffering, frequently took him, as well, to the foot of the Cross of Christ. Yet Fr. Moreau learned over time that he was not merely a bystander at the Cross. Even more than looking through Mary's eyes, he came to see the Cross through Jesus' eyes.

By looking through Jesus' perspective, Fr. Moreau learned that Christ, in his moment of deepest physical, emotional, and spiritual pain, was wholly concerned for us. We, who are so often caught in our own preoccupations, are the focus of his compassion as he gives us his Mother as our own. In the contemplation of this selfless love, our minds and hearts are raised to his sublime love, our burdens lifted, our worries surrendered, our faith increased, and our hope magnified. Indeed, we receive a glimpse of the very kingdom of God.

J. Steele, C.S.C.

February 21

God never permitted me to entertain, for twenty-four hours, a real ill-will towards any member of our dear religious family; and at this moment there is not one in whom I do not recognize some excellent qualities.
—Edward Sorin

SOMETIMES PEOPLE OUTSIDE religious life imagine that everything is always smooth and easy in a religious house. Well, it isn't so. We are human beings, and human beings are frequently in conflict over one thing or another. One of my brothers in Holy Cross captures this reality perfectly, "Where two or three are gathered, there is conflict." While his saying is humorous, it states a truth. The challenge is how we deal with conflict.

Our *Constitutions* speak honestly of the reality of conflict in religious life, reminding us that our disagreements and disputes can and occasionally will unravel the peace in our communities. At the same time, they encourage us to seek frank yet discreet ways to reconcile with one another.

In my own experience, it is rare for me to be in conflict, but it does happen. When it does, I have learned to let the energy and emotion settle a bit before speaking with the other person. Frequently, taking this time and space has revealed to me that the fault is really my own. As a result, whenever I find myself in conflict with another, I go to the person with all the humility I can muster and ask to speak. Often I find that what I thought and what the other person meant were very

different. I have never been disappointed when I have sought
out my brother or sister in this way.

Alan Harrod, C.S.C.

February 22

*The bark of Peter has been assailed before, but has never
sunk. Jesus may seem to sleep in it, and not to mind the
fierce tempest that rages around it; but, let us remember
St. Matthew (8:23): "Jesus said to the disciples: 'Why
are you fearful, you of little faith?' Then rising up, He
commanded the winds and the sea, and there came a
great calm."*

—Edward Sorin

HOPE IS AN essential Christian virtue, and we in Holy
Cross strive to nurture hope in our lives as a central part of
our charism and spirituality. And yet, I must confess, I can
sometimes become a bit anxious about the future of our community, of our apostolates, and even of our Church.

All of these things we hold so dear exist in the midst of
a broader culture that seems constantly to assail our gospel
values and to dismiss our faith. Despite our best efforts, it is
sometimes easy to think that one day soon it simply will be
too much, and finally we will sink under the weight.

At times like that, I like to read the stories of our Holy
Cross forebearers, including Fr. Sorin, who more than one
hundred fifty years ago brought our community's charism and

mission to the wilds of northern Indiana and the swamps of New Orleans. The stories of these intrepid missionaries and the amazing odds they overcame inspire me to have faith and hope as they did. It is a faith and hope not so much in our own abilities to overcome tremendous adversity or to keep the ship afloat and on course, but in Christ's promise that he will be with us until the end of the age, and his assurance that we have nothing to fear. Whatever tempests may rage, however the boat may be swayed or swamped, the One whom even the wind and the seas obey is present in our midst. He will sustain us, and at the last, bring us to safe harbor.

Stephen Koeth, C.S.C.

February 23

Today, more than ever before, Catholic education means for our youth a knowledge of Divine truths, more comprehensive and developed, more visibly sustained by daily Christian practices, cheerfully accepted and faithfully observed by them as an indispensable evidence of their initiation to a Catholic life, of which they may well feel proud all their life.

—Edward Sorin

FR. SORIN HARDLY qualifies as a great educational theorist or intellectual. He was neither a regular teacher nor a serious scholar. He contributed relatively little to discussions regarding curriculum at Notre Dame as it slowly evolved into a genuine institution of higher learning. Fr. Sorin, instead, was an ambitious institution builder and a decisive leader. His courage and iron will ensured that Notre Dame survived and eventually prospered despite fires, a cholera outbreak, and a series of financial crises. Yet Fr. Sorin was much more than this. He was a man of deep faith who believed that God and Our Lady had summoned him across the Atlantic Ocean to undertake a crucial work in Catholic education.

From the outset, Fr. Sorin hoped that Notre Dame would develop as a "most powerful means for good" by preparing young Catholics to go forth and serve well in the world. He understood that Catholic education was not only about training minds but also about forming character and shaping souls. While no great educational theorist, he assuredly got to the heart of the matter.

Catholic educators today at every level might draw inspiration from his example. Our most important contribution to our students is to nurture them in the ways of faith—to provide them with appropriate catechetical and theological formation, to celebrate our faith with them in prayer and liturgy, and to guide them to express it through service of neighbor in the world.

Wilson D. Miscamble, C.S.C.

February 24

*The vow of obedience includes the entirety of our life
in Holy Cross, and through it we hope to discover and
accept the Lord's will more surely.*

—Holy Cross Constitutions

THERE IS SOMETHING about the word "obedience" that is
hard to swallow. For adults, obedience might seem like an
infringement on free will. After all, children obey; adults just
know what to do. When I was issued my learner's permit to
drive, it was pounded into me, "Obey the traffic rules." It
was good advice for a sixteen year old; but now I just know
what to do.

The gospels give the impression that accepting God's will
was problematic for some of the apostles. Jesus had to repri-
mand St. Peter on several occasions for refusing to surrender
his own will to God's. In the end, however, Jesus makes the
most powerful statement about obedience when he asks Peter
three times, "Do you love me?" Obedience is more than bend-
ing our will, obeying a particular command, or agreeing to do
something we really don't want to do. It is about being totally
committed, about loving unconditionally.

I have always been inspired by our Holy Cross religious
who devoted most of their lives to service in the missions. We
say that they went to the missions because they were "assigned
by their superiors." But when we look at the fruits of their
work in Asia, Africa, the Caribbean, and Latin America we
know that their response reflected total commitment and

unconditional love. They teach us that it is not enough for any of us to respond to the Lord, "Okay, I'll do it." Our response has to be, "Yes, Lord, you know that I love you."

George C. Schmitz, C.S.C.

☥

February 25

Our mission is the Lord's and so is the strength for it. We turn to him in prayer that he will clasp us more firmly to himself and use our hands and wits to do the work that only he can do. Then our work itself becomes a prayer: a service that speaks to the Lord who works through us.
— Holy Cross Constitutions

TRANSFORMING OUR WORK into a prayer is much more easily said than done. It is seemingly easier to separate our work from our prayer. Working on staff at our Holy Cross Novitiate in Uganda, however, helped me to realize that we ultimately cannot separate them. The novitiate is an intense year during which religious step back from the world to grow in the spiritual life and discern God's will in preparation for professing the vows of poverty, chastity, and obedience for the first time. The year is anchored in a daily routine of prayer, shared meals, classes, eucharistic celebration, assigned work, and communal recreation.

As a former high school English teacher and dorm prefect, I knew firsthand that I relied on the Lord to sustain me through each day. Yet it was only when I lived at the novitiate that I learned how totally dependent we all are on God. For the simplicity and rhythm of our communal life, the beauty of the Ugandan landscape, and the enthusiasm of our young men inspired me to carry my prayer into my daily work and encouraged me to view my work as a disposition for my daily prayer. I was amazed at the strength the Lord then provided for both my prayer and my work.

When we pray and when we work, none of us is ever alone. Wherever we are and whoever we are, God is there with us and for us. We may be the only instruments God has to accomplish his work, and if we ground our work in prayer, God will give us the grace to do it.

Robert Nebus, C.S.C.

February 26

In order to follow Jesus, it is necessary to deny self and carry one's cross. If we follow Jesus and carry our cross, we will have life. Life is to be found in the Cross and nowhere else.

—Basil Moreau

IN TIMES OF trial, pain, and disappointment, I have often prayed quietly at the foot of the Cross. Knowing that the Crucifixion is just a moment in time makes me realize that my current suffering soon shall pass. Yet moments of suffering are precisely the ones that bring us hope, provided we keep moving forward on the journey of our lives. This is the point that Fr. Moreau is making when he writes of our need to carry our crosses in imitation of Jesus. Since Jesus is the One who calls us to bear our crosses in hope, he is also the One who leads the way in doing so, giving us strength to follow. We also draw strength from our many brothers and sisters who journey side by side with us, carrying their own crosses up the hill of Calvary. Some have already reached the summit while others follow behind, forming a line of disciples living in imitation of their Lord.

Fr. Moreau, however, distinguishes between our own crosses and the Cross of Christ. There is so much of what we do and who we are that is simply us. That is, so much of our pain and our sin are of our own doing. We cannot deny our own crosses, but Fr. Moreau, like Jesus, says we should deny self. Otherwise, we will focus only on our own suffering, which eventually amounts simply to trying to hold up under the weight of the cross without moving forward. But when we carry the very crosses we create, moving forward in procession with Christ and all our brothers and sisters in him, our crosses lead us to the Cross that brings life.

Richard Gilman, C.S.C.

February 27

Let us remain united to one another by the bonds of charity, confidence, devotedness and obedience to our rules and constitutions. Our work here is the work of each and everyone, and we are all, individually and collectively, responsible for it in the eyes of God and humanity.

—Basil Moreau

FR. PATRICK PEYTON, C.S.C., popularized the phrase, "The family that prays together stays together." But when I preach at weddings, I often encourage the couple pledging their vows to eat at least one meal together each day too—without the television on—even if the only possibility is a quick bowl of instant oatmeal before heading out the door. Praying and eating together bound Jesus to his apostles, and they are the essence of what he entrusted to us in the Eucharist.

Community meals sometimes highlight our brothers' failings and cause irritation. There is, however, a sacredness to any table fellowship that encourages us to tolerate idiosyncrasies and, with practice, even permits us to be amused by their repetition. We develop much of our reputations and form many of our opinions about one another from how we interact at table. It is also where we most effectively pass on the lessons of our forebears through stories, much as we do at home and through sharing the word in Church.

As in any family, our primary rules are to pray and eat together, so we do it regularly in Church and at home, for that is to do as Jesus did with his friends. The ripple effects endure for generations as commitments are reinforced, laughter and disappointments shared, and friendships forged, binding us more completely to Christ and to one another.

James B. King, C.S.C.

February 28

Let us bear with everything as Christ did, and unite, if possible, our blood with His Blood, our death even with His death, that we may share in His resurrection—a favor to be granted only to those who shall have been associated with Him in the pains and torments of His Passion.

—Edward Sorin

IN MY EXPERIENCE, the familiar expression, "misery loves company," can convey two separate messages, neither of which is very encouraging. If the phrase suggests that miserable people relish the companionship of those who are similarly pitiful, it offers little comfort, except perhaps for businesses that promote the marketing of antidepressants. If it means that miserable people make the most appealing dinner guests, then the idea of "loving company" needs a new definition, since the problem then arises as to how, by stark contrast, to describe guests who are cheerful, sociable, and gracious.

When Fr. Sorin urges us to identify our blood and our death with that of Christ, we might understandably be tempted to leap ahead quickly to his resurrection due to a reluctance to accept suffering as truly belonging in a healthy community that strives to be happy and caring. But this impulse to try to skip over the pains and torments actually prevents us from coming to know in the flesh that it is love and not misery that brings our company together. We are not called to share misery as if it were, like virtue, its own reward.

Rather, in bearing with everything as he did and in spreading the good news wherever we find ourselves, whether sowing or reaping, we partake in that courageous movement of grace that frees us and all people from the very source of misery.

Patrick D. Gaffney, C.S.C.

February 29

One of the surest and safest means to prevent the collapse of society is to bind and to hold more and more strongly bound the child's heart to the parents' heart, to the family, to home, to primitive and innocent affections.

—Edward Sorin

ONE OF THE strongest values in most African societies is family. I have learned this firsthand through living and working in our Holy Cross community there. Unlike in most Western societies, with their heavy emphasis on thinking, African cultures tend to stress belonging. Rather than, "I think therefore I am," their fundamental understanding of themselves is, "I am because we are."

Every time I am privileged to visit an African family, I strongly experience this oneness. Great reverence is always shown to guests, and they are made to feel part of the family. Upon entering their home, guests are taken to the sitting room, and then all the family members come to greet them, grandparents and parents, uncles and aunts, and all of the children. It is very important for each family member to shake hands and greet the guests by bowing and even kneeling before them. Then the family serves them tea and something to eat. At this point the guests already feel strongly bound to the family.

This strong commitment to family forms the backbone of these African societies. In addition, it has made me value my own natural family even more. It serves not only as an example for us in Holy Cross but for all families as we strive to form the strong and lasting bonds that unite us to each other as communities, societies, and ultimately one human family.

Alan Harrod, C.S.C.

MARCH

March 1

To succeed in the important undertaking entrusted to us, we must be, first of all, so closely united in charity as to form but one mind and one soul.

—Basil Moreau

THE ABSOLUTE IMPORTANCE of being united in charity has become more and more apparent to me the longer I have ministered as a Holy Cross religious. I am reminded of the late Br. Edmund Hunt, C.S.C., who often spoke of the most distinguishing characteristic of Holy Cross as being the "miracle" of bringing priests, brothers, and sisters together in one religious family to fulfill a shared mission. The miracle, however, is even greater because since its founding, Holy Cross also has always collaborated with lay men and women in the service of the Lord. The only way for such a diverse family of people to minister effectively is to remain united and grow evermore in charity.

For over two decades, I have been privileged to be a part of the miracle that God is working at the University of Portland. Together with my fellow religious in Holy Cross, other clergy, religious, lay men and women, and students we are building a community of teaching, faith, and service. What drives and sustains this effort is something greater than a mere group of individuals. For underlying both successes and setbacks, achievements and disagreements, there is a deeper commitment to a common mission and common good.

This is but one example of how the miracle of Holy Cross continues even today. All of us, no matter what our work or station in life, can find inspiration in Fr. Moreau's unfailing resolve that we can make a difference in a world so in need of our many talents if we but remain committed to working together united, mind and soul, in charity.

Donald J. Stabrowski, C.S.C.

March 2

We do not imagine that those who commit themselves in other ways to the following of Jesus are thereby hindered in their service of neighbor. On the contrary, we find in them willing and complementary partners in shared mission. We want our vows, faithfully lived, to be witness and call to them as their commitments, faithfully lived, are witness and call to us.

—Holy Cross Constitutions

SINCE THE FOUNDING of our universities, we Holy Cross religious have lived among our students in the residence halls. As rectors, chaplains, and religious in residence we are role models, teachers, and pastors for them. One of the freedoms that our religious vows provide for us is this very ability to live among our students. Present to them all hours of the day and even sometimes all hours of the night, we help them to grow in their faith and in their learning.

Any married couple who has children whose ages are ten, twenty, thirty, or older will tell stories filled with words like *joyful, energizing, exhausting, mystifying, grace-filled,* and *humbling.* Similarly, any Holy Cross religious who has lived in a university residence hall among eighteen, nineteen, twenty, and twenty-one year olds for ten, fifteen, twenty-five, or more years will tell stories filled with words like *joyful, energizing, exhausting, mystifying, grace-filled,* and *humbling.* And yet both often say they would never want the other's job.

Vows faithfully lived over the course of a lifetime will cause each of us to know grace, joy, sorrow, and total reliance on God. As vowed religious and as vowed married couples we share in the vision and passion of Fr. Moreau, striving to educate the hearts and minds of our youth. Working together, then, as complementary partners in a shared mission, we can continue to draw inspiration from the joyful, energizing, exhausting, mystifying, grace-filled, and humbling character of one another's witness.

Edwin H. Obermiller, C.S.C.

March 3

Jesus Christ is faithful, and He will not permit you to be tempted beyond your strength. If we but know how to awaken Him from His seeming sleep by our prayers, He will command the winds and the storm, and we shall have once more the calm of bygone days.

—Basil Moreau

FOLLOWING IN A long line of Holy Cross priests who served as military chaplains, beginning with Fr. William Corby, C.S.C., in the Civil War, I was a Navy chaplain aboard the *USS Midway*. One night, as howling winds and raging waters muscled waves across the flight deck eighty feet above the sea's surface, I stood above it all on the bridge of the carrier—warm, dry, confident, and unafraid. Among the largest of ocean-going vessels, created and mobilized by the most powerful navy in history, the ship in its eminence insulated me from the tempest below, from all harm. I was immune.

The storm grew in intensity. The nearby captain called out orders, asked for information, and considered his options. With one stark sigh—"this is not good"—he instantly sent a chill through me, washing away all of my confidence. His humility confronted my counterfeit calm. His judgment displaced fascination with fear. The truth he uttered roused me: "This is not good."

Seduced by the loftiness that had conditioned me and lulled by the shell that had cushioned me, I had permitted temptation to take up residence. In such times, when we are distracted by accomplishment and wheedled by privilege, a wake-up call may be warranted. Standing on the bridge, vulnerable, and trembling, I called upon the Lord who seemed aloof and unaware. "Where have you been?" came his reply. "Who's really been asleep here, anyway? Welcome home."

William D. Dorwart, C.S.C.

March 4

Lifelong formation is lifelong growth. As a daily aid for self-knowledge and self-governance, the examination of conscience allows us to find how we succeed or fall short in both our common life and our mission. A grace more powerful still is given in appropriately frequent sacramental confession, whereby each of us opens his conscience to the Lord, to the Lord's minister and to himself and there finds reconciliation with his neighbors and pardon from the Lord, who gave his life lest any of us be lost to him.

—Holy Cross Constitutions

I WILL NEVER forget the first time a priest asked me to hear his confession. I said yes, of course, though with some trepidation. Since then I have been blessed to hear the confessions of many priests and religious. Their humility, holiness, and faith in the midst of their struggles have always given me courage and strength. I see that priests and religious dedicated to the sacrament of reconciliation exude peace and joy in their vocations. Their commitment to lifelong growth inspires me to remain open to God's grace in my own calling.

The example of these priests and religious also calls me to the sacrament. There, as a penitent before the Lord, I confess my own sinfulness and encounter both my human weakness and the wonder of God's infinite love for me. There I find acceptance of myself as I am, and I find peace. There, too,

I discern how deeply and constantly I am in need of God's forgiveness.

The sacrament of reconciliation and the practice of a daily examination of conscience, in which we review our actions and thoughts before the Lord, can help all of us to evaluate our ongoing spiritual growth. And we dare not take that growth for granted because it is the constant renewal of our spirits, indeed of our very lives in Christ, that readies us for eternal life.

Pat Maloney, C.S.C.

March 5

I beg you to walk more and more perfectly in the path of obedience, tightening the bonds of fraternal charity, and meditating frequently on your individual responsibility in the work of Holy Cross.

—Basil Moreau

ON OCCASION, MY students ask me about the life of a Holy Cross brother. After I explain a bit about our life of prayer, ministry, and the religious vows of poverty, chastity, and obedience that bind us to each other in community, a typical student asks, "But do you really have to do what they tell you?"

The vow of obedience can be difficult to understand in a society and culture that exalts individual freedom. I think of the path of obedience as freely and willingly trying to live a "mediated" life. In other words, to know and to follow God's will in my life, I must discern with the help of faith-filled others. My individual actions as a member of a religious community are not isolated; what I do, or do not do, affects the rest of the community. And, my invitation to others with whom I live to help me to discern God's desire for my life tightens our bonds of fraternal charity.

Perhaps this concept of obedience as living a mediated life is not so strange when we consider other life contexts. In marriage, do I have to consult my spouse? At work, do I have to consult my colleagues? At home, do I have to consider my family's needs? Thus, to some extent, we all live mediated lives. The more we open ourselves to each other and to God in the decisions of our daily lives, the more we can fulfill our individual responsibilities with joy and enthusiasm, resulting in tightened bonds of love and respect among us.

John Paige, C.S.C.

March 6

Imitating Christ is not a matter of knowing Jesus Christ, His teaching and His life as we pride ourselves on knowing the story of some famous person. More than this, we must study the details of the Savior's life and know the love which inclined Him to act. We must be filled with the spirit of His example.

—Basil Moreau

WE CAN STUDY a lot about Christ and read a lot of books about him and think through our own personal Christology. But Christ is not bound within the covers of books—no matter how learned their contents. Fr. Moreau understood from his own lived experience that Jesus Christ was different from and more significant than "great figures" from the past, whatever their accomplishments. He grasped profoundly that the fulfillment of Jesus' life on earth came when he freely and obediently chose to suffer and to die so that we in turn might live. Jesus lives beyond books, out among us in the Church and in the world. And he eagerly wants to live within each of us.

Christ's followers today are called to know him such that we might share him with others. In order to do this with any authenticity and conviction, we must deepen our own relationship with Christ. He must be alive in us and we must know him truly as Savior and also as brother and friend, the one who walks with us through life, even amidst doubt, challenge, and difficulty. Our relationship is deepened and strengthened when we spend time with him in prayer and when we seek him out amidst the poor and the sick and the abandoned. This relationship ultimately is confirmed not only when we read the gospels, but also when we live them out as faithful disciples. We cannot sequester Christ into the category of some worthy figure from the past, but we must allow him to enter our lives this very moment and so guide us along his loving way.

Wilson D. Miscamble, C.S.C.

March 7

Lent must be for every Christian a time of reform and improvement in virtue.

—Edward Sorin

THERE'S AN OLD saying that those who sing pray twice. As a community that gathers through song, the Church witnesses music's spiritual power. Yet music is not only words or melody but it is also the silence between them, the stillness that flows in conversation with sound. Without silence, there is no music. Without stillness, there is no melody. Without reflection, there can be no harmony.

Much as an oboe caresses the air, exchanging waves of sound with quiet interludes of stillness, the Spirit of God moves in our lives, speaking to us both in the clamor of daily activity and in the quiet reflection of our own hearts. Each season of the Church year is a hymn of praise. Christmas and Easter inspire us with festive gratitude for the gift of hope in Christ. Ordinary time grounds us in the grace of the routine and the ordinary. And, we recognize our need for renewal in God's friendship through Advent and Lent.

In a special way, the forty days of Lent call us to question our customary habits into which we settle over time. Through taking up the habits of prayer, fasting, and almsgiving, we enter into the silence and stillness resonant with God's presence, leaving behind what crowds out the Spirit's voice within and sharing the fruits of our reflection through service. Above all, the silence of the season of Lent prepares us to sing God's praises all the more humbly, joyfully, and gratefully at the celebration of Easter and in every day of our lives.

Charles A. Witschorik, C.S.C.

March 8

It is at the altar that, in order to console the troubles of our exile, He offers us a manna more appealing than the manna of the desert; it is there that He gives us His flesh to eat and His blood to drink; there that He becomes present in such a way within our soul, His heart speaking to us with all of its affection, and bringing our own hearts to beat with His.

—Basil Moreau

THE STORY OF the Israelites roaming through the desert is one that reminds us how little we human beings change over time. The constant grumbling against God and his messengers has never really ceased. So often, grumbling of any kind occurs when we are hungry. The plaintive cries to God of the Israelites were no doubt imitating the plaintive cries of their stomachs as they searched for food amidst the harsh desert conditions.

Many cries of hunger reverberate throughout the world today. There are still those who cry for the daily nourishment that we tend to take for granted; but in our culture and time, the grumbling, the hunger that we experience more often than not comes from our hearts. The Israelites felt it, too, and

God fed their stomachs with manna and their hearts with the knowledge that he would care for them no matter what. Our hearts seek out this same divine nourishment because money, pleasure, and power—the food that our culture so often serves us—fails to satisfy. The deepest grumblings of our hearts still call for manna. They still call for God.

The Eucharist will fill us. The Eucharist will satisfy our hearts and transform them to love like our Savior's Sacred Heart that loves beyond all telling. It is a feast that God offers us for complete nourishment. Christ draws us to this banquet that we may know his love, be united with his love, and be consumed by his love on the way to eternal life.

Gregory Haake, C.S.C.

March 9

The Lord Jesus was crucified. But the Father raised him to glory, and Christ breathed his Spirit into his people, the church. Dying and rising with him in Baptism, his followers are sent to continue his mission, to hasten along the kingdom.

—Holy Cross Constitutions

THE LOVE OF God revealed in the Crucifixion, resurrection, and pentecost is the source of our hope, the food for our faith, and the catalyst for the zeal with which we pledge our lives to the mission of Holy Cross. How exciting, yet humbling, to be called to this mission which is very simply the mission of Jesus, our Savior. Our efforts, stemming from our prayer, brotherhood, and life in community, are not rooted in who we are but rather in who he is since they are really his efforts. Be it in the classroom, parish, homeless shelter, or in a land or culture foreign to us, we are all missionaries of his hope who proclaim the kingdom of justice, peace, and love.

The mission of Jesus, shared by all the baptized, is often misunderstood, rejected, or frustrated by conflicting values. Indeed, we are walking with him on the road to Calvary when we are mocked, ignored, or reviled for being preachers and teachers of the mission. Hope can be hard for us to sustain when we feel the kingdom impeded rather than hastened. Weariness can dampen our zeal or even create for us a Gethsemane of the spirit. In these times we are reminded that just as the mission is that of Jesus, so also is the strength for it. He sustains us. His unending love for us restores our hope and fires our zeal. And since God loved us first, we are capable of sharing, and yearn to share, that love with others. It is a love that hastens us along in our mission.

David T. Tyson, C.S.C.

March 10

The fast of Lent is instituted for the wisest purpose—to check vices and raise the soul above the desires of the body; to mortify and afflict, but not to disable and incapacitate anyone from duty.

—Edward Sorin

WHILE I WAS greeting my parishioners after the noon Mass on Ash Wednesday, a joyful woman with dust on her forehead gleefully smiled at me and clutched my hand as she was leaving. I quickly questioned her, "Why are you so joyful? There is no smiling in Lent." Pulling me closer, she simply stated, "My birthday was last week, and I don't have to fast anymore. I'm too old." With that, she kissed me and hurried down the steps of the church.

Knowing this woman as I do, I delighted in her spirit. She is a typical "church lady" who always arrives thirty minutes before Mass to recite her prayers and light her votive candle. A widow, she lives alone with her cats in a small house one block away from the parish. I know for a fact she is in her eighties and has been well beyond the recommended age for fasting for quite some time. Her lenten fast is a fast that continues throughout the year. She has given herself completely over to God by denying herself the pleasures of family, status, and material possessions. She embraces life with a smile and kiss because she has never abandoned her hope in the promise of the resurrection. Her lenten fast is a lifestyle that reflects a sincere devotion to and dependence on God. Lent for us, too, is something we ought to embrace rather than endure. How powerful this season can be—in its fasting, prayer, and almsgiving—when we don't merely choose to live it, but live to choose it.

Michael C. Mathews, C.S.C.

March 11

Beyond the liturgy that convokes us into church and congregation, there is the prayer we each must offer to the Father quietly and alone. We contemplate the living God, offering ourselves to be drawn into his love and learning to take that same love to heart. We enter thus into the mystery of the God who chose to dwell in the midst of his people.

—Holy Cross Constitutions

"HOLY, HOLY, HOLY Lord, God of power and might." At every Mass we repeat the words of the fiery angels in Isaiah's vision of the divine glory. In the presence of this revelation the prophet shook with fear because he, a mere human, had risked destruction by gazing upon the divine majesty. Our insignificance before the Divine Power seems overwhelming. God revealed himself to the ancient Hebrews as the Creator of the world, the Lord of the cosmos. He was not one of the gods that pagans manipulated to produce rain or fertility, or to gain victory on the battlefield. He is God, the One who must be adored and obeyed.

Christian faith proclaims that this Supreme Being has entered our world and our history. The Eternal Word "became flesh and made his dwelling among us" (Jn 1:14). We can confidently beseech the Creator because he has become one of us in Jesus the Christ who continues to dwell in the Church. The Holy and Almighty now abides in our midst.

We dare to address God precisely because he has "pitched his tent among us" as John's Gospel puts it. But he remains God, not a god, and so we must first pray that he be honored, that his rule be established, and that his will be done. Jesus has assured us, though, that after these petitions we may appropriately ask that God provide for our daily needs and our physical well-being. For the Incarnation has revealed that God is ever near to hear our pleas.

Louis Manzo, C.S.C.

March 12

The Sacrifice of the Cross is again offered to His Father for the salvation of the world. He renews it, not just on one day, but every day, every moment of every day in the thousands of different places among all people willing to receive Him. The heart of our God at the altar is a blazing heart where a sacred fire always burns to receive our souls.

—Basil Moreau

WHEN I WAS growing up, I was fortunate enough to go to a Catholic school with daily Mass. I can't say that I was always the most attentive person in the Church each day, but one image has always stuck with me. As I sometimes zoned out during the homily or the eucharistic prayer, I always found my eyes drawn to the gigantic crucifix that hung directly above the altar. For me that image made real the love of our God, a love so strong that he was willing to become one of us, to suffer and die on the Cross so that we would have the promise of eternal life. So even though I didn't necessarily understand the theology of the Eucharist, I knew that it flowed from the sacrifice of Jesus on the Cross and that this sacrifice wasn't in vain. The Cross led somewhere—to heaven. And so did the Eucharist.

Even today, when I am at Mass, that early image of the Eucharist flowing from the Cross still inspires me. In times when I feel the weight of the Cross on me, it is the Eucharist that gives me the strength to bear it and go on. For I know that through Jesus, the Cross leads somewhere and the Eucharist is the food that gives me the strength to get there.

Anthony Szakaly, C.S.C.

March 13

And, as in every work of our mission, we find that we ourselves stand to learn much from those whom we are called to teach.

—Holy Cross Constitutions

ALL TEACHERS HOPE that their students will remember what they have learned. Christ the teacher sent the Holy Spirit for this very purpose: "The Advocate, the holy Spirit that the Father will send in my name—he will teach you everything and remind you of all that I told you" (Jn 14:26). According to our Savior, then, true and lasting teaching and learning are fundamentally spiritual activities. And some of my students have taught me lessons I'll never forget.

I teach a subject—college mathematics—that unfortunately seems to bore or terrify more than it inspires. Many find it a challenge or even a cross. Yet every so often, students accept that challenge or embrace that cross with remarkable zeal, determination, or cheerfulness. They don't all achieve the same results. Some scrape by with a barely passing mark; others overcome early setbacks and excel. But in their willingness to strive, all of them remind me of my vocation as an academic and as a Holy Cross religious. They call me to renew my own research, for how can I expect them to work on new and difficult problems if I'm not willing to do the same? They call me back to our motto—Hail the Cross, Our Only Hope—for in their willingness to struggle through confusion they prove their hope for the joy of understanding.

Warning against intellectual and social pretensions, our Lord told his disciples, "As for you, do not be called 'Rabbi.' You have but one teacher" (Mt 23:8) namely Christ himself. Perhaps these words are not only an admonition, but also a divine call. As all of us form Christ's mystical body, so all of us must teach one another.

Charles McCoy, C.S.C.

March 14

Let us take a holy and firm resolution to steep ourselves anew in the religious spirit by generously offering to God

all the little sacrifices demanded by our rules. This is my
most ardent wish for the entire family entrusted to me.
—Basil Moreau

OUR YOUNG MEN in initial formation in Holy Cross often bring a zeal for ministry and religious life that can help us see more clearly the gift that God has given us in our own vocations. Years of ministry and community life and the habits we form can wear away some of our youthful enthusiasm and dull our spirits. Sacrifices that we were once eager to make can come to feel like, well, sacrifices.

If the *Constitutions* that are meant to guide our lives— our call, mission, prayer, brotherhood, vows—are allowed to gather dust, we can drift and lose our focus as individuals and as a community. Only by regularly recommitting ourselves to all of what our *Constitutions* call us to be can we hope to live our religious life in Holy Cross with zeal and generosity.

Similarly, one of the great blessings of parish life is journeying with people seeking initiation into our Catholic faith through our RCIA programs. As they progress and grow in their faith, many of them have an enthusiasm that is apparent and infectious. Their zeal and commitment serve as wonderful reminders of the incredible gift of our faith. The stakes of our lives as Christians are high. Who we are and what we do matters. We live our faith for God and are called as well to offer a witness for God's people. It is important for us, likewise, to return to scripture and the roots of our faith. In this way we prepare ourselves to renew our commitment, to renew our own baptismal promises once again at Easter.

John Herman, C.S.C.

March 15

"May our immortal souls depart in the death of the just!"
And that our last moments may be similar to those of the
Saints. Let our lives, like theirs, prove a long preparation
for death.

—Edward Sorin

PONDERING MY OWN mortality is challenging enough, but caring for a loved one who will likely die before me is worse. The motto of our religious community, *Ave Crux, Spes Unica*—Hail the Cross, Our Only Hope—urges me to keep going when I feel like shirking this particular cross in my life. The anguish and doubt that come from suffering along with someone are real. But, they can be transformed by love into the faith that knows death is not the end.

There is a statue depicting the death of St. Joseph that I pass when opening and closing Holy Cross Church. Jesus and Mary are holding Joseph's dying body. It is not a usual depiction of the Holy Family, but it has brought great comfort and hope to me for I have hugged and held my own dad's body as it writhes from painful spasms. Even though the example of Joseph's peaceful death tells us that dying is ultimately a good thing, that what is mortal must be changed into what is immortal, my heart still has been sorrowful. For I know one day I will be making the Sign of the Cross on his forehead as I do so often at funeral vigils. With that sign, Christ laid eternal claim to our souls when we died to ourselves and were reborn in him in baptism. And it is under the Sign of the

Cross, our only hope, that we can make our lives like those of the saints—a long preparation to meet Christ face to face in peace at the hour of our death.

Bradley Metz, C.S.C.

March 16

We are the children of our heavenly Father. Consequently, we must behave as such, putting into His hand a future which is not our lot to penetrate.

—Jacques Dujarie

WE KNOW THE concepts. God's immense love for us is without limit or depth. We are never out of God's hands. These concepts are really quite simple, and yet they challenge us greatly. For being the human creatures that we are, with faults, idiosyncrasies, and failings, we live in the midst of anxiety. Sometimes anxiety can be good as it motivates us to be creative and to get things done. On the other hand, sometimes it can be paralyzing. Fr. Dujarie reminds us, though, that there is no reason ever to feel paralyzed.

But at the heart of our anxiety lies an enduring difficulty in understanding a love that doesn't count the cost or one that isn't doled out as a reward. We struggle to understand the care that God has for us, a care that envelops and protects. Perhaps we feel that, because of who we are, we are really not worthy of such care. The truth is that we like to think that we are in charge and we like to control, or at least attempt to control, our lives. We are content to let ourselves live in that delusion.

God doesn't seem to mind at all. He lets us live in that delusion and perhaps delights at our silliness, always waiting patiently for that moment of recognition of and total surrender to his love. God delights in us because we are his creatures, created in his image. And so we pray for the courage and grace to live as his children, trusting in the abundant love and care he has for us.

Thomas A. Dziekan, C.S.C.

March 17

From the moment our Blessed Lord came down into the immaculate bosom of His Virgin Mother to His last breath on the Cross His whole life was, above all, an incessant prayer; not only for His devoted disciples, but even for His cruel murderers.

—Edward Sorin

ON TUESDAYS OUR third- and fourth-graders come to daily Mass. One week, as they were walking by me after Mass, I kept repeating to the third-graders, "Be good, and love God." But then a young girl turned to me and said, "Fr. Neil, I know all about that. I'm in the fourth grade!" And hopefully she does. It's a constant challenge to keep grade school children focused—on their schoolwork, on their conduct, and most especially on God. At every opportunity we tell them to look at things through the eyes of Jesus so that they can live as he asks them to live. It's a lesson for us adults as well. For some it's easier than for others, but it's impossible to live well without prayer. If prayer is just something else we have to do, it will be the first thing we don't have time for in our lives. But if our lives are a prayer, then we will live as Jesus asks us to live.

Jesus' life was one of prayer, not only in those explicit moments when he went into the desert for forty days, went up the mountain with his disciples, or retreated to a deserted place, but in every moment of his life. We are called to follow his example and live a life of prayer as well. It isn't enough to be people who pray; we must be people of prayer. For then we are constantly in relationship with God, living the grace that comes from making our lives an incessant prayer.

Neil F. Wack, C.S.C.

March 18

Let us show by our deeds, especially during this holy season of penance and prayer, that we believe in our crucified Redeemer and hope in Him.

—Edward Sorin

WITH ITS FINGER pointing, scantily clad characters, and banishment, the story of Adam and Eve has remarkable currency for an ancient description of sin and punishment. But because a return to Eden doesn't figure as prominently in Christian spirituality as does resurrection, we're better served in Lent by the story of Adam and Eve's children, Cain and Abel.

I learned how relevant Cain and Abel are to our hope of resurrection when a drunken man came to the rectory late one night. The priests were all asleep, I told him, so perhaps I could help. I was a deacon at the time, yet nothing in my subsequent years of hearing confessions has compared to what he had to say. That's because when I asked him what his name was, he declared, "I'm Cain; I killed Abel." As it turns out, his name really was Abel, and in a manner that each of us has experienced, an inner struggle had ended badly. Sin had won out, yet only temporarily, for our Redeemer has risen to die no more. And his resurrection begins to fulfill the yearning of Abel's blood as it cries out to God from the ground (Gen 4:10), not for revenge, but for a spirit recreated.

Like my friend Abel, we can be our own worst enemy at times. So our spiritual task is to make holy again that ground from which we hear the pleas for mercy emanate. To do so, we must heed the appeals for new life that come from others, for our deeds in service of them will render the Cain within us powerless.

Kevin J. Sandberg, C.S.C.

March 19—St. Joseph

The religious spirit consists in the knowledge and love of the duties of one's vocation and has as its effect to make us increase in the love of our vocation, fulfill its

obligations with exactitude, and defend as we ought its honor and interests. The dispositions that I have just mentioned were never better illustrated than by our glorious patron, St. Joseph. Let us then have recourse to him in order that we may understand the sentiments which we should make our own evermore wholeheartedly and obtain, by his powerful intercession before God, the grace of sincere esteem of our state of life, deep conviction of its duties, and the strength to manifest these sentiments in all times and places. If, however, we are to honor him as he desires, it is not enough to invoke him; we must further devotion to him and, above all, imitate his virtues and set them in opposition to the spirit of the world. This it is which makes devotion to him so timely.
—Basil Moreau

AT THE FOOT of Mount Royal in Montreal, there is a statue of St. Joseph that greets the millions of pilgrims who come to St. Joseph's Oratory every year to pay homage to this glorious saint. On the statue's pedestal, we read the words: *Ite Ad Joseph*—Go to Joseph. These words were the mantra of Br. André Bessette, C.S.C., the founder of St. Joseph's Oratory, whose legendary holiness and healing powers gave him the name, "Miracle Man of Montreal." Br. André's stalwart devotion to St. Joseph was partly attributed to the esteemed position that the foster father of Jesus holds in the heart of every Holy Cross religious. It was Fr. Moreau who declared St. Joseph as one of the glorious patrons of his newly formed Congregation of Holy Cross.

But why should we go to Joseph? What is so special about St. Joseph that we, in the spirit of Fr. Moreau and Br. André, should go to him with our aching souls, our hearts' desires, and our longings for holiness?

The answer is simple. In all of his ordinariness, St. Joseph embodies the religious spirit for which all Christians long—integrity, fortitude, fidelity, and yes, sanctity. In living out his foreboding vocation of being the husband of Mary and the foster father of the Messiah, St. Joseph remained unwavering in his loyalty, faithful to his mission, and unselfishly open to the will of God. St. Joseph did this not out of blind obedience or ignorance; he did it simply out of love.

For those who are discerning their vocation in life and for those who are already living theirs out, St. Joseph remains a model of how to live out our baptismal call to holiness and how to do it well. Fr. Moreau recognized this and encouraged us to seek the intercession of St. Joseph so that we, too, may obtain the grace of sincere esteem of our state of life, deep conviction of its duties, and the strength to manifest these sentiments in all times and places. Through St. Joseph's example, we see how a vocation to marriage, single life, priesthood, or religious life requires more than just duty, more than just putting in our time and fulfilling our obligations. It requires love, a love for the One who calls us and a love for those we are called to serve. After all, a vocation not rooted in love is a vocation not rooted in God. Fr. Moreau knew this. Br. André knew this.

That is why we need to go to Joseph, and not just with our prayers of intercession and petition. We need to go to him so that we can learn how to live our own vocations well. By deepening our devotion to St. Joseph and learning how to love as he loved, we will be able to embrace more fully the holiness that is integral to our own vocations. In so doing, in the words of Fr. Moreau, we will honor him as he desires. We cannot wait. We must go to Joseph.

Paul Bednarczyk, C.S.C.

March 20

Has not Holy Communion made us many times more sacred receptacles of Jesus Christ than the consecrated vessels which contain His Flesh and Blood in our churches? Unlike the sacred vessels, we do not merely contain this Flesh and Blood; we really make it part of ourselves.

—Basil Moreau

MASS ON HOLY Thursday has always been one of my favorite celebrations of the Church year. As an altar boy, I had to sign up early and attend two practices to have the honor of serving at this Mass. Our pastor always told us that Holy Thursday was special because it commemorated the institution of both the Eucharist and the priesthood.

The procession around our parish church with the Blessed Sacrament led by incense and candles expressed the solemnity of the celebration. When I was old enough to carry the incense, our pastor told me, "Remember that you are giving honor to Jesus present in the Eucharist. Be slow and deliberate as you bless with incense." And as moving as the procession was, the washing of the feet also stands out in my memory of Holy Thursday. Each year twelve men would take a seat in the sanctuary, and each year there was some uneasiness among them as the ritual began. Like St. Peter, they weren't sure about why their leader would wash their feet. But each year our pastor was "slow and deliberate" as he carefully and tenderly washed and dried the feet.

In our Holy Cross communities, parishes, and institutions we still celebrate the sacredness of the Eucharist with processions and adoration throughout the year. We, like Fr. Moreau, believe in God's real presence in the Eucharist—body, blood, soul, and divinity. In its transformative power, we slowly yet deliberately become more like him whom we receive; we become Christ's sacred vessels, blessing with his presence all those we encounter, slowly and deliberately.

Kevin Russeau, C.S.C.

March 21

By our vows we are committed to single-hearted intimacy with God, to trusting dependence upon God and to willing surrender to God. We wish thus to live in the image of Jesus, who was sent in love to announce God's rule and who beckons to us to follow him. We profess vows for the sake of this same mission of Jesus.

—Holy Cross Constitutions

FROM HIS TERRIBLE deathbed, Jesus cried out, "I thirst." This impassioned cry speaks to each of our hearts because it expresses more than the thirst for water, it voices the very human longing for union with God. We thirst for him. But this cry also speaks of a thirst for other people. Christ was alone on the Cross in death, and he cried out to those around him. We also thirst for communion with each other.

In my life, God opened the path of religious vows to help me quench and deepen evermore my own thirst for union with him and communion with his people. These three vows, chastity, poverty, and obedience, have called me to single-hearted intimacy with God, a trusting dependence on him, and a willing surrender to him. Supported in my thirst for God and his people by my superiors and fellow religious, I have gone in many directions in my ministry as a Holy Cross priest and religious. I recall, in particular, working with the poor in Latin America. In the suffering faces of the children, peasants, the aged, and prisoners there, the image of Christ became clearer to me. It was the image of the Crucified calling out in love for all of his children.

The plaintive cry from the Cross draws all people into the heart of Jesus. Whatever our vocations might be, they are gifts through which we both fulfill and deepen our love and commitment to him. For ever deeper union with God and communion with each other, each of us must say, "I thirst."

Robert Pelton, C.S.C.

March 22

We understand a bit of the emotion called mother-ly love, this love of a mother for the children she has brought to life. Motherly love leads her always to think about them and work to assure their happiness. This is but a faint picture of what Mary feels for all people, and the love she bears for us, since she became our mother and she adopted us as her children.

—Basil Moreau

"BEHOLD, YOUR MOTHER. Woman, behold, your son," uttered Jesus from the Cross. Tradition tells us that this statement in John's Gospel refers to all of us, the members of the Church. In giving his mother to the beloved disciple, Christ gave Mary to each of us as our Mother, too. She thinks of us constantly and inspires us, working to assure our happiness. This is the form her love takes.

Holy Cross priests Fr. Patrick Peyton and Fr. Edward Sorin believed so strongly in the love of Mary that they each took important documents intended to be sent out by mail, placed them on the Marian altar, and prayed their rosary over them. After praying to Mary they would receive some indication of her preference and either rip up the documents or send them according to her instructions. Both of these Holy Cross men were certain of their Mother's love for them.

We, too, can be as certain of her love for us. Those confident enough in a mother's love know that she will decide what is best for her children and their lives. If we lack this confidence, however, we can pray to Mary, and through her intercession, she will help us to trust in her and her Son. She keeps much in her heart, but her deep love is for all of God's children. She loves us because her Son loves us; she loves us because she is our Mother; she loves us in order that we might imitate her Son's love for all her children.

John Phalen, C.S.C.

March 23

Resurrection for us is a daily event. We have stood watch with persons dying in peace; we have witnessed wonderful reconciliations; we have known the forgiveness of those who misuse their neighbor; we have seen heartbreak and defeat lead to a transformed life; we have heard the conscience of an entire church stir; we have marveled at the insurrection of justice. We know that we walk by Easter's first light, and it makes us long for its fullness.

—Holy Cross Constitutions

WITHIN A SIX-MONTH period, a close friend, a colleague at Kings College, a brother in Holy Cross, and my own brother died, all of them at relatively young ages. My brother's death was the most devastating because it came without warning just a few hours after we'd spoken on the phone.

Several months later, I sat with lingering grief, praying and waiting for some relief. I reminded God that I'd had enough of loss and of sorrow. Within a few days, a sense of incredible lightness overcame me, dissipating the weight of pain and loss that had accrued over those dark months. Earlier in life I'd realized that letting go of things, such as success, status, and material goods, was necessary on the journey to becoming an honest self. I still needed to understand the deeper sense of letting go, of handing over to God the direction of my life, which lies at the heart of what living in the resurrected Christ really means.

In the midst of all the daily dying to self, of losing and letting go, God's love beckons for us to lean on him on whom alone we depend. Like the apostles on Easter morning, we cannot fully comprehend the significance of the Paschal Mystery, the passion, death, and empty tomb, until we have lived it more directly. It might be confusing for a time, but when we come to know that all of our dyings and risings occur in the Lord, we will have recognized Easter's first light.

Anthony Grasso, C.S.C.

March 24

Making ourselves all to all must be learned and practiced at home, in order to gain all to Christ, in whom there is neither Jew nor Greek, all having been equally redeemed in His Precious Blood. We know there is no difference of persons with God.

—Edward Sorin

DISCIPLESHIP BEGINS AT baptism but our experience of redemption is deepened by our life experiences. Ministering on three continents over the years—trying to be all to all—I have seen the possibilities of true human community. Though people speak different languages and have different religious beliefs, there is a commonality which makes us all brothers and sisters. Muslim and Hindu children living in poverty in India and Bangladesh can still smile with hope. African children love to sing and dance to celebrate their joy of learning. Children around the world are anxious to enter the adult community, in spite of society's strange prejudices and preferences that confuse them.

The possibility of true human community, our hope for God's redemption, begins with all children deserving to start out on life's journey in a community of faith, hope, and love: learning to share and not simply compete, learning to accept rather than judge, learning to develop their own minds and hearts and not just absorb the habits of others, learning to pray and work and not just expect all to be given to them. Ultimately, all children need to learn that there is no real difference of persons in God's eyes. There is enough divine love for everyone.

Holy Cross men and women and their legions of lay collaborators and students—parents and children together—are fulfilling this vision of education and community in homes, schools, and parishes around the world. It is a gospel vision from the good news of Jesus Christ. And it summons every person to discipleship, for we all have a part to play in God's kingdom.

David E. Schlaver, C.S.C.

March 25

I am blind, and Mary offers me a mother's loving hand to guide me through this pathless wilderness to the gate of heaven! Weak and exhausted from so many falls and wounds, she raises me and promises to support me, through all obstacles and hardships, upon the saving arm of her divine charity.

—Edward Sorin

SO OFTEN I find myself struggling, as we all do, to discover God's will for my own life. At times I struggle to stay on the right path of my spiritual journey, repeatedly falling into the same pitfalls, doubts, and anxieties about where I am going and who I am becoming. I realize that I am trying to depend upon myself alone, but that I am powerless and unable fully to grasp God's vision for me. I simply cannot do it by myself.

At these times, I find myself drawn to Mary, Our Lady of Sorrows and the patroness of the Congregation of Holy Cross. We can all benefit from reflecting on her journey, beginning with the annunciation when she tries to make sense out of the angel Gabriel's message that she is to become the mother of the Son of God. We observe her in the temple when Simeon tells her that a sword will pierce her heart. We walk with her on the journey with her Son when, at the wedding feast, she instructs the servants, "Do as he tells you." We try to feel what is in her mother's heart as she accompanies her Son on the Way of the Cross and sees sufferings and abuses heaped upon him. Finally, we know that we can trust Mary to guide

us through all obstacles and hardships when we hear her Son
say from the Cross, "Behold, your mother."

Charlie Kohlerman, C.S.C.

March 26

*Let us continue to remain thus united in our Lord, and
let us often come together in spirit despite our distance
which separates us. By these relationships of mutual
friendship and dependence we shall help one another
correspond with the designs of Providence in our
regard.*

—Basil Moreau

As MEN, WE can go about our work yearning for accomplishments. Yet when Jesus spoke with his disciples at the last
supper, reminding them that servants though they were, they
were also friends, he then sent them out to "bear fruit." Who
ever sends men out to bear fruit? Men are meant to do great
deeds, no? Indeed, Jesus says, "No." One of the blessings of
the religious community which Fr. Moreau founded is that we
are comprised of men and women, clerics and laypersons. He
wanted us to mimic a family, and so he used the Holy Family
as a powerful model for living together in unity.

What continues to amaze me about Holy Cross, after more
than half a century as a professed member working and ministering across the globe, is how we ordinary men and women
continue to sustain one another in our mission. Whether at

the University of Notre Dame or a new Catholic university in Uganda, whether in the Holy Land or in Bangladesh, we are all called to be and act together. Strengthened by that call and our care for one another, we end up accomplishing incredible things, even though accomplishments are not our goal. At our best, then, the family of Holy Cross—comprised of men and women, clergy and laypeople—becomes an image for the Church. For all of us called into God's family are to work together and learn from one another by serving the people where we are. It is in this way that we live as true friends and bear fruit for God's kingdom.

David Burrell, C.S.C.

March 27

It was a call that came to us from without, but also one that arose up within us, as from his Spirit.
—Holy Cross Constitutions

MY CALL TO religious life as a brother in Holy Cross came through the back door, so to speak. During my junior year of high school, my best senior buddy told me that he was joining the brothers. I was stunned but, at the same time, intrigued. I had no idea that he had been thinking about such a radical move. Certainly, I had not been entertaining such a commitment myself. But the Spirit began to percolate in me, and I joined Holy Cross at the end of my senior year. Now, looking back upon more than forty years as a religious brother, I am aware that the Spirit has been moving me in directions that I never consciously would have chosen.

Perhaps the greater mystery is that I have responded at the very moments when I was unaware that anything positive might occur. The Spirit's gift to me, indeed to all of us, is the courage to move out into the unknown—to step out of the boat onto the waters of uncertainty because the Lord Jesus beckons.

I know in my own life, if I have been effective in ministry, it is because the Spirit has led me to step out of one comfort zone after another. I am who I am right now because of my responsiveness to the Spirit—because I have been able to say, even timidly, yes. True power to be for others, in each of our lives, arises from the Spirit breathing power upon our powerlessness and transforming that into action for the Church and the world.

Philip Smith, C.S.C.

March 28

If we wish to avoid failing, we must do nothing except what is in accord with our vocation and the will of God. We must strive to remain not only in the state of grace, but even more in a state of fervor and in close union with God which makes us want to act always out of love of God.

—Basil Moreau

I RECENTLY ATTENDED Mass with our local community of senior and infirm brothers—men who have steadfastly remained faithful to their vocations and the will of God for fifty, sixty, seventy, or more years. The experience was humbling as only a sacrament can be. Not only had I encountered our Lord and brother, Jesus the Christ, in the Eucharist, but I also felt his embrace in the midst of men who fervently strive with unflagging zeal for a close union with God.

Afterward, as I walked the short distance to my residence, I continued my thanksgiving and reflection on that encounter with Christ. I think the encounter was so extraordinary for me in that it was so ordinary for my brothers who, living in the love of God, are beacons to others to seek union with God. If their ability to minister actively has diminished, their power to reach out to others in prayer and hospitality continues to blossom into an even more transforming ministry. Through them and my communion with them, my own zeal was renewed.

Perhaps that is what Fr. Moreau meant when he uses "we" and not "I" when writing of our wish to avoid failing. Zeal is not a virtue that can be achieved or maintained in isolation. In isolation, it fades to extinction. Zeal, like every other virtue, requires a family of believers to nurture and sustain it. Zeal for the will of God is found in union with God, and union with God is found in union with others who share our journey.

John F. Tryon, C.S.C.

☩

March 29

How sweet it is to abandon ourselves to the love of our
Father who is in heaven and to seek His holy will.
— Basil Moreau

AT THE END of a spring break visit with my family, I checked
my e-mail account as I prepared to go to bed before an early
flight. As I reviewed the subject lines of my e-mails, one
caught my attention. It read, "Sit down before you read this."
As I opened the e-mail I quickly felt my face going pale. It was
from my provincial superior, asking me to accept a new role
of leadership in our province. This new role would require me
to leave the University of Portland, a Holy Cross apostolate of
which I had been a part for over a decade. I turned to God in
prayer, trying to discern what he was asking of me. Could I
truly abandon a place that had become home? I was torn. On
the one hand, I love Holy Cross, so how could I say no? But
on the other hand, I love the University of Portland and our
ministry there as Holy Cross, so how could I say yes? What
was God's holy will? What was my holy will?

When all of us are asked to consider major or even small
decisions in our lives, we are faced with the question of how
we ensure that our needs, wants, and desires do not cloud the
will of God's grace. We have to examine what it will require to
abandon ourselves completely to the love of God. For if we are
not seeking God's holy will in our lives day in and day out, we
will never know how to seek it when the unexpected invitation, e-mail, letter, or phone call comes asking us to abandon

ourselves to something possibly much greater, something maybe only God can see in us.

Edwin H. Obermiller, C.S.C.

March 30

There are many ways of carrying out this imitation which can be summed up as the study of Jesus Christ. When we study Him, we get to know Him; as we get to know Him, we love Him; in loving Him, we are led to imitate Him.

—Basil Moreau

FR. MOREAU WAS an intensely passionate man when it came to the task of teaching Christians to discover and live their calling in life. For many in Holy Cross, the calling as educators in the faith is carried out in institutions of higher learning. For these members, to study a particular field is a lifelong endeavor. They are always immersed in the debates and research of their fields whether they are theology, the sciences, or the fine arts.

The knowledge mined from a life marked by study is vast, but for it to remain mere knowledge, while humanly impressive, would be spiritually sad. True fruit arises when that knowledge bursts into a love for the topic of study and consequently for the God by whom the arts and sciences were created and receive their continued inspiration.

So, too, is it with Christ Jesus who, far from being a mere topic for study, is the very subject of our lives. It is therefore, as Fr. Moreau tells us, the duty of all Christians to study Christ so as to know, love, and follow him. Just as the scholar daily takes up the book, so do we daily place in our hands the word of God in sacred scripture and our breviary, the daily prayer of the Church. We also place ourselves among other believers in the Church's public prayer, the liturgy. How can those unfamiliar with the discoveries of science dare name themselves scientists? Or by what claim can those who fail to view and be knowledgeable of works of art enjoy the title of artist? Likewise, we who hold the title "Christian" must have knowledge of, love for, and discipleship in Christ Jesus.

Michael Wurtz, C.S.C.

March 31

Pray, then, for me, and pray also for one another in order that we may accomplish all the good we can and that the many souls in whose salvation we are privileged to cooperate may at least attain eternal life.

—Basil Moreau

PRAYER WAS FR. Moreau's life. He sought to anchor his entire being in prayer before the Eucharist, devotion to our Blessed Mother, reading of sacred scripture, and willing surrender to Divine Providence. He both partook in common prayer and retreated into solitude in order to strengthen his relationship with the Lord.

Fr. Moreau yearned for the salvation of souls such that he believed that each of us is called to dedicate ourselves completely to extending the reign of Jesus Christ to all people. And it was precisely his deep and fervent prayer life that fueled Fr. Moreau's apostolic zeal to make God known, loved, and served. He is truly my hero because he never wavered in this vocation to serve and love God's people.

That is not to say, however, that Fr. Moreau did not encounter difficulties in seeking all the good he could for the souls entrusted to his care. But he did not see the challenges that he faced as obstacles because he understood them as important and necessary opportunities to answer God's call. Fr. Moreau found the spiritual strength to live in this way first by searching for the spirit of God through prayer, and then letting the rest fall into place.

Knowing that prayer was his very life, Fr. Moreau continually exhorted his religious to anchor their own lives in prayer—both for themselves and for one another. We would all do well to do the same. For it is only in prayer that we will find the spiritual strength that we all need to allow God to lead us and those around us into eternal life.

Thomas Chambers, C.S.C.

APRIL

April 1

*It is in meditation on the great truths of our faith that one
learns to detach himself from the swiftly passing shadow
of the world, which, like a rushing torrent, carries off in
its waves both people and things. It is in such meditation
that we train ourselves to see the hand of God in all the
events of life.*

—Basil Moreau

THE EXPERIENCE OF regret, disconcerting as it is, can have
sublime allure. In a world that is continually passing away, in
a life in which friendships and accomplishments are never set
on sturdy ground, indeed, in our very selves that slip back and
forth between the person we strive to be and the person we
hate to become, we see continual change and loss. The stability we seek in order to counteract this instability, the revival
of those people, things, and attitudes we so desire, is found in
our mantras of regret—or so we think. For it is in entertaining
our regrets that—in the briefest of moments—we relive the
past. But the past can never be restored.

Even our faith does not stop the past from slipping out
from under us. But it does give us reason to hope and not be
afraid. When the storm threatened to overtake their boat, our
Lord Jesus told his disciples not to be afraid. When we medi-
tate on the truth of this statement, that our God is so loving
that even in our darkest moments he rests peacefully beside us,
we come to expose the falsity of regret. It is simple. Regret tells
us that God is removed from our past and present, but the

truths of our faith resound with the "is now and ever shall be." Our healing with the past and hope for what is to come, then, can only be a healing found in God, a healing that begins when we trade our regret for a litany of thanksgiving.

Aaron Michka, C.S.C.

April 2

Nothing is more opposed to the maxims of the Gospel and the spirit of your vocation than fear; nothing is more capable of paralyzing the good which has been so auspiciously begun.

—Basil Moreau

"BE NOT AFRAID." Pope John Paul II opened his pontificate with these words of Jesus Christ, and he repeated them over and over again, in and out of season, as a reminder to the Church and to the world that God's love overcomes all our fears, freeing us to live our callings.

I know the deep truth of Christ's invitation to abandon all fear. God has richly blessed my life and ministry as a priest in the Congregation of Holy Cross. I have even been shocked at what God has done through me when I simply have trusted in Divine Providence. I often wonder how else God seeks to use my life. I don't know. What I do know is that if I let fear govern my life, I will limit the possibilities of what God can do through me because fear restricts us. It inhibits the transformative power of God's love in our lives. But if I trust and take God at his word, there is no limit to the good that he can accomplish in and through even sinners like myself.

When each of us allows God's perfect love to cast out fear from our hearts, we open ourselves to live fully our vocations in Christ. John Paul II was not afraid; members of Holy Cross shed their fears in order to serve the Church throughout the world. We, too, must remember that God is never found wanting in our need. There is nothing to fear. "Be not afraid."

Joe Corpora, C.S.C.

April 3

The doctrine of the Cross is the most mysterious secret of divine wisdom. The Cross, which should be eminently our own, as Religious of the Holy Cross, is the science of the heart more properly than the mind.

—Edward Sorin

WE HUMAN BEINGS typically avoid suffering if we can. Yet the great danger is that our lives become all about avoiding everything that might be a little painful for us. This fear can cause us to avoid risks and to play it safe through life. The Cross, however, reminds us, as it did Fr. Sorin, that there are some things worth suffering for and that the greatest danger in life is not suffering itself, but never caring for or loving others enough to suffer with them and for them. Fr. Sorin believed that God was calling him to serve others through education. At the request of Fr. Moreau, Fr. Sorin left the familiarity of

France to serve God's people in America. He did not play it safe. He was willing to suffer hardships and disappointments in order to found the University of Notre Dame, which he firmly believed God would use to inspire generations to make the sacrifices necessary to learn and to serve.

While our heads may tell us that it is foolish to choose to suffer at all, our hearts and the Spirit of Christ tell us that it makes all the sense in the world to suffer for what is right. For Christians who believe in the death and resurrection of Christ, suffering for what is right is the only option, because they know in their hearts that denying the Cross leads to meaninglessness. While we would rather avoid suffering, if we love as Christ loved we will suffer as he did. But in the end, we will rise as he did as well.

Robert A. Dowd, C.S.C.

April 4

The more we humble ourselves before God, the more God will raise us up and favor us.

—Basil Moreau

AT THE LAST Supper, the night before he laid down his life for us, Jesus gave his disciples a lasting memory of humble service as he washed their feet. In this simple yet deliberate action, Jesus gives us a model of mutual love and service to follow. Called by him to do likewise, we make Christ present today by washing one another's feet.

Over my many years in Holy Cross, I have watched my brothers embody that loving service by responding generously to the needs of the community, the Church, and the world. As educators in the faith, they have accepted the call to serve as pastors, teachers, writers, artists, and chaplains. Whatever ministries they have fulfilled they have gone about the work of making Christ present in the lives of those in need.

The realization that we are called to serve the people of God by washing feet and by saying yes to bear Christ in a variety of ways is both overwhelming and humbling. I remember the first time after ordination that I was assigned to hear confessions. I was scared and hardly slept the night before because I did not want to do it wrong or make a mistake. I spoke with a wise priest in the community who gave me advice that I have never forgotten. This holy priest told me to remember that the sacrament of reconciliation, as well as all other ministries, is about being an instrument of love. Through grace we humbly step out of the way and let God's love be alive and well in the world, raising us and those we serve into his embrace.

Joe Carey, C.S.C.

April 5

Our consecration in Baptism is a departure on a journey that requires us, as it does all his people, to be refashioned by the Lord's creating grace over and over again. Likewise with our lives in a religious community, we must have formed in us by God's enablement the living likeness of Jesus Christ.

—Holy Cross Constitutions

JUST AS YAHWEH would not allow Moses to see his face, but only his back as he strode past, sometimes we only come to see our greatest encounters with the Divine long after they occur when, in a time of remembering, we begin to discern a pattern. After Yahweh passed by, he left proof of the encounter—Moses's face shone. The Israelites saw this and realized Moses had been with the Divine. It was not, however, a sign Moses himself could see, but rather, it was a sign for others. In the same way, we may not have the consolation ourselves of knowing the depth of our encounters with the Divine, but the Lord can work through us to bring the surety of comfort and love to his people.

It takes faith to believe God is always creating us. We don't feel it—at least I don't. Instead, I become immersed in what is happening, and only later, in hindsight, can I see the hand of the Lord refashioning me. When I take the time to look back over where I've come on this journey, I notice that the most intense refashioning has not occurred in easy times, but in difficult.

Beginning with my first consecration in baptism, and more rapidly since my adult consecration as a person set apart for God in religious community, God has used events and persons to carve me closer to Jesus. A fairly quick examination of conscience at the end of each day would be, "God, do I look a little more like you?" Like Moses, we ourselves can't always tell, but we can reflect on what response others around us might give.

Mark Knightly, C.S.C.

April 6

We live our consecration in many lands and cultures. Our commitment is the same wherever we are, but we seek to express it in a manner rooted in and enriched by the varying contexts and cultures in which we live. In this way we hope to make our witness and service more effective for the kingdom.

—Holy Cross Constitutions

IN RELIGIOUS LIFE, I have had the grace of being able to live in different cultures of the world, immersed in diverse Christian communities served by Holy Cross. In each of these places, whether it be South America, North America, or Africa, I have encountered distinct customs, foods, languages, forms of dress, ways of praying, and senses of humor. I have also come face to face with different ways of understanding the poverty, sufferings, and miseries of humanity. It is almost as if each place is a world unto itself.

In the midst of such diversity, however, I have seen and experienced the common meal of the Eucharist; I have seen a race of men and women that originates from the same Father, that has a marvelous and unique way of expressing joys and sufferings through prayer; I have seen only one community thirsty to help, with a common language that transcends external differences. After all my varied experiences, I have come to understand the significance of being a Christian in the world of today, and I know in the depths of my own heart that being a Christian is my only nationality, language, and culture.

In each place, I have seen that the differences—race, socioeconomic condition, political beliefs, age, and many more—are not important in the hour of sharing the body and blood of our Lord. For, nourished and sustained by this flesh and blood, I have come to believe that love carried out in action is our common language, drawing us together into communion with each other and with God.

Simón Cerda, C.S.C.

April 7

Most assuredly, the greatest blessing heaven could bestow this year on our religious family would be to create such an earnest desire in every soul to be a treasure to the Community and a will to cooperate with God's grace and carry out the generous resolve. There is no need of making any exception; in one way or another with a good will, everyone can be in truth a real treasure in the Community.

—Edward Sorin

WE MUST MARVEL at the ability of the early Holy Cross missionaries to endure the multiplicity of hardships that beset them from the time they departed their beloved France for the backwoods of Indiana. Physical, emotional, spiritual, organizational, ecclesial, and political crises confronted the young community in ways that could have easily meant the demise of their important venture in America. What allowed them to persevere in their mission was the link they upheld between the apostolate and their community life.

This pooling of individual talents and merging of skills, this fraternal support in disagreement and common chorus of prayer, this grieving of common loss and sharing of joy in progress all have played a primary role, not only in our foundational years, but throughout our history and to this very day. Our life together and the effectiveness of the mission is not a by-product or accident of some kind of synergy. Rather, it is more of a "holy strategy" deeply rooted in our religious profession and zeal for the mission. It is God's grace and zeal that allow us to possess the good will to become real treasures in community. In this common life, in this union of many members bound by the grace of the Spirit, Holy Cross can be a model for all of us as we seek in our own neighborhoods to form communities of the coming kingdom.

David T. Tyson, C.S.C.

April 8

Consider the great reward promised to those who have taught the truth to others and have helped form them into justice: "They will shine eternally in the skies like the stars of the heavens." With the hope of this glory, we must generously complete the Lord's work.

—Basil Moreau

WHEN I WAS a seminarian, I had on my desk this very passage from scripture about those who lead others to justice and so shine eternally like the stars of the heavens. While at the time I was unaware that this passage was a favorite of Fr. Moreau's, I was aware of the many ways that Holy Cross attempted to engage people on the margins and to work for justice. In our parishes, high schools, social services, and colleges and universities this work for the Lord was being done then and it continues today.

God calls all of us in a special way to the work of justice. Our efforts, which are his, must reach out to the afflicted and in a preferential way to the poor and all those in need. Yet, beyond our own efforts, we must continually seek to draw others into this work. It is precisely through what Fr. Moreau writes about, through teaching the truth to others and helping form them into justice, that we encourage all of our brothers and sisters to walk with the poor and the oppressed. It is a difficult walk, but one that will surely lead them, as it leads all of us, to seek the coming of God's kingdom in our world.

In doing so, we will proclaim the gospel that calls us to bring good news to the poor, liberty to captives, sight to the blind, and freedom to the oppressed. Wherever and whatever our service may be, we all share this mission.

William Lies, C.S.C.

We want to live our vows in such a way that our lives will call into question the fascinations of our world: pleasure, wealth and power. Prophets stand before the world as signs of that which has enduring value, and prophets speak and act in the world as companions of the Lord in the service of his kingdom. We pray to live our vows well enough to offer such witness and service.
— Holy Cross Constitutions

ONE OF THE joys of serving as a parish priest is the sheer diversity of people and needs. The day may start with a school assembly, move through a funeral, and end with adult education classes, marriage prep, or general spiritual counseling. So many souls, and all of us are yearning for the grace of God.

One day a young woman came seeking advice, feeling caught between two relationships. She loved living with her family and caring for her toddler nieces and nephews. But her boyfriend, the man whom she felt was the love of her life, was pressuring her to move in with him. Her family did not approve because they did not trust his shady past and persistent refusal to marry her. To move in with him meant leaving her family behind.

We spent a painful, yet graced hour together. Like many of us, she was struggling with the fascinations of the world, a world that taught her that love is only something we feel rather than also a decision we make requiring commitment and sacrifice. It taught her that her happiness is the most important thing. But there was still something inside her soul—the light of God's grace—that made her hesitate simply to yield to her boyfriend and his promises. I do not know what she decided. I only pray that my vows, faithfully lived, stand as a sign to keep in her heart the fundamental question for all Christians: What will be best for the life of my immortal soul?

Eric Schimmel, C.S.C.

April 10

It seems to me I hear the voice of God, saying to us as formerly to His people: Salvabo te, noli timere—*"I will save you, do not fear."*

—Edward Sorin

As the Israelites stood at the far end of the Red Sea, having just crossed over dry land and witnessed the destruction of Pharaoh's army, they were abundantly aware of God's power to save. They now knew that they did not need to fear their enemies, for God was with them.

We Christians stand at the other side of the Cross of Christ, and so we, too, are abundantly aware of our Lord's power to save. We have witnessed the love of the Father made manifest in the Son: in his actions, in his preaching, in his suffering, indeed, in his very person. We have witnessed the reign of sin and death torn asunder by the passion, death, and resurrection of Jesus. In this we now know that there is nothing we need to fear. We need not fear our enemies; they can do no worse to us than they did to our Master. Indeed, we now know that we can even love them.

There is nothing left to fear in being full-hearted in living out our Christian vocation: to proclaim the good news, to assist those in need, to witness to the call to love, and to invite others to follow. As we unite ourselves to Christ, to his life and to his death, we become one in his way of living and in the salvation he offers us all. To live in Christ is to know of his power to save and to live fearlessly in light of it.

James T. Gallagher, C.S.C.

☩

April 11

Love calls forth love.

—Edward Sorin

JASON WAS INITIATED into our church two years ago. He is a recovering heroin addict. His recovery has had its struggles and relapses. Yet Jason has been clean since the time he joined the Church. And now he is the proud father of a baby girl. She was baptized at our parish on Easter. Her birth has changed him. One morning before Sunday Mass, Jason looked at his daughter sleeping in his arms and said, "She is God's mercy. God is giving me another chance in life." Jason has known the healing of God's love. Now his daughter is drawing love out of him. Love calls forth love.

Mary is one of our volunteers at the hospitality center at our parish. She has lived on the streets. She understands those who are suffering and afflicted; she has been where they are. She does not judge the poor she serves, but encourages them. She loves them by offering hope when they are trying to better their situations. She comes to Sunday Mass with other friends in recovery. Mary's presence in our community, through her prayer, her faith in God's mercy, and her love for the poor, is a witness to the reality of God's healing. Indeed, love calls forth love.

One thing we have learned as a parish staff, serving many people in downtown Portland who are homeless, mentally ill, or afflicted with addictions is that we can't fix people. We can welcome and love them. We place our faith in the center of their human experience and trust that God's love can bring needed change. So often we see how the experience of healing triggers a response to be caring and compassionate. Jason and Mary, and others like them in our community, show to all of us how love calls forth love.

Bob Loughery, C.S.C.

April 12

When I speak of visitations from Divine Providence, whether they apply to individuals, or families, or nations, we Religious readily understand they are always merciful means which our Heavenly Father uses for the salvation of His children. However severe they may appear, if properly received and acted upon, they never fail to create amendment and reach their intended, ultimate result.

—Edward Sorin

SOME YEARS AGO I was serving as the superior of a house of eight priests engaged in various activities. One evening at the supper table, two of the priests got into a rather heated argument, the point of which escapes me now. We all left the table in silence, and an atmosphere of tension pervaded our residence. As the superior, I thought that it was my pastoral responsibility to mediate between the two men who had had the argument, but I had no idea how to go about it. Both men were at least twenty years older than me, and one of them had been my teacher in the seminary. I went to bed pondering my options and slept fitfully.

The next morning we all gathered for Mass in the chapel. Just before Mass began, one of the two priests stood up and said that he wanted to ask forgiveness for anything offensive that he had said at supper the previous night. He walked across the chapel and extended his hand to the other man with whom he had been arguing. The other man accepted the apology.

It is tempting to think that by our wit and wisdom we shall solve all our problems. In this instance it was my brother's welcoming of the grace of God that brought reconciliation and healing.

James Connelly, C.S.C.

April 13

Here is the secret of success for each and for all—a good will. Let us think less of ourselves and more of our God and of our neighbor.

—Edward Sorin

FR. SORIN BIDS us to be of good will by thinking of others first. But this is difficult to do when we are caught up in our own pain. We simply cannot force ourselves to change our feelings and be bright and cheery when despair barges into our lives. Yet being of good will, and not necessarily of good feeling, can work wonders.

Marietta knows this firsthand. A twenty-six-year-old deranged man abducted her seven-year-old daughter Susie from the family's tent during a camping trip. He tortured and killed her. Marietta felt intense rage and the need for revenge, but tried hard not to overburden others with her sorrows and struggles. She was being of good will, thinking of others first. Her doing so helped her to carry her unimaginable grief a little more lightly. It also led her to think of what kind of inner torture the perpetrator must have endured to motivate himself to do such a heinous act. With the help of prayer, such consideration led Marietta to have a phone conversation with the man during which she was able to listen caringly and compassionately. This special conversation led the man to reveal inadvertently information that made it possible for the FBI to identify and arrest him.

Continuing to think of others, she succeeded in getting the man a life sentence rather than capital punishment. She did not want to memorialize her daughter's killing with another death, creating only another victim and another grieving family. Marietta knows that being of good will and thinking of others first heals hearts. She now travels the world, offering workshops on the power of forgiveness made possible by God's mercy and compassion for all of us.

Bill Faiella, C.S.C.

April 14

It does one good to see the wisdom of those great champions of the faith "who chose the better part." They passed from a momentary tribulation into endless joy.
—Edward Sorin

ONE OF THE many highlights of the ordination liturgy to the priesthood is the litany of saints. Just before the litany begins, all those assembled kneel, while those to be ordained lie prostrate on the ground. Once people are in place, the litany begins and for the next five minutes the choir intones the names of saints throughout history, with the assembly chanting in response, "Pray for us."

The litany of saints is a wonderful reminder of God's love for us. From the very beginning of time, God has shed his love upon the earth, and we are reminded of that love through the service of so many faithful men and women. These holy disciples of the Lord were no different from us. Throughout the course of their earthly lives, they experienced difficulty, but they kept their focus on what mattered most—the love of God and his fidelity to his children.

Today, in a world that seems to reject the presence of God, we can be tempted to despair. Yet it is precisely at these moments that we must seek the wisdom and strength of those who have gone before us. The litany of saints is not reserved solely for the ordination of priests or even liturgy in general. It is a prayer that can and should be used in our daily lives. There is no reason that we should act alone on our journeys to discover the Lord, for through the intercession of so many faithful people we already have access to our loving God in so many wonderful ways.

Holy Mary, Mother of God, pray for us. St. Joseph, pray for us. Blessed Brother André, pray for us. Blessed Basil Moreau, pray for us.

Peter McCormick, C.S.C.

April 15

The Savior gently rebuked His apostles for being so slow in believing the Resurrection. He then opened to them a vast field for their zealous efforts. He promised them He was going to remain with them and with all of His future disciples until the end of time.

—Basil Moreau

EVEN THOUGH WE, like the first disciples, have been slow to believe in the power of the resurrection, Holy Cross still finds great strength in the risen Christ's promise to be with us always. Sustained by this assurance, Holy Cross can establish a university in North East India with very little funding. We can journey into areas of Africa where few of us speak the language and establish vibrant parish communities. We can minister through Family Rosary in the Philippines for more than fifty years with no full-time Holy Cross member assigned there and still encourage the people's prayerful and bloodless confrontation with a powerful dictatorship. In these and so many other challenging missions, nothing can separate us from the love of God—not malaria, not ambush, not revolution, not governmental oppression.

Our belief in the resurrection means belief in new life which comes from the Father. Just as Jesus was raised from the dead, so we also can be raised to new heights in the vast fields where we direct our zealous efforts. The risen One is in all of us who are touched by Holy Cross's education in the faith and auxiliary service to the Church. Graduates of Holy Cross institutions can educate the poor in their midst. Lawyers, judges, business leaders, and health workers can mark their work with fairness and justice. All Christian men and women can dedicate themselves to outreach to the disadvantaged. If we believe in the One who is risen from the dead and who remains with and in us, the world will know new life, even peace.

John Phalen, C.S.C.

To maintain ourselves in the sublime vow of chastity we must, as St. Peter says, make our souls chaste by obedience to charity. This means yielding ourselves more and more generously to the law of supernatural love, which refers all things to God and undertakes and suffers everything for His glory.

—Basil Moreau

ALL OF OUR souls long for union with God. And this searching, longing, and desiring ultimately can only be fulfilled in God. In grasping at images to try to capture this deepest of human yearnings, mystics from the Old Testament onward have turned to the image of a bride longing for her bridegroom. In using such sensual imagery, the mystics point to the true intensity with which our souls ache for God.

Fr. Moreau knew this intense yearning of the soul for God, and he taught his spiritual sons and daughters the language of making our souls chaste and ever faithful in seeking God. Fr. Moreau did not dwell on the sacrificial nature of the vow of chastity; he invited his religious to experience the vow as a state of being that allowed a person to be more generous in service and to keep God at the forefront of everything in life. And, as history testifies, this vow has allowed Fr. Moreau and his band of men not to be concerned with comfort and personal needs, but instead to spread the gospel for the sake of the kingdom, making God known, loved, and served.

Our coming to know, love, and serve God, and then making him known, loved, and served by others is a pathway open for all of us to ever deeper mystical union with him. It is the pathway of charity, that in love for our Lord we might be generous in serving our neighbor. In yielding ourselves in this service, we will be evermore united with the God of love.

Tom Eckert, C.S.C.

April 17

Great abilities, unless supported by virtues, are in danger, and seldom prove a blessing.

—Edward Sorin

USE IT OR lose it. We probably have all heard this saying and perhaps even used it ourselves. It expresses our need to take full and responsible advantage of the talents and opportunities with which God has blessed us. For if we neglect our gifts, we will lose what we already have been given. At the same time, in taking advantage of our God-given talents, we must be careful to use them properly because our strengths and gifts can easily become harmful to ourselves and others when used irresponsibly. If we are too strong and confrontational, we may become less compassionate. Our penchant for organization, taken too far, may make us overbearing. In these cases, our great abilities cease to be blessings.

Fr. Sorin thus reminds us that we must clothe our talents in virtue so that we can effectively use these special gifts to support the common good. Through virtues—such as humility, generosity, and charity—we can direct our academic acumen, organizational skill, pulpit eloquence, indeed, all of our God-given abilities, in ways that are welcoming, helpful, and empowering to others. For it is ultimately in uniting our gifts and our talents with Jesus' efforts to build the kingdom of God in our world that they become the blessings they are truly meant to be—for ourselves and for others. Only in such faithful service to God in small matters will we be given greater responsibilities and ultimately be invited to share in our master's joy.

Richard Gribble, C.S.C.

April 18

There is no failure the Lord's love cannot reverse, no humiliation he cannot exchange for blessing, no anger he cannot dissolve, no routine he cannot transfigure. All is swallowed up in victory. He has nothing but gifts to offer. It remains only for us to find how even the Cross can be borne as a gift.

—Holy Cross Constitutions

OUR FUNDAMENTAL SACRAMENT, the Eucharist, is named for Jesus' acts of thanksgiving at the Last Supper. On one level, Jesus simply did what observant Jews always do before they eat: he thanked God for bread from the earth and fruit of the vine. But the Passover was no ordinary meal, and the Last Supper was no ordinary Passover, for the bread and wine

Jesus blessed and shared anticipated his sacrifice on the Cross. Since we offer thanks precisely for gifts, in this meal Jesus first revealed how even the Cross can be borne as a gift.

Just hours later, however, Jesus prayed, asking the Father that this cup might pass from him. Christ himself seemed to want to return the very gifts he had instituted at that first Eucharist. And yet, these two different attitudes—thankfulness and reluctance—reveal the paradoxical truth about suffering. For if we cannot give thanks, we do not bear the Cross as *gift*. But if we do not acknowledge the reality of our suffering, we do not bear *the Cross* as gift. Only in reluctance, only in the plea to God for deliverance, do we really bear the Cross. To bear a cross without fear is an act of extreme denial or inhuman stoicism. If God's gift to us is a real Cross, then our gift back to God is the acceptance of this Cross with our real, unglorified humanity, the very humanity assumed by his Son. For only in light of the eternal Easter will we understand the gift's true reality; only then can we proclaim with the risen Christ that it was necessary to suffer these things to enter into glory" (Lk 24:26).

Charles McCoy, C.S.C.

April 19

Zealous teachers know that all students are equally important to God and that their duty is to work for each with the same devotion, watchfulness, and perseverance.

—Basil Moreau

MOREAU'S ULTIMATE VISION for his congregation was that we be educators in the faith. In our history, this charge has been interpreted quite broadly to include the many and varied ways that we as vowed apostolic religious attend to educating for faith. One of the more direct ways that we do this is as teachers in the classroom. There is in our ministry, apart from the context within which each of us teaches and regardless of our respective disciplines, the demand to see in each of our students their cherished nature. Continued scholarship and professional development inform our ministry on every level. But more even than our attempts to keep abreast of the latest research methods and most effective pedagogy, we seek to root our learning, and that of our students, in an incarnational paradigm—one in which we know and appreciate the power and presence of a living God in and through one another.

Moreau teaches that education is a balance between the heart and mind, between faith and reason. The story is told in the community of a high school teacher released from his contract at mid-year because he could not manage a classroom. Afterward, the department chair remarked, "I don't understand it. In the past, he taught math at the college level." The superior quickly responded, "Ah, therein lies the rub. Here we teach *students*." Like for many of us, it is often easier for teachers to deal with matters of the head than with matters of the heart. As Holy Cross religious we strive to do both and invite others to do the same.

Jim Lies, C.S.C.

April 20

Year after year our faith in prayer has increased. We feel and realize that God has blessed among ourselves nothing but what has by prayer been made His own work.

—Edward Sorin

STOCKHOLDERS ANXIOUSLY AWAIT periodic reports to find out how earnings on their investments have increased. Perhaps for many, Fr. Sorin's report, though showing a steady growth, might be a disappointment. He simply states faith in the power of prayer has increased. This is not a common measure of growth, but for Fr. Sorin brick, mortar, and prayer were inseparable companions for success. He wanted to keep this essential relationship always before his fellow religious and himself. Like many other movers and shakers in the Church, Sorin agonized over whether what he was doing was just his invention in collaboration with other like-minded people or something that came from the God whom he wished to serve by it. The ultimate hope was that they were one and the same. And so they should not be looking for personal gains on their investment but growth in the greater mission. Increase in faith in prayer, therefore, is a good measure by which to judge.

In our daily lives committed to the Lord's service, the same struggle is present—the one with which the psalmist wrestled. If it isn't the Lord who's building the house, our efforts, as dedicated and skilled as they might be, are in vain. We need to remind ourselves that the house is not ours, and so it is best built in conversation with the God who invites us to build it, relying on the fact that from him comes the necessary strength to do it. This conversation takes time and patient constancy year after year. But for restless, energetic people struck with zeal for their mission, that is challenging. So, we must struggle as did Fr. Sorin, but in the fruits of this labor we find hope for ourselves.

Don Fetters, C.S.C.

April 21

We shall have most to share with others by dwelling together as brothers in unity.
—Holy Cross Constitutions

WHEN I REFLECT on my calling to the religious life and priesthood in Holy Cross, I am reminded that what most attracted me was living and working in brotherhood. I wanted to share in and be nourished by the gifts and resources of others while they helped me to develop my own. I wanted to know that I did not have to walk my spiritual and apostolic journey alone, but with others who had forged a path ahead, leading the way. The brothers I now live and work with at our community's assisted-living and medical facility, where I am the religious superior, are living testaments to my goals and purpose as a Holy Cross religious and priest. It is by walking in their footsteps that I strive to follow in union with them.

In religious life we discern God's will in unity together with our brothers, seeking to lead lives of fraternal love and mutual inspiration. We know that what we share is not ours but the result of God's gifts and blessing upon each of us. These individual gifts are then focused and intensified by the lenses of our shared experiences in community.

Yet as in any community, our very God-given uniqueness is sometimes as much a burden as it is a gift. Only through shared reconciliation, then, can we move forward, acknowledging the value of our differences. Often our uniqueness can cause us to become overly judgmental, short-sighted, self-centered, and even angry. Seeing Jesus in each person with whom we dwell, however, will lead us to value our differences and cherish our uniqueness. Then as brothers and sisters in Christ, we can give thanks for the ways in which we help to complete each other's lives.

Charlie Kohlerman, C.S.C.

☫

April 22

The more Divine Providence is pleased to bless the works which it has confided to us and for which we are jointly responsible, the more keenly do I feel the weight of my responsibility and the more deeply I am convinced of the need of personal holiness if I am not to be an obstacle to God's design for each one of you.

—Basil Moreau

DIVINE PROVIDENCE IS neither magic nor attainable by mere human achievement. Instead, it is the marriage between divine initiative and human response. It is the reality we experience when we stop seeing God's design as something foreign to us and begin to see ourselves within that design. Divine Providence is not a suit we must go out to buy, be fitted for, and then live in. It is a reality already at work in us into which we awaken through prayer and attentive listening.

In awaking to the design that God has already inscribed on our hearts, we discover that our only responsibility is to respond. Ultimately, this response does not consist of a list of things to do but is a call to wake up and be—for personal holiness is a way of being in the world. As I discerned my own call to the priesthood, it did not come down to whether I believed I could do everything God might ask of me. The real question that haunted me, the real weight of the responsibility I felt, was whether I could be who he was asking me to be. And that question could only be answered through listening and then responding to what God had already planted within my own heart.

Thus, if we truly seek to do God's will, we cannot rely on our will alone nor can we count on our lives magically unfolding. The only way to fulfill God's designs for us is to listen and to respond continually to the workings of grace in our lives, thereby creating that union between our human response and God's initiative that is Divine Providence.

Jeffrey Cooper, C.S.C.

April 23

I shall have no fears for the congregation, and even if all of you had abandoned me on hearing of our catastrophes, I should have begun all over again as soon as I could, so convinced am I that what I have undertaken is the will of God.

—Basil Moreau

WHEN FR. SORIN returned to Notre Dame from one of his trips to Montreal, he arrived to find the main building burned to the ground with bricks still smoldering. The small university that he and his brothers in Holy Cross had founded was destroyed. His reaction was to gather the community together in Sacred Heart Church. He exhorted and challenged the discouraged religious. They had to rebuild, but even bigger than the previous time, for the fire could only be a sign that Mary had even greater designs for the university consecrated to her name. And they did rebuild. The brothers began pulling the still-hot bricks from the rubble. They made more bricks and rebuilt the Main Building, topping it with a glorious golden dome and a statue of Our Lady.

We might think about how much would have been lost if Fr. Sorin and the Holy Cross community had given up that day. They had no way of knowing how different the world would be because of their resolve. So many lives have been touched, including not only students, faculty, alumni, employees, and supporters, but also people who are simply proud of the most famous Catholic university in the United States.

We all want to be careful in claiming to know and do the will of God. We know there have been cases of people who imposed things on others claiming it to be God's will. But we mustn't be slow to reflect on his will and to be firm in challenging ourselves to be faithful and committed to it. We don't know how much good may be depending upon it.

John S. Korcsmar, C.S.C.

April 24

Just as abyss calls to abyss and one sin begets another, so one grace gives rise to another if we are faithful to the first. Let us then go to the foot of the altar to thank the God of all goodness for the new proof of His mercy, which He has bestowed upon us.

—Basil Moreau

THE MOST IMPORTANT question I was asked while studying for my MBA was put to me by a close friend while walking across the quad. As I was ranting about the crises in the Archdiocese of Boston and how squandered trust was impacting me and future generations in the Church, Lex interrupted me and asked, "How's your gratitude?" My first response was an incredulous bark, so calmly he asked again, "How's your gratitude, Fr. Tom?"

In physics, momentum is a function of mass and velocity. In human organizations, momentum is a powerful, intangible force that can mysteriously propel or thwart progress. Sin and selfishness have a cunning way of self-perpetuating, but they are rendered impotent when confronted with gratitude. Gratitude, with its source in Christ, is the first and fundamental disposition for a Christian. And, when personal gratitude is prayed for, cultivated, and cherished, it proves contagious, spreading rapidly and transforming both those with whom we have contact and ourselves.

The Eucharist itself is the greatest thanksgiving, the greatest act of gratitude, drawing into one and enlivening all who share in Jesus' gift of himself. So it is that when we bring our grateful selves to the altar, and hear the line from the eucharistic prayer, "Lord, we thank you for counting us worthy to stand in your presence and serve you," we and all the world are transformed, one grace after another.

Tom Doyle, C.S.C.

April 25

As religious, we spend daily considerable time before the Tabernacle; these precious visits alone should amply suffice to keep the fire of faith burning in our hearts day and night.

—Edward Sorin

CARDINAL JOHN F. O'Hara, C.S.C., referred to Notre Dame as the "City of the Blessed Sacrament." Today, with sanctuary lamps burning before tabernacles in more than forty chapels, it is easy to see why this name is appropriate. And yet, Notre Dame has been a city of the Blessed Sacrament from its earliest days. One of the most touching letters Fr. Sorin wrote to Fr. Moreau tells of how encouraging it was for the young Holy Cross community to see the flickering of the sanctuary lamp through the window of their simple residence as they returned from hard work clearing the fields each day.

In view of the many trials and hardships that Fr. Sorin and the other priests and brothers endured, and among many graces and consolations they enjoyed, the presence of the consecrated host in their simple tabernacle must have been special. While they always would have the grace to celebrate Eucharist together, the last measure of oil to keep their sanctuary lamp burning would mark the temporary end of their ability to visit Jesus Christ present in the reserved sacrament. I suspect it is not too far-fetched to imagine that the first item on their shopping list even when funds were scarce would have been oil in order to keep lit the lamp that beckoned them so warmly, inviting them to visit their Lord and Savior and be renewed.

So, too, must all of us seek this same spiritual nourishment by making time to be in the Lord's presence before the reserved sacrament. In return, he will keep the fire of faith burning in our hearts day and night.

Richard V. Warner, C.S.C.

April 26

Peter became the Lord's true and reliable disciple not during the days he followed in Galilee but after he disowned his Lord and wept and was given the opportunity not to become as he once was but to serve as he never had served.

—Holy Cross Constitutions

PETER DESERVED TO hear the words, "You're fired." Stubborn, self-righteous, and cocky, Peter made his share of mistakes during his three-year apprenticeship with Jesus. But they had become friends, and Jesus was always able to cast a net deep into Peter's heart and draw out the love and goodness that was in there. It was because of this love and friendship, however, that Peter's betrayal of Jesus was all the more shocking and devastating, and no one felt it more than Peter himself. We can only imagine the guilt and shame this rock of the Church must have felt at what he'd done to his beloved friend.

But as we know, there is always more to the story when dealing with Jesus. What Peter was to discover on the shores of the Sea of Galilee, what we hopefully all discover in our lives, is that love is stronger than all the wrong we might do, that it is stronger even than death. On the beach after his resurrection, Jesus asked Peter the only question that mattered, "Do you love me?" In their exchange, echoed three times, all was forgiven and set right, all was healed and made new. Jesus gave Peter back to himself.

So it is with us. We know what it is like to fail, to disappoint ourselves and others, to bear the weight of sin and guilt. In each of these moments, over and over throughout our lives, Jesus whispers into our hearts his question, "Do you love me?" When we murmur back our yes, however tentative, Jesus heals us and sends us, like Peter, on our way to serve others.

Peter Jarret, C.S.C.

April 27

We must first seek the kingdom of God and His justice and then trust in Providence. That is why I beg of you to renew yourselves in the spirit of your vocation, which is the spirit of poverty, chastity, and obedience.

—Basil Moreau

WHEN I TAUGHT college history courses, my students' first assignment was to write their own obituary. It was not a task most freshmen and sophomores relished, but the exercise demonstrated that everyone contributes to history, even if their names never appear in textbooks. It also made them consider, if briefly, how they might want to be remembered in the end.

Interestingly, none ever bragged about accrued wealth and worldly fame. They did not boast about breaking laws or neglecting responsibilities. The universal theme was that they hoped to be loved. Religious vows are public commitments, but they represent basic aspirations that dwell deep within every heart to be courageous and generous, self-disciplined and accountable. Religious vows, indeed every Christian vocation, drawn out of this desire, seek first the kingdom of God and the love for which we all long. Whatever illusions we hold about controlling our lives in our desire for fulfillment, the details of most daily events and encounters seem quite random and unpredictable. Trusting in Providence, however, we learn to greet the sun, acutely aware that the ultimate goal is salvation, and we are little deterred by trials tumbling into our paths.

We are called to shape our days with prayer, knowing that we are and always will be fully embraced by the Divine Presence, even in our folly, and so we strive to dedicate the hours from morning to night to being selfless, faithful, and dutiful. Our common human longing is to die as we have lived. It is our only hope.

James B. King, C.S.C.

☩

April 28

Let us not forget that it is not money or talents which do great things for God, but faith, prayer and fidelity to the rule.

—Basil Moreau

WHEN BR. ANDRÉ Mottais, C.S.C., set foot on Algerian soil in 1840, he knew little about the country to which he was sent, but he accepted that Fr. Moreau wanted him to use his administrative and teaching talents in this new mission territory. André had been the most important of the Brothers of St. Joseph, founded by Fr. Dujarie, who later became the brothers of Holy Cross. He had served as novice master and spiritual director in the community for fifteen years. Yet when André's new superior, Fr. Moreau, sent him to Africa, he did not hesitate even when it seemed that the place had less use for his talents than he and his superior had hoped. Debilitated by disease and wracked by spiritual darkness, he nonetheless continued on, realizing that talents alone are not the most important things in life. Fidelity to God's will—that is what is most important.

We sometimes think that our greatest obligation to God is to hone our talents for mathematics, or preaching, or counseling. When we find ourselves in situations where our talents are underutilized, however, we must make the greatest act of faith we can and accept with childlike grace what God sends our way.

Like Br. André Mottais, we wait in silence and peaceful reflection for God to manifest his expectations. Then we swallow hard and move forward, trusting in prayer that God knows what is best for us. Faith is a greater gift than any accomplishment of our own doing. Acceptance of Divine Providence makes greater sense than the greatest of talents developed in the absence of God's guidance.

George Klawitter, C.S.C.

April 29

To spend ourselves and be spent for the needs of neighbors; to be available and cheerful as a friend in Holy Cross and to give witness while others hesitate; to stand by duty when it has become all burden and no delight . . . community too can draw us nearer Calvary.
—Holy Cross Constitutions

A LEGENDARY HOLY Cross priest, Fr. Charles Sheedy, C.S.C., left a legacy of many witty and deeply spiritual one-liners. One of his best went like this: "Community life is all about just showing up." Family life is not so different. To come to meals on time and disposed to enter into conversation, to be well dressed and ready to leave for Sunday church, to show up at weddings, funerals, birthdays, and anniversaries, speaks volumes about our love for our families.

If, in addition to simply showing up, we can help out with community tasks and carry the burdens of others, it is a bonus. If we are able to show up, forgetting the grudges and wounds of the past, and be polite and interested with even our unfriendly neighbor, this graciousness will recall the kind of unconditional acceptance God gives each of us every day. Just to do our jobs, completing what is required even if it is not done quite perfectly, remains a mighty contribution.

Our world would grow in peace and love if we all just did our jobs; and it would be all the better if we did them humbly and kindly. For indeed, none of us stands alone. We support one another by our very presence and by our fidelity to what is asked of us. And that will mean, at times, that we will find ourselves at the foot of the crosses of others. But we need hardly speak. Just to stand alongside will be enough.

Nicholas Ayo, C.S.C.

April 30

Each one of us may apply to himself the words said of the Divine Infant by Simeon: "Behold this Child is set for the fall and for the resurrection of many in Israel." None can prove indifferent: all must have either the merit of raising high the flag under which he is enrolled or seeing it dragged to the dust.

—Edward Sorin

THOUGH WE WERE unaware, we were once held aloft as infants by our parents, family members, and friends who pronounced great things that would come from us: "She's going to be a great doctor," or "He's going to be a ball player." Anything was possible, from curing cancer to being a great president or priest. God has equipped each one of us from our birth with the gifts necessary to make a difference in our world, and he expects us to use them. For, as Jesus taught, to whom much has been given, much is expected.

One of the more challenging verses of scripture for me is Revelation 3:15–16, where God says, "I wish you were either cold or hot. So because you are lukewarm, neither hot nor cold, I will spit you out of my mouth." This passage makes it clear that we cannot be mere bystanders in life. Jesus challenged those of his day who were simply trying to get by in life by doing the minimum; and he is challenging us, too.

It is hard when we take a stand or step out in faith. We are uncomfortable with being challenged to live or act a certain way and will resist the one who brings that challenge. Then again, no one ever said that the Christian life would be a comfortable one. We are promised, however, that if we remain faithful to the end and utilize our God-given gifts, we, too, will reign with Jesus in heaven.

Bill Wack, C.S.C.

MAY

May 1

*St. Joseph, who was so noble by reason of his ancestry
and so eminent because of the mission entrusted to him,
lived a humble life, earning his bread in the sweat of his
brow, following the plans of Divine Providence, obeying
the powers of earth, and resigning himself to the most
difficult trials. Behold our model and the model for all
the faithful.*

—Basil Moreau

I DON'T REMEMBER when I first met St. Joseph, but I know
that I was still a boy. The pictures in my children's bible
showed him either walking beside a donkey or working in
his carpenter's shop. My own father had a workbench and
would often help me use the tools. I remember thinking that
Jesus and Joseph were very lucky always to be able to smell
sawdust.

My appreciation for Joseph didn't develop until later in
my life when I was a young adult and relearning that we
don't always get what we want. Pouting and dejected, I ran to
Jesus for comfort, and met Joseph along the way. As I again
read his story, I realized that Joseph had to keep revising his
expectations for his life. Imagine being told, "Your fiancée is
pregnant, but it's not yours." Or, "There is no room in this
inn." Or, how about dreaming of angels who always give life-
changing commands? "Marry the woman." "Flee to Egypt."
"Return to Nazareth."

Joseph, without complaint, took the bumps in the road, the changes to the plan. He didn't need to understand everything, nor did he bargain to do things his way. In the grand drama of our salvation, he was just a supporting actor—without even one line. Silent, steadfast, and reliable, Joseph shows us when our plans disintegrate that God still has a plan—one that includes a role for us. Trustworthy, loyal, and just, Joseph shows us how to carry on despite initial disappointment, believing that God will finish the good work that he has begun in us.

Brent Krueger, C.S.C.

May 2

We never have enough of good hands. The humblest and most unpretending, if animated with a good will, will give glory to God.

—Edward Sorin

WHEN MEETING SUCCESSFUL people, I tend to come away with one of two very general impressions. Some strike me as overbearing, carrying perhaps a prideful confidence stemming from their successes. Other individuals are unpretenious, seemingly more attentive to conflicting viewpoints, and thus, less imposing. By most standards, both types of people are equally intelligent, confident, and passionate about their work. Yet, more often than not, the less pretentious people are those who leave the more lasting positive marks on us.

Successful people who exhibit humility and lack pretense are not necessarily meek or dispassionate. As talented and as important they may actually be, they recognize that others could fulfill the same duties with equal proclivity. Thus, they bring a certain strength and honesty to daily interactions that communicate the conviction that their truest, most confident self abides in something greater than their work. Simply put, they recognize their transient place in the world.

We, too, are called to live with such humble conviction, always animated by a good will that seeks to do God's. Both our humility and our conviction deepen as we come to recognize God's omnipresent goodness. In seeking a greater good than our own, we allow God to transform our will into our most prominent, yet unpretentious, quality. In this way, we are given the blessed opportunity to be humble prophets heralding Jesus' message through the very work of our hands.

Jesus Alonso, C.S.C.

May 3

Brethren, how happy I find myself to be able to offer the sacrifice of my whole being for souls for whose salvation I have so many times made the same sacrifice.

—Jacques Dujarie

THE BIG SACRIFICE of our lives only follows upon smaller sacrifices made along the way. Over and over again, we want to do the will of God. We want to say yes. We want to be instruments in God's hands. But, if we go forward with too predetermined an idea of what he intends for us, we might miss the very invitations he gives us to say yes to his will.

I came to Holy Cross from a family of four generations of educators. My great-grandmother taught elementary school for more than five decades. My father is a university professor. I pictured myself being a priest and professor at the University of Notre Dame. God, however, opened another way for me. My saying yes to that unexpected invitation first led me to South America, then Arizona, and then back to Indiana. Serving souls in parish ministry has been a gift that I never anticipated. In less than eight years, I have baptized more than one thousand six hundred infants. I have married more than two hundred couples. I have buried more than four hundred people. I have celebrated at least two thousand five hundred masses. In all of this, I am left more thankful and joyful than ever for my vocation as a Holy Cross priest.

Before God changed my plans, I understood vocation as my gift to God. Now, however, I understand that all Christian vocations are God's gift to us. Through fidelity and repetition, the little "yes" of each day, wherever it leads, becomes the supreme "Yes" to the God who loved us into being.

Christopher Cox, C.S.C.

May 4

In the Holy Eucharist, He is joined to matter; and by this wonderful act of His love, He left us His Body and Blood until the end of the world.

—Basil Moreau

"BEHOLD, I AM with you always, until then end of the age" (Mt 28:20). With these last words, Jesus promised that he would not leave us orphans. He would remain with us in his words and works. And so he instituted the seven sacraments as signs of permanence, as sources of strength, and as channels of grace. Indeed, they maintain his presence among us.

And primary among the sacraments is the Eucharist. In the Mass, in that simple ritual with a few spoken words, a tremendous transformation takes place. For when Jesus took bread and said it was his body and took wine and said it was his blood, he indicated that the immensity of the Divine is captured and contained in this now-consecrated bread and blessed wine. In other words, Jesus was telling the apostles and all of us that he will be with us, body, blood, soul, and divinity, in the blessed host and the sacred wine. Yes, through the words of consecration Jesus truly is present in our midst today. What a tremendous gift.

If we keep the Eucharist in mind, we don't have to look far when we hear Jesus summon us: Come to me all you who are hungry, all you who are thirsty, and all you who are lonely. For we will know where to find him: on the altar during the Mass, in the sacred host in the tabernacle, in the monstrance during exposition. There is Jesus the Son of God, the Son of Mary; there is Jesus true God and true man; there is Jesus our teacher and friend, with us until the end of the world.

Alfred D'Alonzo, C.S.C.

May 5

The pagans called the first followers of Jesus "Christians" because they saw that the disciples followed what Christ did and said. When we become Christians, we become children of God by grace as Jesus Christ, the Son of God, is Himself by nature.

—Basil Moreau

IN THE CHURCH, we often speak of all human beings as the children of God, for God has revealed himself as one who loves each of us as Father. But we also speak of baptism as the sacrament by which we become children of God. It is by God's grace, free and unmerited, that we enter into the relationship of faith that makes us his own. What does it mean to be God's sons and daughters? Jesus tells us that our love must be transformed beyond the natural loyalty and affection we give to family, friends, and those who share our nationality. We must love even our enemies. It is then that we will "rightly be called sons of the Most High, since He Himself is good to the ungrateful and the wicked" (Lk 6:35).

While in one sense we become God's children in an instant, in another sense it is a process that unfolds over a lifetime. More and more, God's grace calls us out of our preoccupation with ourselves and into a new perspective in which we look upon the world through his eyes. We see through God's eyes when our primary concern is the salvation—the total wellbeing in this life and beyond—of every human being. We see through God's eyes when our first concern is to uncover, even in the case of people we find difficult or even evil, signs of God's hidden grace at work in them. For to become children of God is to be transformed into the image of Christ. To the extent that such transformation takes place, our attitudes and actions will allow those who encounter us to encounter Christ.

John P. Reardon, C.S.C.

May 6

If we are not animated by the spirit of the saints, the important work of Holy Cross will come to naught, and our efforts for the sanctification of youth will be vain and useless.

—Basil Moreau

THE SPIRIT CHANGES everything. Water becomes the wellspring of everlasting life. Oil becomes the bearer of the seal of God's abiding presence. Bread and wine become the body and blood of Christ. The Spirit indeed changes everything.

The Spirit changes everyone. Immersed in the waters of baptism, consecrated with the oil of gladness, and nourished with the eucharistic bread and wine, we are invited into the life of the Father, Son, and Holy Spirit. In these sacred mysteries of love's extravagance, we are conformed to Christ and drawn into the fellowship of his Body, the Church, the communion of saints.

The Spirit changes every work. Recreated by the grace of the sacraments and animated by the spirit of the saints, we no longer live merely ordinary lives. For our ordinary labors become extraordinary as the Spirit enables us in the way of God's own, self-emptying love. All our works, imbued with God's love, become a prayer—a prayer that calls forth the Spirit who lives in us and beyond us. Thus, enlivened by this same Spirit, our human work becomes the means of the sanctification of youth and of all for whom and with whom we labor.

The Spirit changes everything, everyone, every work. Both the work of Holy Cross and the work of all God's children depend on this sanctifying power of the Spirit. If truly we are grounded, transformed, and sent in his life-giving Spirit, our efforts will never be in vain.

Thomas P. Looney, C.S.C.

May 7

It is essential to our mission that we strive to abide so attentively together that people will observe: "See how they love one another." We will then be a sign in an alienated world: men who have, for love of their Lord, become closest neighbors, trustworthy friends, brothers.

—Holy Cross Constitutions

IN OUR RELIGIOUS life in Holy Cross we do not choose those with whom we live and work. There is a danger in that. We could treat our brothers in community with civility, yet remain aloof. And, indeed, the work may get done and the life may get lived, but by not truly loving one another, we run the risk of disliking our life and work together, even of compromising our very mission. People would observe nothing extraordinary here.

Our Holy Cross mission is more demanding than a job; it requires that we do more than tolerate each other. Mission requires attentive abiding. A respectful, loving group is more effective in ministry and certainly less tense than a bickering crowd. But there is an even greater fruit than this. When we abide attentively together, we not only work together for the Lord, but we witness the Lord's very presence in our midst through our love for one another.

We all have a mission in this alienated world in which we often divide ourselves into different groups of them and us. Even as our societies struggle to become more integrated, we can still tend to associate only with those people who are like ourselves, distancing ourselves from those different from us. Striving to abide as closest neighbors, trustworthy friends, and brothers and sisters with all people, therefore, is a prophetic sign that our modern world sorely needs. And so we all share the call along with Holy Cross to be hopeful signs in an alienated world, willing to cross borders of every sort to love one another.

John Paige, C.S.C.

May 8

Education is the art of helping young people to completeness; for the Christian, this means education is helping a young person to be more like Christ, the model of all Christians.

—Basil Moreau

IN MY LIFE journey as a teacher and administrator in Catholic education, I have discovered, after many years of trying to bring about great success in the classroom and in leadership, that getting to know Jesus is the only achievement necessary. For Jesus himself questions his disciples, "What profit is there for one to gain the world and forfeit his life?" (Mk 8:36). And what profit would there be for us to educate young people without inviting them into a personal relationship with Christ Jesus?

I know from my own education that I profited the most from those teachers who passionately provided me the necessary support and nourishment to model my life on Christ. I recall in particular one scripture teacher who awakened in me a yearning to know God's universe, a yearning that has remained with me throughout life and inspires me still today. Then, in my own teaching, the most graced moments have been those in which I have witnessed this transformation of students as their cloud of unknowing becomes the brightness of understanding, filling their hearts with hope, and preparing fertile ground for the seed of Christ's love to grow.

Yet the work of transforming young minds and hearts is shared by all. For as we witness and give witness to Christ's love in the world around us, we are teaching young people by our very lives how they too might model their lives on Christ. For it is through our quest to follow Jesus and our teaching of his example that God will open our hearts and minds, educating each of us in the grandeur of his love.

William C. Nick, C.S.C.

May 9

Jesus went to heaven to prepare a place for us, and what a place! There, as He does now, we will one day have no more pains to suffer, no good thing to wish for, no change to fear. God Himself will wipe away the tears from our eyes. The source of tears will be forever dried up. All capacities of our soul and body will be satisfied.
—Basil Moreau

I HAVE HAD the privilege of presiding at the Mass of Christian Burial for a number of significant people in my life. Thinking of them, I continue to be moved by the words from the Mass that assure us, "Lord, for your faithful people life is changed, not ended." The place that Jesus is preparing for us in heaven is our ultimate destination—the one for which we live our lives in service of the kingdom of God. In heaven our lives will be transformed; we will become the fullness of what we have strived to be in living out our baptismal promises. Eucharistic

Prayer III reminds us, "On that day we shall see you, our God, as you are. We shall become like you." In other words, as we strive to live our lives in imitation of Christ we become like the Father whom Jesus images for us.

This same eucharistic prayer assures us that "every tear will be wiped away." Thus, we shed tears not for those who die in the Lord, but rather for ourselves and our loss. We find ourselves in this valley of tears where the imperfections of this life cause us suffering and trials. But Fr. Moreau reminds us of that day when we will suffer no more. All capacities of our soul and body will be satisfied. And to this degree, we live our Christian lives in joyful anticipation of that day when we will rest in the fullness of life in heaven.

Jim Fenstermaker, C.S.C.

May 10

The spirit of the congregation is a spirit of peace and charity; the brothers shall live together in the most perfect union, loving each other and helping one another equally. If any dissension arises, however small, they should come to reconciliation before evening prayer.

—Jacques Dujarie

WHENEVER I ATTEND a community function—a profession of vows, a celebration of a feast day, or, most notably, a funeral—I look at the members of the community and reflect. I will be here to bury most of these men, and some will bury me. For me, this is not a morbid thought, but a life-defining experience. We are part of a brotherhood that's larger than each one of us. Besides being colleagues in ministry, we are partners in discipleship, sharing a particular response to the Lord's summons. It is clearly a call to do something, but it is perhaps more importantly a command to be somebody, along with others called to do likewise.

More than thirty-five years of community life have yielded many ups and downs for me. There have been disagreements with and even estrangements from some members. But that does not change the fundamental dynamic of life in community—brothers living in perfect union.

Community life is primarily this sharing of individual lives lived in imitation of the Lord. In that regard, the dynamics of a Christian family, business, or parish are no different from those of the religious life. All of these require the same give and take that aims for perfect union, including the realization of our solidarity with each other and the will to reconcile with those we have hurt. Perhaps that's why I look upon Holy Cross as I do when we are together. Just like any of us, I am not who I am without my community. Nor are my fellow community members who they are without me. We are brothers.

Joseph H. Esparza, C.S.C.

May 11

We must above all have recourse to grace, to the Holy Spirit, and hence to prayer which is, as the apostle says, good for all things. This was the mind and practice of all the saints.

—Basil Moreau

I OFTEN THINK back to when the Lord is leaving the apostles. He's risen from the dead and has been with them for forty days. Now they're on the Mount of Olives again, the place where he experienced his agony in the garden. Jesus instructs them to go out into the whole world and spread the good news. But they are flabbergasted. Most of them are unschooled, not knowing how to read or write. They do not even know what the whole world is. They live in a little backwater called Judea and speak a language very few people know. Yet Jesus tells them not to worry, that he will not leave them orphans. He promises to send them an Advocate, the Holy Spirit, who will tell them where to go, what to do, and what to say.

Then, on the day of pentecost, a great wind fills the Upper Room where they had been praying for nine days. Little flames of fire appear above their heads. And Peter, a fellow who had denied that he had even known Christ a few weeks before, goes out on the balcony inspired by the Spirit and gives a sermon so powerful that all those present hear him in their own language. Thousands ask to be baptized right away, and the Church is born.

Now there are well over one billion Catholics in the world and over two billion Christians of all sorts, all because the Lord has given to us his Holy Spirit. The Holy Spirit continues to work today as it did among the apostles, guiding us where to go, what to do, and what to say. We are never orphans as long as we have recourse to the Holy Spirit.

Ted Hesburgh, C.S.C.

May 12

In vain will we consume our energy in building up a house which God does not help to raise for His own glory.

—Edward Sorin

GROWING UP IN the Great Depression, my parents learned to work hard in order to survive. I inherited from them this same work ethic. When I add in my stubborn, perfectionist temperament, I've always found it easier to depend on my own strengths and efforts than to trust in God or in others.

All of that changed, however, when I went to Mexico to learn Spanish and to work in our Holy Cross parish there. For the first time in my life, I felt completely helpless. I couldn't even ask for directions to find a bathroom. Mexico forced me to depend on others, and even more importantly, on the Lord. I clearly remember when the pastor asked me to lead a Bible study. In my heart, I cried out, "Lord help me. Give me the words to speak, for I hardly know the language." I arrived at a dirt-floor house with my bible in hand. A tiny tree grew in the living room, and chickens ran wild at my feet. I clung desperately to the words of St. Paul, "When I am weak, then I am strong" (2 Cor 12:10). And, miracle of miracles, I was able to teach the Bible in Spanish. Although my speech was halting and imperfect, I was helped by God's Spirit and the graciousness and patience of those wonderful Mexican parishioners.

Recently, I have been working at our Holy Cross parish in Coachella, California, serving a largely Hispanic immigrant population. Our parish is growing rapidly, and we are working to build a new church. In times past, I would have tried to build this new church on my own strength, and the project probably would've given me an ulcer. But today, thanks to that transformative experience in Mexico, I know that the Lord is the real Master Builder.

Bruce Cecil, C.S.C.

May 13

There stood by the Cross of Jesus his mother Mary, who knew grief and was a Lady of Sorrows. She is our special patroness, a woman who bore much she could not understand and who stood fast. To her many sons and daughters, whose devotions ought to bring them often to her side, she tells much of this daily cross and its daily hope.

—Holy Cross Constitutions

SHE WAS A twenty-three-year-old mother, and this was her firstborn. The child was fine his first two days of life, but within hours of going home he had to return to the hospital, not as a newborn, but as a life-or-death patient. For seven months he continued on the edge of life, and every day his mother was there. On the eleventh day of the seventh month it became obvious that he would not survive. His mother was distraught. Within moments, the doctor came into the room and advised that she withdraw the many tubes that were keeping her beloved son alive.

She looked to me for an answer, but all I could do was grasp her hand and put my arm around her. She wailed, moving back and forth. My heart ached for her. Then, with the calm that only grace and faith can give, she looked at me and then at the doctor and said, "I have had him these seven wonderful months. It is time to give him back to God." I could hardly control my tears. I walked her to the crib of her firstborn, arms around her shoulders. She reached down, kissed her beloved son, held his hand, and began a slow prayer, silent but more sincere and profound than any prayer I had experienced. Then, as if to confound all who were present, this woman of sorrows quietly uttered, "Into your hands I commend him." As if previously orchestrated, the tiny body with a full head of hair and tubes protruding, looked directly at his mother, smiled, and breathed himself into the arms of God.

John Gleason, C.S.C.

May 14

Consider in relation to ourselves, the Heart of Jesus is of a friend, a brother, a father, and a Savior. It is a Heart of mystery, wherein justice and peace have given each other a kiss of union, and worked out those prodigies of power and mercy which have renewed the face of the earth.

—Basil Moreau

ABOUT SIX MONTHS into my first term as pastor, I made a decision that was not met with universal enthusiasm. One of the strongest voices of criticism came from a rather burly and imposing man with a loud voice who had a habit of regularly barging into my office without an appointment. Right on cue, he walked in one day, shut the door, and said softly, "I know your heart. You would never do anything to hurt this parish. Everybody knows that. We know your heart." He then turned around and walked out of the office.

The human heart reveals who one truly is. We give our hearts to each other in friendship and in love. Our hearts betray our deep-rooted desires. Our hearts compel us to bold action when our minds tell us to cower in fear. Our hearts harbor the divine light of God and brilliantly illuminate the world with their warm glow.

The Sacred Heart of Jesus reveals who God truly is. God gives his Heart to all people through the flesh-and-blood person of Jesus Christ. The Heart of Jesus calls us into a deeper relationship with God. The Heart of Jesus consoles us in our despair and inspires us in our faith. The Heart of Jesus invites us to share in the love of God that renews the face of the earth. For God knows our hearts, just as even the most surprising people do. Through their help, we start to plumb the mysterious depths of our own hearts, our deepest motivations and desires, where our union with the Heart of Jesus begins.

Michael C. Mathews, C.S.C.

I beseech you by our most sacred common interests to strive and imitate the true Religious in every community in "their newness of life, modeling their conduct after that of the risen Savior who dies no more."

—Edward Sorin

THE CHRISTIAN LIFE is a life of imitation. We strive to imitate the example of Jesus Christ and live as he did. One way we do this is by imitating other people who truly model their lives on his. As children, we learned a lot about our faith by watching what our families did, not just what they said. That doesn't change when we grow older. We learn new ways of praying and serving others by watching how other people pray and serve. We learn how to be Christlike by watching others who imitate Christ.

If we look for evil and despair in the world around us, we will surely find them. But if we look for Christ, we will find him, too. We just have to learn to recognize Christ when we see him. We will find him in people who somehow find hope in the midst of their many crosses. We will find him in people who joyfully perform acts of kindness and generosity without counting the cost or seeking recognition for their good works. We will find him in people who pray faithfully and help others to do the same. Not only are we called to follow these examples, we are called to provide them, too, through the witness of our lives. Just as we can recognize Christ in others at countless times each day, so also should others be able to see Christ working through us in the smallest actions of our lives.

Steve Lacroix, C.S.C.

May 16

Before I lose faith in prayer, I should certainly lose my mind.

—Edward Sorin

LISTENING IS NOT something I do particularly well. I am the classic "type A" personality. I tend to do more of the talking. As an associate superintendent of Catholic schools in a large diocese, I continually find that my time is often demanded by several people simultaneously. More often than not, it feels like everyone wants an answer immediately. In my rush to get to the next item on my agenda, I will sometimes cut people off and answer the question that I think they are going to ask. I can be a harsh critic of myself and others.

As a vowed religious, I commit myself to a daily pattern of prayer. Without prayer as my point of departure I am working, not ministering. When I pray, I discover a quiet place in myself where God dwells. When I manage to listen and let God get a word in edgewise I find myself a more patient, caring, and loving person.

Prayer isn't always easy. There are times when I pray while fighting traffic on the New York City highways, while working at my desk, or while sitting through an endless meeting. Other times, I am able to steal away and sit quietly in the chapel of the building where my office is located. Sometimes I pray the rosary, the psalms, or the readings from the Mass for that day. Sometimes I just sit. The thing that always amazes me is that when I do pray, God does listen, and so do I.

William Clifford, C.S.C.

May 17

Education, in its proper sense, implies the expansion and cultivation of all the faculties, mental and physical —the cultivation of the heart as well as the mind; and of these the formation and enrichment of the heart is undoubtedly the most important of the two.

—Edward Sorin

MY HEART SANK as I read the quotation assigned to me for this reflection. In my experience, the language of not educating the mind at the expense of the heart often has been used within religious life to promote a lack of aspiration for excellence in academic quality and effort. I still remember one of my fellow religious telling me, "You know, what is more important is what your heart teaches you, not teachers." Afterward, I promised never to let the heart and mind dictum pass my lips. And so, my heart sank even further when I learned that not only Fr. Moreau, but also Fr. Sorin, the second founder of Holy Cross, said the exact same thing.

So much of education is in fact cultivating the intellect, cramming ourselves with knowledge. In my own case, early on, this was the hard work of understanding the structures of foreign languages and, even harder, memorizing vocabulary without having acquired it from the surrounding culture since birth. Simply put, what Fr. Sorin calls "filling up the mind" is much of what education is. Indeed, the very pursuit of knowledge through study is a reflection of what it is to be human, because such intellectual curiosity about all things reveals both our incompleteness as humans and our desire to be with God completely.

Yet the importance of the formation and enrichment of the heart comes to us later, after we have had experience. It comes to us within the struggle to know God with our minds. And so it is that any education moves toward completion in God having cultivated both the mind and the heart.

James E. McDonald, C.S.C.

May 18

In Baptism, we received the seed of spiritual life which must grow and be strengthened until Jesus Christ is formed in us. In this way, we become other Christs and His life is made manifest in ours.

—Basil Moreau

DURING MY TERM as pastor at Christ the King parish in South Bend, Indiana, a seventh-grade student in our elementary school was suffering from a rare form of leukemia. Numerous radiation and chemotherapy treatments left him so weak that he was unable to attend classes. To the boy's surprise, his uncle asked him to be the godfather for his first son. The young cancer patient was excited to be chosen for this honor and responsibility. He sincerely said, "I hope that I can be as good a godparent as my uncle was a confirmation sponsor for me."

That young seventh-grader clearly understood the importance of baptism and growth in the life of Christ. Baptism is important because we are who God says we are: beloved sons and daughters of the Father, beloved brothers and sisters in Christ who share in his mission. What God does for us in this sacrament has unique and cosmic significance. It is more than a naming ceremony because through baptism the tiny seed of God's love is forever planted in our souls.

This seed, however, requires nurturing and cultivation if it is to grow and bear fruit. The examples of others living lives in Christ—sponsors, godparents, parents, teachers, and mentors—teach us what it means to be people of faith, gratitude, and service. We in turn, like the young student with leukemia, are then called to model Christ to others. For by baptism we are forever changed in a way that summons us to be agents of hope for others who live in the little acre of the world which we call home.

Tom Jones, C.S.C.

We pronounce our vows in a moment, but living them for the sake of the kingdom is the work of a lifetime. That fulfillment demands of us more than the mere wish, more even than the firm decision. It demands the conversion of our habits, our character, our attitudes, our desires.

—Holy Cross Constitutions

HAVING HAD THE privilege of working with several hundred couples preparing for the sacrament of marriage, I have experienced one inspiring constant in the great majority of cases. Aware of the increasing percentage of divorces and oftentimes having felt its effects personally, most couples express a sincere, even passionate, commitment to "making this marriage work." I want always to affirm the inherent rightness of this desire. At the same time, I challenge the couples to place this desire in the context of grace. I speak about the reality that any genuine vocation breaks those who are called to it. I share my firm conviction that marriage, like religious or dedicated single life, demands every ounce of their energy; and once they have expended this effort, there will come a time when they discover it just isn't enough. At that point, they can either give up, or give themselves up to God.

In Holy Cross, we believe that all vows to God are tried and refined through formation and transformation. Whether preparing for religious life or marriage, we owe it to each other to form ourselves in the great wisdom of these vocations as they are handed on to us in our Catholic tradition. Yet, in the end, the living of vows—in religious community or in marriage—will always depend on the grace of ongoing conversion. Conversion is transformation. It demands consent of the will, and then it demands a surrender of the will. Formation is what we can do; transformation is what only God can do in us.

Don Dilg, C.S.C.

May 20

God has breathed his very breath into us. We speak to God with the yearning and the words of sons to a Father because the Spirit has made us adopted children in Christ. The same Spirit who provides us with the energy and impetus to follow after the Lord and to accept his mission also gives us the desire and the utterance for prayer.

—Holy Cross Constitutions

FOR ONE GASPING for air, wanting for the very breath of life, resuscitation is the only hope of being raised, revived, restored, and renewed. We think of paramedics or other emergency workers breathing their own breath into someone on the brink of death. So, too, with God. In a desperate state, needing support for our every breath, God tenderly revives and renews us with his own, thus sustaining us with the same breath that gave life in the beginning of time. For the Lord blew his Spirit into the nostrils of Adam, formed from the dust of the earth, so that he might become "a living being."

We, too, all live as children of a divine Father whose breath is creative and life-sustaining. Because we have been given this gift of life in the Spirit, we live no longer for ourselves, but for God. This breath of the Spirit, this breath of life, provides us with the energy and impetus we need to rise from our prone and helpless state and to take on the mission that the Lord has given to each of us. It also inspires us to praise God and to seek guidance in prayer, that our words and work might be the Lord's very own. Our words and our work—in education and parishes, for families and communities, with the poor and afflicted, at home and abroad—indeed, our every action, should be simply a continuation, or really an exhalation, of the breath of life that created, saved, and sustains us still.

George Piggford, C.S.C.

May 21

Human life is like a great Way of the Cross. We do not have to go to the chapel or church to go through the different stations. This Way of the Cross is everywhere and we travel it every day, even in spite of ourselves and without being aware of it.

—Basil Moreau

SO OFTEN I wish that life itself was not a great Way of the Cross, that discipleship and the Cross were not so intimately related. I prefer, like most, to flee from suffering, difficulty, and hardship. I prefer a God whose love saves me from sin, death, and the suffering that links them.

And yet, each day I find the invitation to take up the Cross—in the boredom of life's everyday tasks, in the neighbor whose very presence is an affront to my serenity, in a news item that details the suffering of another, in unrequited love, in tasks beyond talents, in the realization of my own pettiness, and in the battles that persist within. At times, I find myself taking up the Cross in spite of myself; it is hoisted upon my shoulders before I realize it. Love—not simply being human—requires it. At times, I run from it, only to fall exhausted into bed, the Cross nestled beside me preventing me from falling asleep. Other times, I willingly take it up, my heart moved by a love beyond my own loving.

And so, I do not have to find a church to go through the different stations, for I am aware that I walk with him already; rather, he walks with me. I am accompanied by Love itself, a love that has born my infirmities and guilt, a love that saves me from sin and death. I am aware that the Cross, and its daily way, though not my preference, is my salvation. As the Cross is offered to me each day, I beg for the grace to echo the prayer of Jesus, "Father, if it is possible, let this cup pass from me; yet, not as I will, but as you will."

Thomas P. Looney, C.S.C.

May 22

If I could have foreseen the development of the Congregation of Holy Cross at the outset, I could then have regulated and coordinated everything in advance. If such were the case, however, the congregation would have been a merely human combination and not the work of Divine Providence.

—Basil Moreau

FOR THOSE LIKE me, we plan and prepare and like to think that we are somewhat in control of things. But thanks be to God, he is really the one in charge. When I began my life in Holy Cross, I felt that I was called to the ministry of teaching, and so I planned and prepared to enter the high school classroom one day. Even with all the things I have done as a Holy Cross religious in more than two decades in the community, I have never once set foot in a high school classroom. God's plan for me was to teach in other ways. Whether it has been guiding a college retreat, hearing a confession, serving as chaplain for a college sports team, serving as rector in a university residence hall, offering counsel to a student, or preaching at Mass, the Lord has provided me with countless ways of "teaching" that have been far greater than any for which I could have planned.

In our lives it is good to have plans and dreams and aspirations, and it is good always to bear in mind that these dreams find their origin in the One who gives us all. And the One who gives us these great dreams and aspirations will be the One to bring them to fulfillment. So we continue to plan and dream and prepare. But in the end, we surrender it all to our loving God, who will fashion our hopes into the most life-giving gifts possible.

Tom Gaughan, C.S.C.

☥

May 23

Before the Lord we learn what is his will to be done, we ask that no one lack daily bread, we dare to match forgiveness for forgiveness and we plead to survive the test. We desire that his name be praised, that his kingdom come and that we be his faithful servants in the planting of it.

—Holy Cross Constitutions

LET GOD BE God. This is the heart of the first half of the Lord's Prayer. We are not in control; it is God's world and religion is about what God is doing more than about what we are doing. "Hallowed be Thy name; Thy Kingdom come; Thy will be done." I believe God wants what we want, just as good parents want their children to lead their own lives. God, however, wants what we want at the deepest and truest depths of our beings. Alas, we are often bewildered and confused about what we want because we try to mimic what our culture tells us we ought to want. But at heart, we all do want to give our lives to God and for God.

The second half of the Lord's Prayer says in effect: Let human beings be human beings. I look at a small child, and it reminds me of my human needs. I need to be fed: "Give us this day our daily bread"—which includes both emotional and spiritual food. I need to be cleaned up when I make a mess: "Forgive as we are forgiven." I need to be secure and protected: "Do not put us to the test or lead us into temptation"—be it divorce, cancer, death of a child, loss of a job, or any other trauma. We thus pray not to be given a cross heavier than we can carry, and we know that this prayer, prayed by the Lord himself, will always be heard.

Nicholas Ayo, C.S.C.

May 24

The Holy Spirit alone can form and reform religious con-gregations as He formed the Church, after first forming the humanity of Our Lord in the womb of the Queen of Virgins, the masterpiece of His influence and love. Hence, I beg you to invoke Him frequently.

—Basil Moreau

THE HOLY SPIRIT moving among us is an amazing, even down-to-earth phenomenon. In the beginning, the Spirit hovered over the waters and life began, creating human beings whom God called very good. Then in the fullness of time, the Spirit overshadowed the Virgin Mary and God's Son took on our same human flesh. Ever since, the Spirit has continued to fill our world and our Church with divine grace.

Men and women fall in love, families take shape, and children are born and raised into a relationship with the loving God. The Church grows, the sacraments are celebrated, and its members show forth God's love to the world by the example of their lives. Religious communities are formed and re-formed to carry the gospel to the ends of the earth. Come Holy Spirit.

Parents find support to bring up children even in difficult circumstances. Teachers feel strength to challenge their students to reach their fullest potential. Preachers stand up with courage to face the injustices of their times. Believers are amazed at what they can accomplish through the power of faith. Come Holy Spirit.

We've all seen the smiling faces of the poor, ready to hope and believe that they can overcome. We've watched the energy of the young, ready to conquer the world. We've marveled at the fortitude of the bereaved, the sick, the abandoned, and the abused as they continue to pursue their dreams. Nothing moves us quite like the Holy Spirit, and his presence is everlasting. Come Holy Spirit.

David E. Schlaver, C.S.C.

May 25

By our vow of celibacy we commit ourselves to seek union with God in lifelong chastity, forgoing forever marriage and parenthood for the sake of the Kingdom. We also promise loyalty, companionship and affection

to our confreres in Holy Cross. Openness and disci-
pline in prayer, personal asceticism, compassionate
service, and love given and received in community are
important supports toward the generous living of this
commitment.

—Holy Cross Constitutions

FOREVER FORGOING MARRIAGE and parenthood for the sake of the kingdom is a commitment involving both a promise and a gift. For our celibacy as religious does not find its meaning in what we do without, but in what we open ourselves to receive from God. We promise to be there for those who are lonely or hopeless, those who have suffered the loss of a loved one, and those nearing the end of their earthly journey to God. We promise to be there for those following the Lord in the single life, those seeking to confirm their love in marriage and family, and those searching for God's plan in their lives. And in this promise lies the gift. God's grace provides that we might serve and care for all whom we encounter. In love, he draws us into their lives; and in love, he draws them into ours.

For all of us need to love and to be loved. It is our deepest human longing. We celibates also need the loving support of our brothers and sisters in religious life and of our co-workers in the Lord's vineyard to remain faithful and generous in our promise to God. And yet, the only way for any of us to find love is by making and keeping a promise. For it is in making and keeping a promise—whether in religious vows, marriage vows, or single faithfulness—that we open ourselves to receive not only the gift of each other's love, but ultimately the unparalleled gift of God's love.

William B. Simmons, C.S.C.

May 26

In the fullness of time the Lord Jesus came among us anointed by the Spirit to inaugurate a kingdom of justice, love, and peace. His rule would be no mere earthly regime: it would initiate a new creation in every land. His power would be within and without, rescuing us from the injustice we suffer and also from the injustice we inflict.

—Holy Cross Constitutions

THERE IS A huge gap between the values of this world, so firmly rooted, and the values of Jesus spoken in the Beatitudes, the charter of the kingdom. Both sets of values pull at our hearts although they stand in such contrast—competition and loving care, sophistication and childlikeness, revenge and forgiveness, dominance and humility, self-centeredness and service, individualism and community. Uprooting the first and tending the second can be excruciating. Yet scripture tells us never to grow tired of trying to do good, of trying to be part of that new creation.

Then I meet people here in Bangladesh—good people, usually poor and uneducated—who have so little and suffer so much, but are clearly children of that new creation. These are people who daily carry heavy loads, but continue to love, to smile, and to be generous and peaceful. Their lives quietly proclaim that the kingdom of God is among us, close at hand. They are the children of the Lord, who does not trample on the bent reed or extinguish the flickering wick.

I have seen the kingdom in them and I am often in awe. The kingdom of God is not a place; it is people. My experience here is that when we share the lot of the people, they bring us to the faith. We can all think of those special graces of God, the people who have shown us the new creation—through a smile, a kind word, a gentle touch—beautiful glimpses of the kingdom among us.

Frank Quinlivan, C.S.C.

May 27

Triumphant and glorious, victor over death and hell, the Divine Redeemer mounted up to heaven. He rose up to his Father; He sat down at his Father's right hand. Yet, He does not cease to live and dwell in our midst. He makes this the joy of His heart.

—Basil Moreau

I REMEMBER WHEN my nephew, Steve—a brilliant, gentle and thoughtful young man—was diagnosed with Lou Gehrig's disease. This incurable illness gradually undermines muscle function and is ultimately fatal. It was painful to watch Steve's struggle, as he was unable to speak, unable to eat except through a feeding tube, and unable to walk without labored steps. It seemed so cruel and unfair. His courage, however, was remarkable and his death peaceful. He died in the arms of his loving and attentive wife. His son was with him as well and bid him a gentle goodbye.

During his illness, we as a family began to realize ever more profoundly that Jesus was in our midst. For no matter our position or status, no matter how important we think we are, or how insignificant we portray ourselves to be, the work of caring for others brings us ever closer to the right hand of God. It was the Lord and Fr. Moreau who comforted Steve and the rest of us. Steve kept a relic of the founder of Holy Cross with him throughout his illness. Through Steve's grave disease, our family became holier and far more prayerful. We prayed for healing, we prayed for comfort, and finally we prayed for peace, all the while knowing that the Lord was in our midst comforting us and letting us know that he was at our right hand. I always marveled at Steve's courage and strength. Each day now, I pray to him, trusting that he is enjoying God's good graces. I ask him to be with me, joined in courage, to face whatever challenges come my way.

Jerome Donnelly, C.S.C.

May 28

A common burial ground will guard the ashes of the various members of the association. It is there that we shall await together, under the protection of the Cross, the hour of the final awakening. For us who have the gift of faith, the cemetery, which in our language means the sleeping place, is truly the spot for that rest which is a little longer than an ordinary night, and which will end with the radiant dawn of eternity.

—Basil Moreau

IN THIS MEDITATION on the resurrection, Fr. Moreau writes of how a common burial ground, analogous perhaps to our common mother Church, can be a powerful sign of our common hope. As he accepted the Church's invitation to send Holy Cross religious to Algeria, the United States, Canada, and India, the possibility of one common burial ground for his religious family eroded. Since then, Holy Cross has had to leave some of the places where it served, has endured in others, or has spread to new countries. Wherever we have been, are, or will be, there is or will be a cemetery for those Holy Cross religious who have died there.

This dispersion of our lives and deaths, however, is itself a powerful sign of our common hope. Guided by the hand of Divine Providence, the congregation which began as a tiny seed in France grew into a giant tree spanning the globe. Our growth has been organic, dying out in some places but flourishing in others.

For all Christians, whatever our calling and wherever it leads, our common hope in the resurrection binds us together. The gift of faith enables us to see that just as we and our brothers and sisters cross borders of every sort, together we also will pass through death into eternal life.

Thomas P. Gariepy, C.S.C.

☧

May 29

All of us are involved in the mission: those who go out to work and whose labors sustain the community itself, those in fullness of their strength and those held back by sickness or by age, those who abide in the companionship of a local house and those sent to live and work by themselves, those in their active assignments and those who are still in training. All of us as a single brotherhood are joined in one communal response to the Lord's mission.

—Holy Cross Constitutions

THE PAST, PRESENT, and future of Holy Cross have all come together in our community at Stonehill College—from young men in formation to some of the venerable patriarchs of our Eastern Province. Not every member has been able to be as active in ministry as others, but all, regardless of age or infirmity, have contributed what they can to the house, the province, and the local Church. In some cases this might have been simply helping to clear the table after a meal, sorting mail, or providing spiritual direction to our seminarians. Our senior members provide us with oral history and insight into our past while our younger brothers bring fresh ideas and youthful zeal. Together, as a single brotherhood, we then face issues in the present and plan for the future.

In the scriptures we find that God uses people of all ages in his plan of salvation. In the Old Testament, we see both the young shepherd David as well as the aged Abraham and Sarah invited to share in the formation of God's people. In the New Testament, we find the young Virgin Mary along with her older cousin Elizabeth both participating in the events which would finally bring Christ into the world. There are no limits to whom God will call to bring about the kingdom. Each of us, no matter our age or ability, has something to offer, whether it is through prayer or serving God's people in a more direct way. All that is needed is our yes.

Thomas C. Bertone, C.S.C.

May 30

Whether He afflicts or consoles, whether He leads to the gates of death or brings back therefrom, let us praise the Lord.

—Edward Sorin

EVERY DAY AT Portland's Downtown Chapel, I learn that I cannot control people's lives. I cannot fix the heroin addict to make him love himself. I cannot change the decisions of the mentally ill who cling to patterns from childhood abuse. I cannot influence our guests to search for housing and to seek employment. I can suggest nothing to motivate my friend to move out of his depression, his anxiety about never feeling loved. These can be days when the inconsolable suffering of people turns me toward fear.

On these days, God alone points me in a new direction. Faith allows me to trust God and not the gifts I think God should be bestowing on those who suffer. This awareness brings me great humility and profound patience. It teaches me to learn from other believers. I now understand the leper who waited for Jesus on the margins of his village. I see the mother who begged Jesus to cure her daughter. I empathize with the man whose withered hand was cured on the Sabbath.

The profound treasure that the Holy Cross tradition passes on to all believers is an unwavering trust in God's presence, regardless of life's circumstances. We grow in faith through life's adversities and seek God's love even in despair. We demonstrate perseverance when uncertainty brings us low. We worship with full hearts when we let go of the illusion that we are in control. And we grow in gratitude when we move beyond ourselves and finally seek God.

Ronald Patrick Raab, C.S.C.

May 31

Visits from above are not always of gladness and of joy, but much oftener of pain and sorrow; we must be prepared to receive them all with faith and merit. Children never turn more quickly to their mothers than when in danger or in suffering. When does she receive and press them to her loving heart more tenderly than in their fright and pain?

—Edward Sorin

MY TWENTY-FIFTH ANNIVERSARY celebration as a priest was approaching, and I was not feeling very spiritual. God, however, provided me with just the visitation from above that I needed. While visiting Chile, one of our Holy Cross Associates invited me to accompany her as she brought communion to a blind woman named Lucia, whose apartment was in a poor area of Santiago. Upon entering her home Lucia proclaimed, "Thank you God for the blessing of this spiritual priest visiting me." We had an engaging visit. Before leaving I asked for her blessing.

I returned to Lucia's apartment for many more visitations before leaving Chile. Through her challenging persistence, I shared with her deep feelings about the death of my mother six years prior after an eight-year struggle with Alzheimer's disease. I was able to express my pain to this blind woman of faith and see more clearly why it was that I was not feeling spiritual. Her daily prayers and our other visits and phone calls since 1991 continue to be graced and joyful moments in my life.

In addition to Lucia, my ministry and spiritual life have been nourished by countless women, from Holy Cross sisters to women faculty, staff, alumnae, and students at the University of Notre Dame. Like Fr. Sorin, I have discovered that the mystery of God's unconditional and compassionate love can be likened to the love of a mother for her child, tenderly embracing us in all moments of our lives.

Don McNeill, C.S.C.

JUNE

June 1

Happy those who understand this spirit of denial; happier still those who have tasted its sweetness and opened their hearts to it. For them, obedience becomes easy, and subjection to rules and superiors, sweet and light. Each subject does the will of God and not His own.

—Basil Moreau

WHEN WE ARE asked to accept assignments we would rather not take or to leave a place we have come to love, obedience can be the toughest vow. As effective ministers, we often give our hearts to the people we serve. When asked to go elsewhere, the letting go can be difficult. And yet it is in the surrender, in obedience to the will of the community as expressed through our superior, that we grow in freedom and give life to others. It is a lesson taught to us by those who loved us first and who in their own obedience to God's will let us go so we could be free to become the people God was calling us to be.

I still remember the early morning when I said goodbye to my mother and left for the seminary. As I drove off I could see her silhouette framed by the light of the open garage door. My father had died when I was just sixteen, and as the youngest, my departure meant my mother would now live alone. I did not fully appreciate it then, but her encouragement of my journey to Holy Cross and subsequent letting me go was an example of her surrender—of her obedience, really, to God's work in my life. It would have been far easier for her to keep me close, to ask that I not venture so far away and into a new family, but she let me go as a gift to God and to Holy Cross. Her surrender reminds me of the Widow's Mite. In obedience to God, the widow gives from her want what little she has, trusting that God will use it. That is the surrender that is freeing and life-giving for us all.

Peter Jarret, C.S.C.

June 2

Ingratitude, says a great saint, dries up even the source of Divine favors. Common sense tells us the same, and daily experience proves it

—Edward Sorin

FR. TED HESBURGH, C.S.C., proclaims that his best day, the most important event in his life, and his greatest honor was his ordination. I, too, look upon my ordination as the ultimate defining moment in my life. It was the culmination of my years of study and formation, the fulfillment of my lifelong dream, and the beginning of my public ministry. Yet who I am today is a result not only of my ordination but of every day of my life. I draw strength from my family and my many experiences of growing up with their love. Over the years my friends have supported, encouraged, and challenged me. I am able to do what I do because of God and because of my family and friends. God has given me many talents and gifts. My family and friends have provided me with the vitality and richness that makes those gifts and talents radiate God's goodness.

To recognize our dependency on God and on many others is the beginning of gratitude. We do not accomplish great things independent of others or of God. Any attempt to isolate ourselves and our achievements from the influence of others is to isolate ourselves from the source of what makes us God's greatest creation. Instead we express our thanks, we acknowledge our dependency, and we seek to strengthen ourselves so as to continue becoming a better and stronger reflection of the God in whose image we have been created. For everything that has been, thanks. For everything that is to come, yes.

Mark B. Thesing, C.S.C.

June 3

The legitimate love of neighbor comes from love of God and leads back to love of God.

—Basil Moreau

I LIVE CLOSE to the fishing village of Moree in southern Ghana. Like many typical fishing villages in Ghana, lack of basic infrastructure makes life difficult and sometimes unbearable. Yet in spite of these harsh realities, the villagers have an overwhelming sense of joy that overshadows the poor living situation in which they find themselves. The villagers' steadfast trust in God can easily shame the rest of us. Never is this more apparent than when groups of American students from Holy Cross College visit Moree as part of their international study program. The village fascinates and disturbs them as they come face to face with the deprivation and helplessness of the people, experiencing life in a manner they have never known. The students cannot help but think of their own vulnerability and dependence on God.

We are fragile creatures dependent on our Creator and on one another. Like the students, whose Moree experience changed their perspective on life, inspiring them to help the people in their helplessness, we too can become instruments of God's providential care. We only have to pray for an increase of our faith and trust, the things often abundant in the lives of the impoverished people whom we serve. For we, too, can cultivate a deeper faith and trust in God that are not only the product, but also the source, of our love and service. In doing so, Divine Providence finds concrete expression in our hands and feet as we serve the coming of God's kingdom on earth. And so it is in the midst of all the complex connections of life that we discover God is the One holding it all together.

Paul Kofi Mensah, C.S.C.

June 4

The disciples followed the Lord Jesus in his ministry of proclaiming the kingdom and healing the afflicted. Jesus also spent long days alone with his disciples, speaking to them of the mysteries of his kingdom and forming them to the point when they too could be sent on his mission. Later they would return for his comment and for a deeper hearing because of what they had expe-

rienced. We too are sent to his mission as men formed
and in need of lifelong formation for his service.
—Holy Cross Constitutions

AT GRADUATION AND at profession of vows, my brothers in Holy Cross and I thought we had come to the end of our personal formation. Now, having lived not a few years after both, I realize beyond any doubt that my formation continues in everything I do. I continue to learn and to grow spiritually each day of my life.

Both my library and my prayer life continue to expand. In my intellectual life, I try to keep up with new thoughts and theories evolving from professional research. Every day, every class, every counseling session has taught me something about myself, about others, and about God. My prayer, too, has changed through the years. As I grew inwardly, I began to spend more time alone with Jesus, to listen to him, to learn from the inner silence and darkness. Like the Psalmist and the disciples, my flesh pined and my soul thirsted more and more for God.

So it is that my learning has grown and my spirituality has deepened. Formation in the Christian life, whatever our calling, is a never ending story taking us from the kingdom of this world into the kingdom of God. It is with anticipation that we can all look forward to the great adventure of stepping through the veil of death and into the open embrace of the compassionate Father of Jesus.

David H. Verhalen, C.S.C.

June 5

The more we come through prayer to relish what is right, the better we shall work in our mission for the realization of the kingdom.

—Holy Cross Constitutions

IN OUR DAILY lives, we need to care for so many things that it is not always clear that we are directly working for the realization of the kingdom of God. Doing research, teaching, going to meetings, living in community, joining in household chores, and raising children might not at first seem to be clear images of serving the mission of Christ and ushering in the kingdom. However, the core of our mission both as baptized Christians and as Holy Cross religious, does not reside so much in what we do, but how it is that we do it. Since we are called to carry out Christ's mission, we first of all are called to have the same sentiments as Christ Jesus, no matter what the task or labor at hand.

Yet we all know the difficulty of being of one mind and heart with Christ. It is impossible without prayer, for our thoughts are not easily God's thoughts, nor our will his will. Our union with God through prayer brings us deeper into the mystery of his presence within us where we can discover his will for us. For to know his will is to hear the call, as Fr. Moreau describes it, to lead with our Lord a life hidden in God. Then, grasping more clearly the will of God for our lives, we come to relish more and more what is right. That is, we seek to live our every action with the same sentiments as

Jesus Christ. Then we, too, shall contribute to the realization of his kingdom.

Gérard Dionne, C.S.C.

June 6

If the teaching body in the Church exhorts, so powerfully and unanimously, all Christians to seek salvation in the Sacred Heart, we, consecrated as we are by our own constitutions to this Adorable Heart, should be foremost in this solemn act by the fervor of our souls and the entire offering of our whole being to the loving Heart of our Divine Savior.

—Edward Sorin

TO SPEAK ABOUT the heart is to speak about the very core of who we are, the very center of our being. Traditionally, the heart is also the symbol of the emotions, most particularly the symbol of love. In a rich and powerful way these two ideas come together in the Sacred Heart. For, devotion to the Sacred Heart draws us into the core of who Christ is, which is ultimately divine love.

Fr. Moreau chose the Sacred Heart as the patron for the priests of Holy Cross because it drives at the heart of who we are called to be—men who are drawn to the Lord and his divine love and men who offer our lives to him in service of the Church.

Throughout most of my formation and early priesthood, I wondered if I had what it took to be a Holy Cross priest. This question was probably the strongest in my mind as I lay on the floor at my ordination while the litany of the saints was sung. What was I doing? What did I have to offer? And as I listened to the words and the beating of my own heart, it slowly came to me: right there on the floor was what I had to offer—only me and my beating heart. And in the end, that is all any of us has to offer to God—our very self and our own heart beating in time with Christ's.

Jeffrey Allison, C.S.C.

June 7

Bear in mind and do not forget that just as Divine Providence has willed its greatest works to begin in humility and abjection, it has also decreed that they should expand only at the price of difficulties and contradictions, trials, crosses, contempt, calumny, and detraction. Its purpose in so decreeing is that the first materials of these spiritual edifices may be tried as gold in the fire.

—Basil Moreau

FROM THE PERSPECTIVE of the Christian faith, encountering the Cross is more than a probability, it is an inevitability. Trials—of whatever kind and in whatever dimension of life—will not rank among our favorite moments, but neither can they be avoided. In fact, consciously trying to avoid these difficulties might be the worst thing that we could do. For, as

Fr. Moreau points out, God's greatest works usually begin in small, humble circumstances. Scripture testifies to this truth; we need only recall the stable in Bethlehem to remember the power hidden in unassuming beginnings. And, as Fr. Moreau goes on to say, these works progress and expand through trials. Scripture testifies to that also; we need only envision the hill outside Jerusalem to bring to mind the saving victory wrested from seeming defeat.

These are not merely the truths of scripture, they are embodied in the very history of Holy Cross, and they are experienced daily by all who follow Christ. Yet we live in settings that often deny pain and pretend it away. We ourselves may even try to discard or erase the memories of our encounters with the Cross. The great risk in this is that we also discard the grace that accompanies painful, difficult, or confusing times. We might, instead, reflect on the graces that God is offering us through these trials and thus find the strength to embrace them. For each encounter with the Cross is the Lord's invitation to us to grow ever more fully into the persons God made us to be.

Joel Giallanza, C.S.C.

June 8

In consecrated celibacy we wish to love with the freedom, openness and availability that can be recognized as a sign of the kingdom.

—Holy Cross Constitutions

THE MAN POUNDING on my rectory door looked crazed. Often homeless folks call on Sunday afternoons. I wondered, "Do I open the door?" Tired from a weekend of Masses, a wedding, and several baptisms, I knew I had to make a choice. I turned the lock, opened the door, and invited this man and his chaos into my life. The first thing that came out of his mouth was, "Father, I need a priest."

Soon we were telling his four-year-old daughter that Mommy had gone to live with the angels so she could be her guardian angel. Her mother's death had been sudden and violent, but we had mediated an annunciation that was peaceful and prayerful.

Divine Providence had placed me in their lives. My witness to God's faithfulness had to be called forth, shaken from me by the insistent pounding of a stranger. Yet the decision was a free and conscious one. The decision to love can never be recognized in the abstract; otherwise it would be only the desire to love. Authentic love, true love, only exists in the concrete reality of our lives. To love freely, openly, and with availability is a sign of the kingdom, to which not only religious but all of God's children can witness. Yet the gift of consecrated celibacy flowers in due season when the self-possessed divest. When it blooms in selfless love, it enriches and inspires all who love. For only if we are truly free can we decide to love, to be open, and available. This decision to give ourselves radically to others is our prayer, our worship, and our consecration.

John Donato, C.S.C.

June 9

Whatever they may be, let us not forget that the heaviest crosses contribute most to the general good of our work and to the welfare of each one of us.

—Basil Moreau

PREACHING AT MY grandfather's funeral is still one of the hardest things that I have done. He taught me how to garden, fish, play cards, pitch horseshoes, catch night crawlers, and cheer for all the Detroit teams—whether winning or losing.

I was able to say goodbye to Grandpa although I didn't know it at the time. He was the first person to whom I showed the chalice that my parents had bought for my ordination. Because of his stroke, Grandpa didn't say many words, but as he lifted up the chalice, he did so purposefully, as a priest would. He said, "Good, good," and gave it back to me with a tear in his eye.

My tears came in preaching the funeral. It was, for me, a powerful experience that has helped me to realize the Cross as a precious treasure. Like the Cross of Christ, our crosses lead to something; they are not the end for us. Our pain, hurt, suffering, and losses lead to resurrection experiences just as Jesus' did. My grandfather's death taught me deeper compassion and empathy, which have helped me to walk with others in their times of grief. His death also led me to trust in his eternal life. To this day when I hear the clink of the horseshoe or watch the bobber go down while fishing, I remember Grandpa—both as he was to me then and as he is to me now. The crosses in our lives are certainly painful, but my grandpa has taught me that they are not all bad. In fact, for the Christian, they become "good, good."

Kevin Russeau, C.S.C.

June 10

Strive to be ever mindful of your vows and, once you have consecrated yourselves to God, do not look back.
—Basil Moreau

LOOKING BACK HAS a bad reputation. We're taught when running a race never to look back because in doing so we inevitably slow down. Baseball teams have base coaches to protect the runner from looking back to see where the ball is and thereby losing a critical step. Most tellingly, the Lord Jesus said, "No one who sets a hand to the plow and looks to what was left behind is fit for the Kingdom of God" (Lk 9:62). Farmers know that unless they keep their eye on where they're going, they'll wander off and the furrows will no longer be straight.

Fr. Moreau seems to have a similar idea. As religious, we spend a long time, years actually, preparing for the moment that we promise to live the vows of poverty, chastity, and obedience forever. We study them, we examine them, we parse them, and we practice living them, renewing them each year until we reach the point of maturity to decide that indeed the Lord wants us to allow those vows to shape the rest of our lives. Once we take vows, Fr. Moreau would have us live them, not wondering about life outside them, about all the infamous "what if" and "grass is greener"–type things that attempt to distract us.

Is this really all that different from the lives all Christians are called to live? Don't the vows of baptism to which we are all bound require us to look forward and plunge into the Christian journey? If we're married, doesn't our marriage have a better chance of success and final happiness if both spouses are single-minded in devoting themselves to making it work? Living the Christian life in any of its forms requires of all of us who go by that name to live passionately and single-heartedly, attentively and determinedly.

John H. Pearson, C.S.C.

June 11

O Jesus who has said "Let the little children come unto Me," and has inspired me with the desire to bring them to You, deign to bless my vocation, to assist me in my work and to clothe me with the spirit of strength, charity, and humility, in order that nothing may turn me aside from Your service.

—Jacques Dujarie

SOME OF MY students are hungry for everything I offer. Others are just too full, or too empty, before they even walk through the door. Most are in between. But I am supposed to teach them all and do it every day. I have read, studied, and researched, and I have composed important lessons. On good days they inspire and make all of us a part of something greater than any one of us can be alone. As we all are students, we have the responsibility to open ourselves to be challenged and inspired, building upon the legacy of those who have gone before us, and hopefully learning from their mistakes. As teachers, we are to be catalysts for that learning, and expect our students to respond with equal effort and success. Isn't that why we teach and learn, after all?

An adage states, "Education is what we remember after we have forgotten everything we learned." I have found it to be a good reminder every time I begin to get stressed about my lessons in my class with my students. It reminds me that it is usually not about me. I am simply the instrument. And when I am most tuned in, it reminds me just whose instrument I really am.

I am grateful for the blessings I encounter each time I realize that one of my students has learned the important lessons—which are sometimes close to the content I taught and, in the best times, much closer to the lesson God wanted them to learn. That is why we teach and we learn.

Kenneth Haders, C.S.C.

☨

June 12

The mission is not simple, for the impoverishments we would relieve are not simple. There are networks of privilege, prejudice and power so commonplace that often neither oppressors nor victims are aware of them. We must be aware and also understanding by reason of fellowship with the impoverished and by reason of patient learning.

—Holy Cross Constitutions

THE IMMENSE SUFFERING in our world today demands that we take it seriously. If we have the courage to do so, we discover that suffering is complicated, not easily explained, and that a great deal of it results from injustice. As followers of the One who innocently suffered and died for our sake on the Cross, we are called first to awaken to the suffering that can lie hidden from our eyes. Then we must neither run away from it nor avoid it.

In standing and facing the impoverishments of our world, we become more deeply aware of the pain and suffering that is the result of injustice, ignorance, and indifference. With this awareness comes the summons to let God work through us to bring about change—a change that will remove the obstacles that prevent both the poor and the wealthy from making the most of their God-given potential. If we are to do this effectively, we must know well the problems we address and avoid self-righteousness. The head and the heart must work together.

Although we seek to be constructive in our critique of the world around us and to act only out of a deep love and concern for all of God's people, there will be times when others will be offended by our work for change. Our own limitations may even get in the way of the good for which we are striving. But with Christ as our model, we must be both courageous about proclaiming the truth and faithful in always seeking to live the Father's will.

Robert A. Dowd, C.S.C.

June 13

We learn that formation and transformation are both the Lord's gifts which we as a community can help one another to receive.

—Holy Cross Constitutions

FORMATION IN THE Christian life never ends. We always can be transformed more fully into Christ. The person who rests satisfied has missed one of the deepest truths about human life—our hearts are restless until they rest in God. Even Fr. Sorin realized his need for help in this continued transformation, so he asked Br. Vincent Pieau, C.S.C., to be his spiritual monitor in Indiana. Each month, Br. Vincent would counsel Fr. Sorin, giving feedback, even constructive criticism, on his leadership of the nascent Notre Dame community.

It is not easy to accept correction, but if it comes from a trusted friend it can be transformative. We cannot know ourselves well without the mirror of an outside commentator, someone who can point out to us the things that impede our transformation into godliness. In fact, we owe each other such simple admonitions. For if we are to progress together, whether as a family, community, school, or parish, we all have to grow in the same direction of faith. None of us can be exempt from continual formation.

The result of our opening up to others is a freshness of heart, a cleansing we cannot achieve in isolation. Among the greatest gifts we can give to our brothers and sisters is to look out for one another. We need each other, not only in good times, but also in times of sickness, spiritual wandering, and even darkness. For we build each other up in the light, coming to our full stature in the one Body of Christ. Together we are formed; together we are transformed.

George Klawitter, C.S.C.

☧

June 14

People who live according to the will of God, even though they do only the most ordinary things, things with no attraction in the eyes of people, they are the people who will enter the Kingdom of Heaven and will receive a full reward.

—Basil Moreau

FAMILY AND OLD friends often tell me that I look like my father. Be that as it may, I hope that I resemble him in his gentleness and patience, his good judgment and quiet dependability. While he never missed Mass on Sundays and Holy Days, supported the local parish financially, and sent my sister and me to Catholic schools, my father was not a "churchy" person. His approach to the externals of religious practice was summed up in the parable of the Pharisee and the Publican. His model was the Publican.

Among other things, my father taught me that piety could be a manly thing. When I went into my parents' bedroom to say goodnight, I often found them kneeling beside their bed saying their prayers. As long as I can remember, my father went to confession and received communion on the first Friday of every month. Before I had even made my first communion, I started to accompany him to early Mass on those Fridays. It's a devotion that I still keep today.

My father was initially disappointed when I chose to become a priest and religious of Holy Cross. He would have preferred that I succeed him in his business and give him grandchildren, but he respected my choice and eventually came to endorse it. I have met people who rebel at speaking to or of God as Father, rebel at asking that the Father's will be done in their lives. My father modeled God for me, and fear of the Lord for me means fearing to disappoint God.

James Connelly, C.S.C.

June 15

It is necessary to be humble, docile, fervent, to take courage and not look behind you, always to move forward until you are in the possession of the glory of God.
—Jacques Dujarie

ALL OF US have something to be humble about, no matter who we are. After all, we are finite. None of us can claim great wisdom, yet we try to grow in wisdom as we grow older through our education and our life experiences. And the fact is that we do not and cannot move forward without a certain basic humility. It boils down to this: We must realize that we are simply instruments. The instrument does not do the job. The person who uses the instrument does the job. In this way, we open ourselves to the Spirit; we allow ourselves to be instruments in the hands of God. And we give him the credit for what we do because it comes from his inspiration.

The older we get, the more we tend to simplify things, even the religious life. I have read dozens of religious books, but when it all got boiled down and I was on the firing line, the inspiration of the Holy Spirit is what I found most important. Ultimately it is not just a question of being docile, but being docile to the Holy Spirit. We need to know and to trust that the Spirit is working through us by virtue of our baptism. We today have lost a sense of the active, living influence of the Holy Spirit in the life of the Church. We need to be more attentive to the promptings of the Spirit, following his lead. It is then, when we are obedient to the Holy Spirit, that courage comes. For we receive true courage only when we know we are in the hands of God, when we know that God is acting through us for his glory.

Ted Hesburgh, C.S.C.

June 16

*To struggle for justice and meet only stubbornness, to
try to rally those who have despaired, to stand by the
side of misery we cannot relieve, to preach the Lord to
those who have little faith or do not wish to hear of him
. . . our ministry will hint to us of Jesus' suffering for us.*
—Holy Cross Constitutions

EACH MORNING IN my bedroom, I pray with gratitude before
more than two hundred photos on my wall. Every photograph
is a link to people who have affected my life and ministry in
Holy Cross. Several of the photos remind me of the people of
Chimbote, Peru, with whom I spent three months in 1976.
There I daily witnessed our Holy Cross religious with lay
companions standing by the side of those in misery and trying
to rally those in despair. In their struggle for social justice I
experienced many hints of Jesus' suffering for and with us. I
returned to the University of Notre Dame, where I was on the
faculty, filled with passion to teach in new ways. Collaborators
and I developed programs to invite members of the campus
community to serve and learn in cross-cultural settings.

Charlie Kenney was one of the students who participated
in many of our programs, including in Peru. Desiring a deeper
ministry experience, he returned to Peru a few years after
graduation as a lay minister. Soon he met and married
Caridad Marchand, a Peruvian parishioner and teacher at our
Holy Cross parish and school. My photo of them and their
four children calls me to pray *gracias* for our friendship and

shared mission. Their faces remind me that struggling for social justice bears fruit through personal and community connections. All of us can be challenged through such relationships in mission to make and keep the commitments that will continually transform us into people with hope to bring.

Don McNeill, C.S.C.

June 17

God's help will not be wanting in our hour of need. Providence never fails to provide for all the necessities of those who, by fidelity to their duties, abandon themselves to its guidance, even if it becomes necessary to send angels to help them.

—Basil Moreau

MY JOURNEY AS founder and pastor of a parish in Duchity, a poor village in a remote area of Haiti, tells a vivid story of God's love and Divine Providence. When I first arrived there one Sunday morning, I was like a builder on a big construction site. I was ready to build, but I lacked plans or resources. In the depths of my heart, however, I had much more than any of those material assets. I had the burning desire to love and serve the Lord through those simple people. I wanted to share the many gifts that God's love had given me.

That Sunday morning I did not have a penny to begin even one of the many buildings that the new parish, then just a clay chapel, desperately needed. One parishioner took me in until I had a place to live. I could only follow God and listen to him day by day, praying that he make me an instrument of his love. Today this parish in Duchity, which is part of the Diocese of Jeremie, is a well-known community where people from both Haiti and abroad go on a regular basis to live their faith and share with their brothers and sisters in Christ the gift of love God has granted them. All that the Lord accomplished through us—shepherding souls, helping people grow in faith, and bringing pride to that neglected village—was made possible by our unfailing trust in him. For wherever we are, unless the Lord builds the house, we the builders labor in vain.

Fritz Louis, C.S.C.

June 18

If we drink the cup each of us is poured and given, we servants will fare no better than our master. But if we shirk the cross, gone too will be our hope. It is in fidelity to what we once pledged that we will find the dying and the rising equally assured.

—Holy Cross Constitutions

I'VE LOST TRACK of the number of weddings and final professions of religious vows in which I've participated. Each is unique, yet there are common elements—joy, hope, excitement, the support of community and family, and a sense that everything is indeed possible with God's grace. Yet we veterans of life know something that the young often do not. Fidelity to one's commitment, which in the moment seems so forever easy, will eventually reach a point where what we once pledged has to be confirmed again and again, and yet again.

Life is not static. We change—or resist change—and must honor and obey our growth and experience. Our spouses or communities change—or refuse to change—and we must remember our promises, for better or worse. Neighbors and co-workers change, as do parents and children, and we must somehow remain faithful to them. The Church changes, as does the world in which we live. Even God seems to change, in the sense that the One whom we thought so close and so supportive now seems absent and unheeding.

There is no doubt that fidelity will sometimes tear us apart, as it did Jesus on the Cross. Hard choices may be necessary as we seek to balance the demands of being faithful to God, self, and others, whether in family or religious community. All we know for sure is that God will be with us, every step of the way. Somehow, someway, that which is torn apart will form the fertile ground for yet one more renewal of our fidelity.

Herbert C. Yost, C.S.C.

June 19

The brothers shall remember always that the children in their charge are given to them by God Himself to teach them to love and serve Him; and by consequence, their principal care should be to form them in virtue.

—Jacques Dujarie

FOR MANY YEARS, I had the privilege of living with and caring for youth in the Hogar Santa Cruz, a home for abused children run by Holy Cross in Santiago, Chile. I don't know who profited more from our time together, them or me. They certainly helped me to learn a lot about myself through their open and frank observations. Although they still had a great deal of their lives ahead of them, these children came to our home laden with memories they did not willingly wish to examine. They carried the heavy burdens of abuse and neglect. Those of us who worked with these children had the responsibility of helping them gain positive experiences that would be more colorful and pleasant to recall.

Many of the children with whom I lived at the Hogar Santa Cruz have now grown to become young adults. When they come to visit me now, it is clear that it was not so much what I said to them that made a lasting impression, but the manner in which I spoke. My tone of voice, my facial expressions, and my gestures are what left the more enduring mark on them.

For all of us who raise or work with children and young adults, it is critical that we welcome them into our hearts so that they can experience a true concern for their well-being. This loving care is the expression of the dignity that they deserve. In this way we can hope to make a lasting, positive impact on the young who are entrusted to our care.

Donald Kuchenmeister, C.S.C.

June 20

We grow close to one another as brothers by living together in community. If we do not love the brothers whom we see, then we cannot love the God whom we have not seen.

—Holy Cross Constitutions

MADE IN THE image and likeness of God, we are called to communion with God and neighbor. Intimate relationship is at the heart of God's own life and ours as well. In marriage, husband and wife live out this image and likeness in a pledged love that is open to the sharing of new life. In Holy Cross we live out this image and likeness in a pledged love to live together as brothers. It is through, with, and in our shared life—whether as brothers in community, husband and wife, or neighbors—that we are called to experience, celebrate, and proclaim God's love for the world.

The longing for communion—for intimate relationship with God and neighbor—that the Lord has placed in the depths of our being is not easily or readily satisfied. It continually beckons us to sacrifice and to self-emptying love so that we make in our hearts a space of welcome for both God and neighbor.

We must dare, then, to allow our longing for God to turn our minds and hearts to the needs of those with whom we live. We must dare to allow our gaze to recognize in our brothers and sisters a mirror image of ourselves as fellow pilgrims on the journey to a communion of life and love that knows no end. We must dare to allow ourselves to see in our neighbors the image of the Father such that in loving them we love God and even ourselves. We must dare to allow ourselves to grow close to one another so that our communion with each other becomes a sacramental sign of the communion God desires for all humankind.

Thomas P. Looney, C.S.C.

June 21

But we do not grieve as men without hope, for Christ the Lord has risen to die no more. He has taken us into the mystery and the grace of this life that springs up from death. If we, like him, encounter and accept suffering in our discipleship, we will move without awkwardness among others who suffer. We must be men with hope to bring.

—Holy Cross Constitutions

HIS WEEKLY COLUMN in the university newspaper was called "Letters from a Lonely God."

As an official chaplain at the university, he opened a simple, "well-lighted place" where the uncool and the unconnected arrived late into the night to find someone who would listen to their demons. As an unofficial friend of the city, he spent holidays on the backstreets with the poor and the broken, buying cups of sacramental coffee and hearing hours of not quite sacramental confession.

"Are you happy?" he always asked, seeming to hope that someone would finally say yes. His tired eyes invited trust; his wounded spirit called for truth; his fierce loyalty gave strength. The stories of faith and fear and love and doubt and passion and pain were all gently heard and woven back into the one gospel story—of life and death and again new life. He wanted them to know that he and his lonely God really loved them.

The life of this son of Fr. Moreau had carried its own share of pain. His health was never good. Struggles with depression took a toll. He was often misunderstood. But he knew better than most of us that we are all walking wounded. He knew that loneliness and fear touch each one, and he used his honest, lonely spirit as a passkey into the hearts of many. When they opened their dark spaces, he entered gently, with care and with love, bringing his personal witness that the Good Lord has not lost even one of us.

Thomas McDermott, C.S.C.

June 22

Fear not to consume yourself in the service of Him Who at all times protects the just and frustrates the vain efforts of the impious.

—Jacques Dujarie

WHILE I WAS growing up, my uncle owned a motorcycle, which he would often ride to family gatherings. Once while my cousins and I were playing basketball in the back of my grandparents' house, he rode up on his motorcycle and parked near where we were playing. Realizing the potential danger, he looked us all in the eye and said, "Do not touch the pipes. They are extremely hot." Being a curious young man, I simply could not ignore such an invitation. I only touched the exhaust pipe with a small part of my hand, but it was enough to send shoots of pain up and down my arm.

Although few of us have been foolish enough to touch hot exhaust pipes, many of us have experienced the sudden attraction to explore the divine life, but found the experience difficult or even painful. Sometimes we are drawn to faith by the hope that our lives will get better, and when our experience remains the same, we feel compelled to try something else. In a way we may feel as if we have been "burned" by the whole experience.

The experience of feeling burned is an invitation to enter more fully into the service of our loving God. We can be tempted to play it safe in our spiritual lives, doing just enough to get by, yet through baptism we have been consecrated to God. It is left to us, then, to believe firmly that we have been called by the Father and led by the Spirit to offer our lives and our work in the service of the Lord for the needs of the Church and the world.

Peter McCormick, C.S.C.

June 23—Sacred Heart of Jesus

No matter what the cost, let us remain united with our superiors through obedience and united among our-selves by the bonds of that love of which the Sacred Heart of Jesus is the burning center, and which, so to speak, should form a chain linking together all the mem-bers of Holy Cross. This, moreover, is the recommendation of our Divine Lord to His apostles. It was the object of His touching prayer to His heavenly Father for us when He said: "Holy Father, I pray that they may be one, in the unity of one spirit, one faith and one love, and that just as Thou art in me and I in Thee, so also they may be one in us.

—Basil Moreau

EVERY SUMMER, WE in Holy Cross gather to celebrate jubilees of our brothers who are marking twenty-five, forty, fifty, and even more years of vowed life or priestly ministry. These powerful occasions of reminiscing and rejoicing—the joys and sorrows, the achievements and trials, the grace and the sin—invite us to rekindle the dreams of our youth and our hopes to make a difference. For us in Holy Cross, they are dreams and hopes inflamed with the love of the Sacred Heart of Jesus. Fr. Moreau chose the feast of the Sacred Heart as the patronal feast of the priests of Holy Cross precisely because of the powerful image of Jesus' human heart aflame with love for all sinners. We ground our model of priestly love in the Sacred Heart of Jesus—that heart pierced by the soldier's lance in the final proof that Jesus offered all, every last bit of his life substance, for us. His open heart is a burning center from which flows life-giving blood and water, hope for the world that we strive to embody.

To love in this same way—unreservedly and sacrificially, creatively and redemptively—is a challenge for us each day and draws us into a whole new priestly identity. For those of us who are ordained priests, the image of the Sacred Heart of Jesus holds up for us a model of the complete and unconditional love that must be the heart of our ministry of bringing Christ into the world. Yet we are all a priestly people, anointed as priest, prophet, and king in our baptism. There is no room for any of us to hold back, to hesitate, to shrink away in fear. There is no place for self-absorption or self-protection, no way to hide from the costs of such incredible love, no way to make this love self-serving. It must be the total gift of self.

Jesus' compassionate and merciful love, a fully human love, leads to and builds unity among people. There is room for everyone in the Sacred Heart of Jesus—every sinner and every saint. In his heart the sinner finds forgiveness; the saint finds glory. The sinner is led to conversion; those striving for the perfection of holiness learn the lesson of self-giving. Both in conversion and in self-gift, our hearts will be broken and pierced. But from a broken, contrite heart flows a steadfast spirit and an enduring love.

Jesus indeed brought to the world a truly impossible love. He wanted us to love each other with the same love he experienced in the Divine Trinity, a love that unites all as one. And so our own love must be much more than any natural love of kinship or friends. This love, manifested for religious in obedience to community and for all people in their regard and care for their neighbors, can be costly. It underscores that a total gift of self is precisely a total gift of self for the sake of others. But Love himself draws us from independence and self-sufficiency to interdependence. Inflamed by the Sacred Heart, we live and love, beyond our own capabilities; we become convincing signs that our ultimate destiny is union with one another in Christ.

Wherever two or three are gathered together—in families and in religious communities, with kin and with stranger—there we will find Jesus in our midst, inspiring us all to be imitations of his Sacred Heart—living witnesses of love's unifying power.

Bob Epping, C.S.C.

June 24

To each and to all a star appeared, and moved on, and rested over the mysterious spot where every faithful follower found all he had desired—the Child and His Mother and St. Joseph. What more could be wished for?
—Edward Sorin

POETRY ABOUT TRAVEL resonates with me. T.S. Eliot wrote that "the end of all our explorations" is to return to the place from which we began and to know it for "the first time." Shakespeare writes that love "is the star to every wandering bark." Each of these poems reminds me of the journey of the spirit, following a star and ultimately seeking to rest. So it is that our lives are often marked by periods of movement and periods of rest.

My own life in Holy Cross has been marked by this very rhythm—from one assignment to another, one ministry to another. I have moved from the city to the country and back again. I began in New York City teaching high school. I then moved from there to Rochester, from Rochester to Maryland, Maryland to Boston, Boston to New Orleans, and New Orleans to Des Moines. Each place on my journey has provided its own sense of home through friends, worship, community, and daily routine.

Although each of these moves has not been easy, external movement and settlement has provided the opportunity for interior growth and reflection. This interior journey is a deepening of life, a finding of God at the heart of things. Intimacy with God is our place of rest only found under the surface in movement to the inside. This movement within comes through the recurrent practice of quiet, silence, and communication with God. The Child, his Mother, and St. Joseph are our companions in that sacred place, in that moment of epiphany. There we can all dwell together and find a delightful rest.

David Andrews, C.S.C.

June 25

Oh! The folly of the world! Oh! The wisdom of the Cross! Here is our study, our hope.

—Edward Sorin

IN MY FIRST parish assignment, one of the first home visits I ever made was to a woman with a degenerative disease that had liquefied her muscles. By the time of my visit, she had been reduced to unbearable pain as her spine compacted upon itself. She looked at me and said, "Deacon, Jesus did not suffer as I have suffered. Three hours on a cross is nothing compared to twenty years of intense pain. Why do I suffer so?"

Pious platitudes seemed empty and even cruel to speak, yet I sputtered them anyway, desperate for something to say. Watching me, she shook her head and said, "Oh, Deacon, stop. I suffer. I don't know why bad things happen in our world. But this I know—God didn't cause this suffering. He's the one who gets me through it." She then described how God's love had filled her through the years of her illness and how his abiding presence comforted her, even as she ranted at him.

In life, we will all face crosses of our own. The world tells us to avoid, sanitize, or eliminate them. But should we shirk our cross, we will miss the opportunity to encounter Love itself and experience God's gentle embrace. There is no need to romanticize human suffering or make of it a virtue. But when, in faith, we accept our suffering and shoulder the burdens of our lives, we open our hearts to God. Such is the hope of the Cross—the ultimate school of love.

Gary S. Chamberland, C.S.C.

June 26

Let us be one, just as our Lord Jesus Christ asked this unity for us of His Father. It is only on this condition that God will give us His own strength. This strength is that which flows from charity, mutual harmony, oneness of mind, and the sweet bonds of brotherly love.

—Basil Moreau

IN MY MORE than forty years of working in Holy Cross education, I have been blessed to witness so many miracles in the lives of young people. Through these years as a teacher, school counselor, coach, principal, and now president of a school I have seen truly extraordinary happenings. Graduation day in June seems to bring it all to light. That day is always a testament that God's miracles find their way into youthful lives through the attention and care given by so many of my colleagues in our shared ministry of forming minds and hearts for Christian life.

No matter what ministry I've been doing, I have often had to confront the temptation to go solo in my efforts, thinking I have the strength and wherewithal to do it all myself as if the miracles were mine to perform. As I reflect back on the numerous circumstances where I have tried to play "superman," they become laughable at best and pathetic at worst. Thankfully, a sizeable number of my colleagues in ministry have had the care to challenge me in my foolishness. Since the day I first stepped into the classroom, my brothers in Holy Cross, alongside numerous lay men and women, have empowered me to be all that I have been able to be for so many youngsters. More importantly, however, they have taught me the great truth that being one in mind and heart, united together in the sweet bonds of charity and mutual harmony, is the way to miracle. It is only in this condition that God will give us his strength.

Jim Branigan, C.S.C.

June 27

Let us be the tabernacle where God dwells since His Kingdom is within us. In our hearts, may the mysterious lamp be fed unceasingly by the oil of good works, and may it be kept constantly burning.

—Basil Moreau

EACH HUMAN BEING in the world is called to be God's tabernacle, a holy place where God might dwell. Each person, without exception, from the greatest to the smallest, from the proudest to the humblest, is called to be holy. We are called to embody God's love and pardon, to be fertile lands where the reign of God might grow and thrive.

God's reign is already in our midst, here with us, and it grows to its fullness in God's love for the most unprotected, outcast, and abandoned. It is the love that visits a thief in prison without judging him for what he did, that welcomes a refugee, an undocumented, an exile. It is the love that adopts children orphaned by war, that waits in watchful prayer with those who suffer. It is the love that reaches out to those of a different race, ethnicity, or sexual orientation, that extends hands in solidarity to victims of violence and natural catastrophe. It is, above all, the love that forgives even the very ones who would take away human life.

To this love and to no other we are called. We are all capable of it. When we live the very love of God, we feed the lamps of our hearts and God's Spirit comes to dwell within us. Then we truly become places of refuge amid so much indifference, holy tabernacles, beacons of hope in the midst of darkness, proclaiming to the world that the kingdom of God has not died.

Simón Cerda, C.S.C.

June 28

Our vows bind us together as a community. We commit ourselves to share with one another who we are, what we have and what we do.

—Holy Cross Constitutions

TRAVELING ACROSS THE country to spend our summer vacation with my cousins, we finally arrived at the campground, exhausted from the journey and the heat. While setting up, my father called to my mother, "Where are the tent poles?" Bags were checked, looks were exchanged, but nothing could change the fact that the tent poles had been left at home a thousand miles behind us. Where would we sleep for the next two weeks? The adults came together and made a plan. One child could go with that family, another with those cousins; and so each of us would find a place to lay our heads. A potentially terrible vacation had been averted by the ingenuity and generosity of family.

I have often thought of our vows—chastity, poverty, and obedience—in terms of the familial ingenuity and generosity shown on that vacation. For it was sharing that bound us closer together as a family that summer, and it is sharing that binds us ever more closely as brothers in a religious community. Anchored in the ground of our Christian faith and commitment, our shared vows lift up and support our common life. We come knowing perhaps only a few members of the congregation, and each of us brings our own unique backgrounds and gifts. Over a lifetime we weave together our diverse talents and dreams to create a community that is a sign of hope in an alienated world.

Each of us, as followers of Jesus, first by our baptismal promises and later by the particular vows we make, is called to support and build up the Christian community. In this community, under our tent, all of God's children find welcome—family, friends, strangers, and even those who have forgotten their tent poles.

Jonathan Beebe, C.S.C.

June 29

*Our thoughts are not easily God's thoughts, nor our
wills his will. But as we listen to him and converse with
him, our minds will be given to understand him and his
designs.*

—Holy Cross Constitutions

IN THE GOSPELS there are few, if any, more strong-willed than
Simon Peter. The evangelist probably has kindly edited Peter's
response to Jesus' request that he row back to deep waters
for the catch that the apostle was certain was not there. Luke
tells us that Peter simply said "Master, we have been hard at it
all night long and have caught nothing." I can only imagine
Peter's response was really a bit lengthier and perhaps more
colorful before it ended with his gasp, "But if you say so, I
will lower the nets." This is classic Peter, obstinately sure of
himself but finally given to temper his own steely will with
Jesus' persuasive insistence that he let go of it.

The *Holy Cross Constitutions* recognize the Peter in all of
us. They tell us that our thoughts and wills are not easily
God's but do not rule out the possibility that they could come
to be so, just as Peter's became evermore like God's. But first
we need to be humbly honest and recognize that we cannot
know God's designs unless we are given to understand them.
Otherwise, the more we try, the more frustrated we become
because often our own designs, superimposed upon God's,
are what we see. So perhaps we need to take being given to

understand literally and let Jesus lead us to be given to know God's will.

Letting go of our will is not a loss, but a gain. When we allow it to become part of something greater, something greater becomes part of it. And in the process, God's greatness overcomes our pettiness and self-interest, and his breadth and depth fill the shallowness of our understanding.

Don Fetters, C.S.C.

June 30

We know that hope never confounds; that we must glory in the hope of the glory of the children of God; and that, even against hope, we must believe in hope— hope against hope.

—Edward Sorin

GIVEN THAT HOLY Cross in the Americas had its birth in Indiana and that a large community continues to serve there, we can tend to think of the congregation as a Midwestern community—landlocked and surrounded by cornfields.

But for those of us who live in coastal Holy Cross, the emblem devised by Fr. Moreau of a cross flanked by a pair of crossed anchors has a nautical resonance that fits our vernacular. The first Holy Cross house in the eastern United States, a stately mansion in the town of North Dartmouth, Massachusetts, served as a novitiate before becoming the home for the mission band and a place of recreation. For many classes of novices, Sunday afternoon recreation involved walking several miles to the small village of Padanaram on Buzzards Bay. Passing by small boats anchored in the harbor, the novices enjoyed an ice cream before walking back to the novitiate for prayers. Often on summer afternoons, I brought my Midwestern classmates to that same village harbor, though unlike our predecessors we bicycled or drove. Those boats, in the tossing waters of the bay, were visible reminders of anchored stability that helped to form in our imaginations an appreciation for the virtue of hope.

Fr. Sorin reminds us that hope never confounds; rather it anchors the Christian in a tumultuous world. That does not mean that hope is always clear, because like the Cross, hope is paradoxical. Submerged, weighty, sharp, and rusty, hope anchors us even when we don't see much promise, when we hope against hope. Often when the reasons for hope are most absent from our lives, it is then that hope is holding us fast.

Peter J. Walsh, C.S.C.

JULY

July 1

Loss may soon be called a real blessing, if it brings every Religious of Holy Cross to resolve earnestly to be, now and forever, a model of regularity and devotedness, of obedience and humility; a cheerful lover of actual poverty.

—Edward Sorin

THE LOSS FR. Sorin speaks of here was the near destruction of a fledgling Notre Dame to fire. It must have been catastrophic to see a promising dream smoldering in ashes. Yet the dedication and resolve of our Holy Cross brothers saw the phoenix rise from the ashes. Notre Dame continues to be a blessing to the congregation, the Church, and the world. Indeed, it is a blessing far beyond the hopes and dreams of the young Holy Cross community in America. And it was dedication and resolve, a true model of regularity and devotedness, that changed this painful loss into an enduring blessing.

Loss is inevitable in life and in ministry. We suffer the loss of loved ones who come and go in our lives. There is, for example, a certain dying when we religious are called from one ministry to another. It is always difficult to leave those for whom and with whom we have lived and ministered to embrace a new challenge, a new opportunity, and to discover a new blessing. There is a certain painful poverty in any letting go, but the blessings of the people who have enriched our lives and ministry endure and continue to bear fruit long after we have moved on.

The paradox of dying and rising, of loving and letting go, is a daily reality in the Christian life. It is only when the grain of wheat falls into the ground and dies that it can bear much fruit; and it is our collective resolve to transform every loss into a blessing that will enable us to remain strong for the future.

Ed Kaminski, C.S.C.

July 2

I am not the least bit surprised by all these trials. Thanks be to God. They have only increased my confidence in Him who alone has founded and maintained this congregation. He it is who will expand it more and more.
—Basil Moreau

AT KENYATTA NATIONAL Hospital in Nairobi, Kenya, I visited a woman with a very serious condition on her face and in her eyes. I was serving as a chaplain at the hospital with one of my brothers in Holy Cross from Tanzania. Each week, we visited and prayed with the sick. To do this, I had to learn *Kiswahili*, the local language of many of the patients. Yet, even with my newly acquired language skills, I was at a loss for words in conversation with this particular woman. She explained, "I yearn to cry, but I have no tears. I endure the pain." Given the severity of her condition and the anguish of her words, I felt helpless. At first I got caught up in what I could say or do in order to lessen her pain. Then I realized that what really mattered was that I simply was there for her and could share my tears. Breaking through the silence, she said, "Your being with me speaks volumes. Thank you."

To endure pain, disillusionment, and setback in our lives can be trying, but it should not be surprising. These things are a part of all of our lives. The grace is to see these trials, as Fr. Moreau did, as opportunities to increase our confidence in the Lord. This is the grace that comes as we stop searching for what to say and what to do and begin simply to rest in God's presence with us.

Ronald M. Kawooya, C.S.C.

☩

July 3

Let us forget past wrongs. Let us bear in mind the reply of our Divine Lord to St. Peter who, after asking how many times he ought to pardon, received from His sacred lips the equivalent of these words: Always and without ever tiring.

—Basil Moreau

WITHOUT FORGIVENESS THERE can be no community. Without forgiveness human societies and nations fall apart. Holy Cross exists because our founder, Fr. Moreau, understood why Jesus made forgiveness such an important part of his life, both in story and in action. Jesus himself forgives not only his friends the apostles for their cowardice and betrayal, but also his Roman enemies who ultimately put him to death. He extends this forgiveness to them when they do not ask for it or even know how.

In this world all too full of conflict, exploitation, and ethnic cleansing, forgiveness can be unfortunately dismissed as a sign of weakness, and even as an injustice. How could we ever forgive a betraying neighbor, a torturer, or a killer? Jesus, however, teaches otherwise, calling on us to forgive always and without ever tiring. For him forgiveness is a sign of strength, the only kind of strength from which true justice can come.

And yet, the power of forgiveness is so subtle that only a child can do it with grace and love. Maybe that is why Jesus continually invites us to be like little children. We adults must work hard at forgiving and asking for it. Even then, it does not always come easy or end very well. But when it does, it is a pure gift, a divine gift making our very life together in human communities possible.

Claude Pomerleau, C.S.C.

☧

July 4

If we wish to love one another more, then let us develop an ever greater love for the common Master of us all, our common Father, our joy and our reward. By coming to know Him we shall come to recognize our own dignity, and, by that very fact, the dignity of our brethren also; by loving Him we shall learn to love others.
—Edward Sorin

THE LOVE OF a father is an empowering and freeing love. A father works to instill confidence in his children so that they feel free enough to leave home, to explore the world, and to become what they are destined to become. Perhaps Edward Sorin's own father helped instill in him the freedom and confidence that let him leave everything behind in France to become founding father of a great Catholic university.

Above all, what sustained him in his journey to America was his unshakeable faith in our common father. This is the father who gave Jesus his Son the freedom and courage to leave behind the glory of heaven for the most difficult and risky mission—the salvation of the world. This is the father of the prodigal son—loving unconditionally, looking out of the window day after day along the dusty road, longing for just one glimpse of a wayward child and celebrating his return with a kiss, an embrace, a ring, sandals, a new cloak, and a fatted calf. Such is our dignity in God's eyes, no matter what we've done.

In coming to know this God, in making our own homecoming in faith, we shall finally recognize our own dignity and that of our neighbor. Then we can move out in freedom and confidence to welcome the stranger, the poor, the immigrant, the prisoner, the person of viewpoints or of a faith very different than our own. The salvation of the world depends on our loving the common Master and Father of us all—so much does he love us and free us to love in return.

Patrick Neary, C.S.C.

July 5

We must be contented to be treated as poor. Should we gain nothing else by this new general effort but to conform ourselves to the spirit of poverty, we might well congratulate one another; for the spirit of poverty is the greatest riches of a community.

—Edward Sorin

THE GREAT DANGER of riches is that they can fool us into believing that we can make it on our own, that we don't need to depend upon others, let alone on God. Conversely, by our vow of poverty we in Holy Cross pledge dependence upon one another as we hold all our goods in common and share them as brothers. This disposition requires and thus expresses a true confidence in one another. For our poverty is not merely our own; by its very nature it draws us closer together and binds us into community.

Our renunciation of the independent use and enjoyment of the goods of the land causes us to acquire riches not of this world. They are the riches of a deeper connection with, and dependence on one another—riches of deeper connection with, and dependence on God.

Yet for all Christian believers, our spirit of poverty should not express or exhibit a disdain, or even contempt, for the material riches and the blessings of the earth. Rather, it should express a yearning and eagerness to share the bounty that the Lord has placed in the world. It is this sharing of the earth's abundance that draws us together and binds us as the human family. We liberate our very hearts in order that they might be possessed entirely by each other and by God. Our graciousness, then, is an imitation of the abundant love with which the God of the universe created us—the love that is truly the greatest of riches.

Fermin Donoso, C.S.C.

July 6

The God of Justice and Mercy may, and often does, afflict His faithful servants here below in order to reward them hereafter with an eternal happiness.
—Edward Sorin

EACH ONE OF us is caught up in the ageless fight between good and evil. It is a struggle for which we are ill prepared because we cannot predict the afflictions that will come our way. Moreover, we live in a world well beyond our immediate control. And so it seems that the only match for evil is our omnipotent God, who is just and merciful.

And yet we must face our imperfect human situation, filled with weakness, illness, accidents, and tragedy. The ravages of nature—tsunamis, tornados, earthquakes, fires, and floods—also burst suddenly upon us, disrupting our lives. And we honestly wonder why these things happen to us. Then there is sin, our own personally chosen affliction. So much of our interpersonal turmoil and sadness stems from ill-chosen words and acts of unkindness. Their consequences can heap bitterness and resentment onto our already trying lives. In our suffering, caused both by the course of nature and by our own free choices, we cry out to God asking where he is. Has he really conquered evil?

When we face afflictions and are tempted to give up, we are peering directly into God's inscrutable ways. Even Jesus prayed in anguish to the Father, seeking to understand his ways before he endured his passion and death. Yet Jesus' faithfulness was ultimately rewarded in the glory of the resurrection. All God asks of us, too, is faithfulness. And so even when we fail to understand God's ways, we can "boast of our afflictions, knowing that affliction produces endurance; and endurance, proven character; and proven character, hope; and hope does not disappoint" (Rom 5:4–5).

Bob Epping, C.S.C.

July 7

Honor and glory to the teachers who will bear me out in this engagement and especially to those who will impart, besides a real religious instruction, a true sense of piety in the young hearts entrusted to their care. In proportion as they will have taken God's own interest to heart, Heaven's blessings will follow them.

—Edward Sorin

AS I WAS finishing my years as president of a large Catholic high school founded in the Holy Cross tradition, I was reminded on several occasions that those who teach, and especially those who teach from the heart, give a great gift to young people. It is always touching to know that the efforts expended to reach the heart of a young person are often repaid with truly personal and profound gratitude. It is the small things—the kind gestures, the thoughtful remarks, the offers of assistance, and the promise of prayers—that make all the difference.

A student of mine from more than three decades ago stopped by my office one day to say thanks. My memory was vague and I did not recognize him. Yet he clearly and vividly remembered what I had said that supported him in his formative years of adolescence. His sentiments were so genuine and appreciative that I realized that somehow, someway, I had been in the right place at the right time. It is true that more often than not teachers never know how much they matter or how important they are in the shaping and molding of their students' characters. It is a great prize when it is revealed in unexpected ways.

We are all teachers. We are all capable of touching hearts. When we invite God to dwell within us we become teachers and instruments of his generous love. Yes, I am certain that God's blessings do follow.

Jerome Donnelly, C.S.C.

☩

July 8

His delights are to be with us; our greatest happiness is
to live for Him and with Him, to follow Him and obey
His holy will.

—Edward Sorin

ONE SUMMER, WHILE working as a seminarian at our camp
in Maine, twelve of us were returning from a three-day canoe
trip when a terrible storm came up on Lake Sebago. Thunder,
lightning, and high waves threw us into a panic. I spotted a
small island several hundred yards away, and we focused all of
our attention on paddling to it. Two hours later, we reached
it with our hands blistered and energy sapped, but we were
eternally grateful for the ability God had given us to stay
focused on our goal.

When I began my ministry at Holy Cross Parish in South
Easton, Massachusetts, I had never served as a pastor in my
more than three decades of priesthood. In taking the job, I felt
at first like I did that day on Lake Sebago. I suppose I could
have allowed myself to be overcome with fear and uncertainty.
Instead, I decided to take each day as it came, to stay close to
God, and to do all in my power to help others to do the same.
In all honesty, I am not always certain in my ministry there.
But as long as I keep myself focused on doing what God has
called me to do, I am filled with gratitude and happiness.

If we are going to be true to our God-given callings, the
challenge for all of us lies in keeping our sights set on Christ,
especially in times of fear and uncertainty. He will always live

in us if we live in him. And therein we will find our greatest happiness.

R. Bradley Beaupre, C.S.C.

July 9

We must be responsible—each of us—for the conformity of our lives to the Gospel and for the harmony of our ministries with the mission of Christ. The Spirit of the Lord may choose any of us to speak the truths we all need to hear. Our vow of obedience itself obliges each of us take appropriate responsibility for the common good.

—Holy Cross Constitutions

CONFORMITY, OBEDIENCE, OBLIGATION, common good— generally speaking, these are not popular words in today's western culture. In order to make it in the world, we are trained at a young age to be self-reliant, ruggedly individualistic, and independent in our thoughts and actions. As a result, unfortunately, it is easy to be duped into believing that life and the world is all about me. Nothing, though, could be further from the gospel truth. A true follower of Jesus Christ knows that it cannot be just about me. It can only be about us, together.

From the beginning, Fr. Moreau aligned the mission of the Congregation of Holy Cross with that of Jesus Christ. For his mission to be successful, Fr. Moreau knew that he needed men and women united and rooted in their faith, so that they would have the courage to preach and to witness to the gospel truth. Fr. Moreau realized early on that it had to be more than just about him. It had to be about everyone, together.

As we look at the dire needs of our world, our planet, and the human family, we cannot think just about "me" any longer. More so than ever, and for the sake of the gospel, we must take appropriate responsibility for the common good so that together we can ensure our future.

Paul Bednarczyk, C.S.C.

July 10

God is faithful; He will not suffer you to be tempted above your strength. He will always give you the means to resist your temptations in such a way that you will be able to overcome them. Hence, laying aside the burden of sin which can retard our advance, let us run with constancy in the way which is opened up before us.

—Basil Moreau

HUMAN LIFE IS no stranger to temptations and trials. Our brother Elijah was ministered to by an angel so that he might be given strength and consolation before he departed for a journey lasting forty days and forty nights. We recall that even our Lord experienced temptation. Situated in the desert for forty days and forty nights, Jesus felt the mental and physical pain and anguish of temptation, but did not succumb. Afterward, he was ministered to by angels.

It is out of this scriptural history that Fr. Moreau wrote this letter of encouragement. He knew then, and communicates to us even now, that we are not strangers to temptation and trial. But Fr. Moreau, always a man rooted in the hope of the Cross, reminds us of the grace of God that is ours. This is what is meant when Holy Cross religious profess their vows and say, "May the God who allows and invites me to make this commitment strengthen and protect me to be faithful to it." We are not ministered to by angels, but by Christ Jesus himself. And this is a great consolation to all Christians who strive daily in discipleship, our own forty days and forty nights.

God does indeed give us the means by which to resist temptation and, more importantly, to live well our Christian lives of discipleship with joy and freedom. The task, then, for we Christians who are beset daily by temptations and trials is to accept the gift of grace as it comes to us with joy and faithfulness.

Michael Wurtz, C.S.C.

July 11

Resist the evil one stoutly, having frequent recourse to prayer, constantly imploring the aid of our dear Lord and His Holy Mother.

—Jacques Dujarie

THERE IS AN insightful scene at the end of the often unedifying film *The Devil's Advocate*. After watching more than two hours of the protagonist's having surrendered to temptation and abandoned his personal and professional ethics, we learn it was a dream, or rather a nightmare. In an inspiring final scene, the hero announces to a packed courtroom that he must abandon his client, whose guilt he had come to discover, come what may. Moments later though, the hero is interviewed by a newspaper reporter, promising him fame for his virtue. The reporter then turns to the camera, his face morphing into that of the devil himself, who notifies us that vanity is his favorite vice. In an instant, we are brought back to the knife's edge between sin and grace.

This clever twist upon a twist at the end of the story portrays a truth all too easy for most of us to forget—evil lurks around every corner because it lurks within ourselves, even when we are doing the right thing. Rarely are we able to act out of unmixed motives. For, as the prophet Jeremiah reminds us, more tortuous than all else is the human heart. Therefore, we need the constant vigilance of a sincere prayer life to help us to stay true to the voice of our Good Shepherd. Fidelity to the life of prayer is no guarantee of a sinless life. On the contrary, by keeping us honest before our God and mindful of our consciences, it keeps us aware that, in the midst of our sinfulness, grace abounds.

William R. Dailey, C.S.C.

July 12

We forgo the independent exercise of our wills in order to join with brothers in a common discernment of God's will as manifested in prayer, communal reflection, scripture, the Spirit's guidance in the church, and the cry of the poor.

—Holy Cross Constitutions

WE PRAY IN the Our Father, "Thy will be done." And in baptism, all of us are called to be disciples, to help in building up the kingdom of God. For religious of Holy Cross, giving ourselves to the Father's will and following our baptismal call to serve the kingdom are lived out radically in our profession of vows. Our vow of obedience, by which we forgo the independent exercise of our own will so that together we might discern God's—allows us the freedom of being at the service of our community wherever we are sent. We are disciples working in and with the Church. We trust that our superiors will use our gifts and talents together with others to spread the good news.

For all seeking to do God's will, our example should be that of Mary who responded so generously and freely to God's invitation to be the mother of Jesus. Like Mary, we too might point out our limitations when we are requested to do something for which we feel unprepared, but then we should trust in the Holy Spirit. In my own life, I have found that the assignment I would not have chosen, the one I felt unprepared to accept, has brought me the greatest joy. And this same joy awaits all of us if we but generously and freely respond to the promptings of the Spirit in our daily lives—in the needs of our neighbors, in the faces of our loved ones, in our own prayer and reflection. For indeed, God's will is our joy.

Carl F. Ebey, C.S.C.

July 13

Allow me to hope that yours will be the heritage of Jesus Christ, the heritage which His saints, our fathers in God, have bequeathed to us. It is a heritage of humiliation, poverty and suffering; of trials, temptations, labors, and persecutions of all kinds. In vain shall we seek any way leading to heaven other than the road to Calvary.

—Basil Moreau

THE HERITAGE LEFT to the Church by Fr. Moreau is that of Jesus Christ himself, the heritage of the Cross. It is the same heritage handed down to us by the other saintly men and women in Holy Cross, a heritage that was their daily bread. It is not a heritage of money, fame, or earthly power. But it is a solid inheritance, made to last. It rests on the continual cultivation of a virtuous life and a deep, disinterested love of God and neighbor. Anything keeping us from acquiring this heritage must be put aside. Everything that can increase our possession of it must be favored. It is here that we encounter the Cross.

The Cross does not consist in seeking privations or suffering. Rather, the Cross flows from our love of God and of neighbor and our seeking after a virtuous life. The Cross is the result of such a choice, and it is a measure, if not an indication, of our efforts to acquire this virtuous life. The higher we aim, the more certain we can be that we will find the Cross.

There is the question of the stakes involved. Is it all worth it? What, if anything, awaits us beyond these crosses? Heaven is the answer. It is the final goal. It is the summation of our call to follow Christ and to embrace his Cross—to become truly the image and likeness of God.

Mario Lachapelle, C.S.C.

July 14

If God is our only hope, we must try to deserve His protection.

—Edward Sorin

"WHAT'S KEEPING YOU from leaving the priesthood?" The question startled me. But in fairness to the young man who asked it, I recognized how troubled he was by what he saw in the Church of the late 1960s—priests and religious leaving, liturgical experimentation running amok, and Church authority flouted or ignored. Those turbulent times were understandably upsetting for someone discerning a vocation to religious life and priesthood. Could he commit himself to a life so many were abandoning?

Upon further reflection, I might have answered differently, but in the moment I responded, "I'm no prophet and I have no idea what the future holds. But I'm ready to walk into darkness, if only accompanied by one or two of my brothers in Holy Cross." They were brave words indeed. And many dark days did come along in my religious life and priesthood to test my resolve, just as they had tested the resolve of the men who had gone before me and will test those who will come after me. I admire the generations of Holy Cross men and women who have lived and worked in the shadow of the Cross with little more to sustain them than hope itself—hope in God, hope in the Cross. For it was, after all, in this hope that they found their way to the Lord. Their example inspires all of us who are seeking our way to the Lord to let go of everything that clutters our lives and finally put all of our hope where it rightly belongs, in the Cross of Christ our Savior.

Leonard N. Banas, C.S.C.

July 15

The Sacred Heart of Jesus is the chief source of the affections of Our Lord, and the center of the most perfect virtues which ever existed: a veritable treasure-house of sincerity, innocence, purity, meekness, patience and humility. In a word, the Heart of Jesus is a living mirror of the most admirable human perfections, and of the choicest gifts of grace.

—Basil Moreau

As THE STORY goes, Fr. Patrick Peyton, C.S.C., was giving an address in Uganda, speaking in his Irish brogue about the foundational experience of praying the rosary with his family as a child. The crowd was immense and hushed as he spoke, urgently begging them to take up the practice of the family rosary to strengthen and save their families.

Among the thousands of rapt listeners was a man from a tribe that did not speak English. One of the many reporters spotted him and studied his countenance. The man could not have been more riveted upon the glowing face of Fr. Peyton. He was hanging on every word that came from the Holy Cross priest. Bemused and curious, the reporter spoke to the man in his native dialect.

"Do you agree with that fellow?"

"I certainly do," came the immediate reply.

"But you do not speak English, do you? No members of your tribe do. How can you agree or disagree?"

"You are right," admitted the tribesman. "I cannot speak or understand a word of the English language. But I know I agree with this man."

"How can that be?" the reporter questioned.

"I can read his face. This man is sincere, innocent, meek, and humble. I don't understand the exact words, but I know they come from someone close to God, so I agree with them. When I stand before the judgment seat, I would be privileged to stand next to such a holy man. Why, he has the heart of Christ!"

This, too, is our call—to put on the Sacred Heart of Jesus.

John Phalen, C.S.C.

July 16

We will live so that our faith might be so simple, so strong and lively that it not only enlightens the spirit but also inspires our thoughts, feelings, words and actions.
—Basil Moreau

WHEN I READ Fr. Moreau describe the ideal faith as simple, I must admit that a part of me bristles. I associate "simple" with negative words like "simpleton," and so I hesitate to endorse the simplicity of faith. And yet, religious philosophers like Augustine and Aquinas remind us that God is by nature simple. How can this be? In what sense can the source of all the universe's complexity be simple?

God is simple because of his essential and eternal unity. God is so pure that his word and his love share his very being. We admire people whose words and actions are consistent with who they really are. God's being and speaking and doing are so consistent that they are truly one. It is in this sense that God is awesomely simple.

And so Fr. Moreau rightly asserts that our simple faith in this simple God will affect a similar unity in us—a unity of spirit, thought, feeling, word, and action; a unity of mind, heart, soul, and strength. Far too often, unfortunately, we endure the frustrations and struggles described by St. Paul as he laments the predicament of a divided self, "For I do not do the good I want, but I do the evil I do not want" (Rom 7:19). When I am divided against myself, I waste so much energy fighting myself that I have little left to give to God and neighbor. By contrast, Fr. Moreau understands that a simple person, a united person, is lively and strong, because that person is an image of the living God.

Charles McCoy, C.S.C.

July 17

We know to us are addressed those words of Jesus Christ: "Suffer the little children to come to Me," etc., "for it is to them, and to those that resemble them, belong the kingdom of heaven."

—Edward Sorin

AS A YOUNG religious, I often wondered what in the world these words of Jesus might mean for me as an adult. Wasn't I to put aside the things of childhood, eat the food of adults, and live the life of a mature religious? A lifetime of experience, though, has brought me to a new understanding of Jesus' words.

I travel quite a bit and spend a good deal of time sitting in airports where I enjoy people watching. Very small children, if they are not fussing, are wonderful to watch. They have a bright, welcoming smile for everyone. Everything they see is filled with wonder and joy and they accept it with a welcoming heart. On one overseas trip, I sat in a row behind a seven year old who was sitting with his mom. As the plane was taking off, he grew excited: "We're taking off, we're taking off.

We're flying, Mom, we're flying!" His joyful shouts filled the whole cabin with smiles.

As we grow up we can lose our sense of wonder in the seemingly ordinary. Jesus teaches us how to rediscover the simple joys of our youth, how to enter into his kingdom. In living out our ordinary, humdrum existence, Jesus blessed it, and even in his last years, could still find beauty and delight in the ordinary—the lilies of the field, the birds of the air. Everything speaks of awe, of God. Perhaps the kingdom is for those who, like little children, can still find wonder and joy disguised in the ordinary, the face of a stranger or the taking off of an airplane.

Raymond Papenfuss, C.S.C.

July 18

If the imitation of Christ is our duty, it is also our glory.
—Basil Moreau

AS A NEW kind of apostle, struggling to lead a fledgling congregation in making Christ known and the gospel lived across the globe, Fr. Moreau understood the need to put on Christ. Like the apostle Paul, whose putting on Christ required a new way of seeing himself and the world around him, Fr. Moreau had to suspend fears and judgments in order to devote himself, and lead his followers, to see as Christ saw. If the need presented itself in India or America, there the congregation would go; it was the path the Lord had selected.

In my work in a college setting, God asks—often prods—me to put on Christ, to suspend my human and intellectual judgments about what knowledge I might impart in favor of seeing with the heart. Rather than judging how well prepared I think a student is, should I not be more concerned with how I will reach that questioning or indifferent student in the third row? I need constantly to identify and to refuse to surrender to the self that impedes compassionate action, which is motivated by the other's need rather than my own.

Fr. Moreau taught that our goal as Christians is to understand others as God sees and accepts each one of us. It is not really a "duty," except in the sense that we must work at it each day. Rather than being a loss of self, the rooting of our will and ability in the heart of Christ's saving mission enables our fulfillment. When we put on Christ and let God lead our hearts and minds, our lives and our service become a transforming—indeed a glorious—experience of his grace-filled presence.

Anthony Grasso, C.S.C.

July 19

It is this union, the fruit of sanctifying grace, which will strengthen us against the world and the devil, while being at the same time the source of our success and consolations. It is like the mortar which holds and binds the stones of the building we have undertaken, for without it, everything will crumble and fall into ruin.

—Basil Moreau

EACH OF US is unique and free to make the most of our God-given potential for good. Yet without a connection to each other in community we may never discover that wonderful uniqueness and God-given potential. Through the interactions that community fosters, we come to learn about ourselves and about the God who created us. Community, at its best, helps us to celebrate good work but also prevents us from becoming vainly proud over our accomplishments. And, when we fail or make mistakes, as all of us do at times, it is community that consoles us, prevents us from giving up, and encourages us to keep reaching out to serve others.

Without community our work and our lives become directionless. We become isolated individuals, unable to recognize how God seeks to unite our gifts to our neighbors' in greater service of his kingdom. Whether in a religious community or in any other community that unites people of faith, we are more effective in mission together than we are apart. So God builds us up into living walls, made of individual stones but bound up together into a spiritual house.

Yet while community holds us together, it must never confine the creativity of the individuals who form it, for God seeks to harvest, through the community, the fruits of individual creativity. It is the community that should cultivate this unique creativity in individuals and it is the through the creativity of individuals that God will always renew it, bringing it to the fullness of life.

Robert A. Dowd, C.S.C.

July 20

For those who live by faith the Cross is a treasure more valuable than gold and precious stones. If we were truly worthy of our vocation, far from dreading these crosses, we would be more eager to accept them than to receive a relic of the very wood which our Savior sanctified by His Blood.

—Basil Moreau

WHEN A BIT of debris becomes wedged in the flesh of an oyster, the irritated mollusk responds by coating the offending fragment with countless layers of a substance called "nacre." In time, a pearl is produced. What began as a source of pain to the shellfish ends as an iridescent jewel. Of course, if the oyster had kept its shell firmly closed, the debris could never have gotten inside in the first place. But an oyster needs to open its shell in order to breathe and feed. So, if the oyster hadn't taken the risk of opening its shell, it would have suffocated and starved, and there would have been one less pearl in the world.

Fr. Moreau's reflection on the Cross suggests that something analogous is true of us. If we respond to the sufferings of each hour by enfolding them within a life of patient, generous love, we will in the course of time become jewel-like adornments of the kingdom of God. But if fear of suffering causes us to withdraw from others and the world, we will be spiritually stifled. And someone beautiful, with whom God intended to adorn creation, will never come to be.

In at least one respect, though, the analogy fails. For while a pearl is precious, the fragment of debris at its center, considered on its own merits, is valueless, whereas the suffering that occasions a Christian life well-lived is itself a priceless reminder of the saving Cross of our Lord Jesus Christ.

Charles B. Gordon, C.S.C.

July 21

Certainly we celebrate the love and affection of the people we love. Even greater is our joy and love toward Jesus who has loved us so much more.

—Basil Moreau

YES, WE ARE loved by those who love us, but it is in experiencing this love from others that we also experience a greater love, the love of God that surrounds us and challenges us to go beyond what we are content to do.

As a Holy Cross priest I have found love from others and from God present at every step of my ministry. This was certainly the case at my very first funeral when I was unsure of how to minister to the family and the larger community. Just how do we reach out to many different people who are all suffering from the aftershocks of a double murder? I had to rely on the love that I had received from others and trust that Jesus would guide me. I do not remember what I said, but I do know that the love of Jesus did embrace all of us during the tragedy. Love was also present when I later moved to Mexico to minister among the people there. Just how do we reach out to people with a language, culture, and way of living so different from our own? It was the love that I had received and given in my previous ministries that helped me to move on to this next challenge in my faith journey, and it was the love I encountered there that helped me to fulfill it.

Jesus continuously provides all of us with opportunities to walk in his steps, to face the unknown, and to share the love that we have received from him and from others in new and unexpected ways. It's when we have shared this love, his love, with others that we realize just how much love Jesus shares with us.

Joseph Moyer, C.S.C.

July 22

We find prayer no less a struggle than did the first disciples, who wearied of their watch. Even our ministry can offer itself as a convincing excuse to be neglectful, since our exertions for the kingdom tempt us to imagine that our work may supply for our prayer. But without prayer we drift, and our work is no longer for him. To serve him honestly we must pray always and not give up. He will bless us in his time and lighten our burdens and befriend our loneliness.

—Holy Cross Constitutions

MARRIED PENITENTS REGULARLY confess that their primary sin is the failure to nurture their relationship with their spouse. They acknowledge working long hours for mortgage payments, food, and tuition and know that carting children around town, preparing meals, and keeping house are acts of love for their family. Yet amidst this activity, they have failed to cherish, engage, compliment, or simply talk to the one person who means most to them in this life. One senses guilt for their omission and a longing to recapture what it has taken from them.

If we are prone to avoid meaningful interaction with those whom we love, how much easier is it to fall out of conversation with the Lord? We can slide quickly into a relationship with God where we are about his work, yet never give him a moment of our time, never let him into our heart. And yet, what God most wants with each of us is to have the whispered conversation of lovers, to know our heart's desire and to lend us strength. Be it murmured rosaries, focused meditations, anguished petitions, or stolen minutes simply basking in his presence, prayer strengthens and refreshes us for the joys and trials of life. Together with the other true conversations of our lives, prayer binds us more deeply in the web of love, which is God himself.

Gary S. Chamberland, C.S.C.

July 23

Our mutual respect and shared undertaking should be a hopeful sign of the kingdom, and they are when others can behold how we love one another.

—Holy Cross Constitutions

WHEN ANOTHER BROTHER and I were visiting our Holy Cross high schools to assess the effectiveness of our mission there, we set up meetings with randomly selected groups of students. We asked them to tell us what was special about their school. At one of the sessions, a young woman spoke up, saying that at some schools one only gets respect if he or she is smart, athletic, or popular. She then added, "What I like about our school is that we are respected the minute we walk in the door on the very first day."

Jesus came among us preaching about a kingdom where mutual respect and understanding are central. And indeed, these qualities are indispensable elements in spreading the kingdom of peace and justice, in which everyone will have life and have it to the full. Mutual respect and understanding only come about when we do what Jesus did, that is, when we look at the world around us through the loving eyes of the Father.

I've thought often of the young woman's remark. It spoke so well about that school and made me proud of our mission as Holy Cross educators. But the reason that it has really stuck with me is because it challenges me to love ever more deeply. For if any of us are to help extend God's kingdom on earth, we can't size up a situation and then act. We have to be open to giving every person respect and understanding when they come through the door for the very first time.

George C. Schmitz, C.S.C.

July 24

Only this Holy Spirit can make us real Religious, as He alone has made us Christians.

—Basil Moreau

THE HOLY SPIRIT has led me step-by-step along my life's journey. That is not to say, however, that there haven't been major surprises along the way. My childhood days were blessed by the constant support of friends and family, Church and community. Everything seemed stable and my future predictable. But the Spirit summoned me, through the wise advice of my pastor, to enroll as a student at the University of Notre Dame. This prodding of the Spirit continued to guide me until I found myself anchored in the safe harbor of my vocation in Holy Cross.

In my religious life and priesthood, God's holy Wisdom has continued to walk step-by-step with me along my journey. Through countless men and women, the Spirit has slowly but surely communicated God's loving guidance to me at every twist and turn of my life. Seminarian classmates and saintly pastors, dedicated teachers and inspiring writers, civil leaders and retreat participants, and indeed so many more, have all shared with me the sparks of their own burning love for God, sparks which have, in turn, fed the fire within me.

And so we should not always anticipate surprises from the Spirit, even though they do come. More often than not the work of Divine Providence is slow and sure, imparted to us through daily encounters with the people around us. Yet it is the Holy Spirit that is always at work in us, ever continuing to fashion us into the Christians God has called us to be.

Robert Pelton, C.S.C.

July 25

Let us march with courage under the banner of the Cross.

—Edward Sorin

IN THE EARLY hours of July 25, 2000, on the feast of St. James, three Holy Cross priests and their driver were hit by gunfire directed at their vehicle by insurgents in North East India. Bullets struck Fr. Victor Crasta, C.S.C., in the heart and head, but he prayed aloud: "Forgive them Lord for they do not know what they are doing." As the brave son of Holy Cross breathed his last, he encouraged his fellow priests to move ahead and stay true to their mission.

I was one of those priests in the car. I also was hit by the insurgents' bullets but survived the attack. Holy Cross's profound faith, courage, and hope in the face of the Cross give me the strength to move on in spite of losing an eye in this assault. Lack of sight in one eye reminds me every day that it is the Lord who works through me and through us all. As St. Paul reminds us, God's grace works through each of us, especially when we are weak.

I continue to live my life in Holy Cross, trusting in Divine Providence and in hope. In this life, each of us faces challenges. Some of them are small and others are large and difficult to bear. Fr. Sorin reminds us that these daily crosses, if we but bear them with courage, will strengthen us to be effective disciples of Jesus, whom we continually experience and radiate in our lives. The death of a loved one, a car accident that cripples, the diagnosis of an incurable cancer, or the deviant behavior of a son or a daughter are all heavy crosses that some among us may have to bear. The Cross, however, becomes light when we are rooted in the Lord and march under his banner.

Paul Pudussery, C.S.C.

☩

July 26

Let us all try, more earnestly than ever, to consolidate our hopes of an endless union in heaven by a faithful discharge of our respective obligations and, above all, by a daily increasing union of hearts upon earth.

—Edward Sorin

A GROUP OF parents at Saint George's College in Chile asked me to assist them in their annual weekend retreat. On the retreat team, I met parents who were hungry to know more about Holy Cross, not just what they had experienced in Chile, but more about the history, mission, and the international character of the congregation. We decided to place the retreat participants into thirty groups, each bearing the name of a Holy Cross religious to serve as an inspiration.

As I worked to identify the thirty names and to write their brief biographies, I realized how many Holy Cross men and women were worthy of imitation. The list included those who took the gospel to distant places and those who served faithfully in their own homelands. The images of great teachers, servants, preachers, administrators, community leaders, and pastors filled the list. The prayers and conversations of that weekend retreat celebrated the lives of Holy Cross religious like McCauley, Ganguly, Peyton, Bessette, and McGrath who through the years have said yes to the Lord. They, along with Victor Krasta, the Rwandan Brothers, and so many others who laid down their lives for the gospel, trusted in God in times of great challenge, even in the face of their own mortality. Through their inspiration and example as witnesses to the faith, they unite today, in service of the gospel, all of us who learn and know their stories. Our lives, then, faithfully lived in their footsteps, can in turn unite the hearts of those we are called to serve across the globe today and for generations to come.

Michael M. DeLaney, C.S.C.

July 27

To understand the doctrine of the Cross we must love the Cross after the manner St. Paul loved it when he said: "May I not glory unless in the cross of our Lord Jesus Christ!"

—Edward Sorin

EVERYONE WHO HAS been to the University of Notre Dame has some favorite places on campus.

Like many in Holy Cross, I was ordained a priest at Sacred Heart Basilica. For me, this place holds a special draw, reminding me of my first dreams and hopes as a priest. Like many others, when I return to campus I pray at the Grotto amid the light of hundreds of glowing candles while asking our Lady of Notre Dame for help.

A visit to the Holy Cross Cemetery on the road to Saint Mary's College, however, is a must. I find great strength and hope walking through the neat rows of simple crosses marked only with the names and dates of birth and death of generations of teachers, confessors, collaborators, and friends in Holy Cross. Each visit seems to evoke a different series of memories. Sometimes memories of painful, protracted choir practices in summer heat can still produce a sweat, even after so many years. These professors, classmates, and friends are now all united in this quiet field of crosses after years of dedicated ministry and service throughout the world. They all have come home to rest together.

No one really knows, apart from God, every detail of their earthly lives. In general, from the ones we knew best, we know that life was filled with fun, laughter, struggle, some success, and sometimes failure not unlike what befalls each of us. In silence they call out, reminding us that the true wisdom and holiness of Jesus is the way of the Cross. They assure us by the lives they lived that indeed the Cross is our only hope, our genuine success, and our authentic glory.

Jack Keefe, C.S.C.

July 28

Truly, we cannot sufficiently admire God's plan in our regard. After sending us crosses and trials, He now crowns us with success and consoles us with peace both within and without. It is an indubitable proof that He wishes to guide His work himself according to His own admirable designs.

—Basil Moreau

THERE ARE NO individual examples of God's care for us, if by this we mean special moments when God provides for our needs. At the core of our Christian faith is the trust that every moment is part of God's design. As Fr. Moreau wrote, trials and successes, crosses and consolations are all part of Divine Providence in our lives.

This faith does not lead us to disdain the material world or to abandon our efforts to accomplish something. We are called to dedicate ourselves to some useful task, and we all share the same human responsibilities—to worship God, to lead an honorable life, to love our neighbor, to be of some service. In all of these we often fail. But life's ultimate significance does not depend on our worldly successes and failures. Our salvation is the final value, and this is in the hands of God. Fr. Moreau put his hope in the Cross because he found there the revelation that God had rescued us from sin and called us to himself.

Everyone who has lived many years learns the truth of the saying that life is what happens while we are making other plans. But even though our plans are not accomplished, we can be sure that we are part of a greater design not of our making. God's shaping of our lives remains a mystery, yet each day we can lead lives of thanksgiving because Christ has opened for us the gates of heaven.

Louis Manzo, C.S.C.

July 29

We could never complain of the sacrifices demanded by our vow of poverty, if we reflected on what the Gospel tells us of the sacrifices which Jesus Christ imposed on Himself for us and if we had a true love of Him who for love of us became the poorest of people. Oh, how edifying would be our language and our conduct on the score of poverty if we kept our eyes always fixed on this divine model.

—Basil Moreau

MY CURRENT PARISH assignment is quite a bit different from my childhood home in sunny southern California. When I was growing up, everybody drove shiny new cars. My friends lived in large homes overlooking the Pacific Ocean. Weekends were spent at the malls. Restaurants were a regular part of the weekly routine, and nothing was ever beyond our grasp. Surveying the streets of my parish neighborhood, I observe dented and rusted-out cars that squeal and squeak as they rumble along. Dilapidated old homes seem to slouch under the weight of their many years. The local strip mall and liquor store bustle with activity around the clock. Fast food boxes and bags litter the streets, and people of all ages linger on porches and sidewalks with apparently nothing better to do.

For some, this dichotomy might seem depressing. But as religious of Holy Cross, as men with hope to bring, the vow of poverty calls us into the neighborhoods of the poor and working class. It challenges selfish displays of wealth and consumerism that characterize many parts of our society. If we want to follow truly the example of Christ, we must embrace the same self-sacrifice and poverty Jesus endured for us. For a life of simplicity and sacrifice is a requirement for all who dare to follow Christ. Whatever vocation we embrace, our poverty must be a response of the heart to the teaching of Jesus: if any want to become my followers, let them deny themselves and take up their cross and follow me.

Michael C. Mathews, C.S.C.

July 30

I am so sorely in need of prayer! In it rests all my hope and consolation. Let us pray, then, and pray much. Let us gather before the throne of God, united in the hearts of Jesus, Mary, and Joseph.

—Basil Moreau

IT WAS 1975, a Jubilee Year. I was excited that I would be traveling to Rome to celebrate the occasion with more than twenty parishioners from St. Ignatius, Martyr, Parish in Austin, Texas. Many of the pilgrims had never been to Rome, so excitement was high among the group. After an eight-hour plane flight, we landed in Rome. Upon arriving at the hotel, I found a message from our Holy Cross Generalate, our headquarters in Rome. I called and was informed that while I was en route to Rome my mother had died in Dallas. She was fifty-eight.

My mother had suffered for a number of years from emphysema. During her illness I was fortunate enough to be able to visit her and my dad on a weekly basis. But now, in Rome, thousands of miles away, I felt guilty that I had not been at her side in her final moments. I was crushed. Alone, I returned to the States. I cried much of the way home. What gave me strength in this terrible time of loss was prayer, knowing and believing with all my heart that God would help me and the rest of my family, especially my dad, through our sorrow and pain. I knew I was not alone on that plane, but that God was traveling with me.

I have probably never prayed so much or so hard as I did on that fateful return trip. Without prayer, without the Lord at my side, I don't know how I'd ever have survived that long, arduous flight. The hope and consolation I experienced through prayer carried me through the difficult days that followed. In the Lord, indeed, is our hope and consolation.

Peter D. Rocca, C.S.C.

July 31

As a teaching body, here is our first duty clearly revealed: we must excel by a special care to place at the head of all sciences that of religion; hence our chief end is to make of our pupils good Christians before they are learned scholars.

—Edward Sorin

IN THE THREE Holy Cross schools of which I have been a part, I have found that Fr. Sorin's words of wisdom echo in the hallways. Respecting the personal beliefs that our students, teachers, administers, and staff might have, our campuses are anchored in the work of being good Christians.

At Notre Dame Sherman Oaks, this reality begins with our students' sense of family and their welcoming spirit, which allows them to excel in their academic and civic responsibilities. It extends to the ways in which our students model Christian values in their commitment to service in their local communities. My experience has been that the students find means to work hand in hand with those they come to serve. Whether it be putting on a prom for renal patients or laying cement in Tijuana, Mexico, they embrace the people with whom they are working. By their actions, the students continue to spread the message of Christianity. Most importantly, our students' work of being good Christians is grounded in their commitment to their spiritual lives. I am renewed every time I attend a retreat with them. Gathered with our Catholic students are their Jewish, Muslim, Buddhist, Protestant, and Hindu classmates who eagerly share with one another their life experiences and how God has brought them together at that time and place to work with and help each other.

Our students, through the communities they build, the service they do, and the beliefs they share, thus confirm that our most important task as educators, parents, and community members is to teach those God has entrusted to us to explore and live out their faith.

Joseph Moyer, C.S.C.

AUGUST

August 1

What we call a loss is often, in Heaven's design, a gain, even to those who cannot see it immediately.
—Edward Sorin

I'M AN ELDER member of the Holy Cross community. If a younger member suggests that I have done something wrong, I might easily become offended. I might think that I've lost the proper respect owed to me as an elder. I might even have the pain of loss. It is very hard for me to understand how God might be trying to bless me by helping me to see my shortcomings. I may even view the other more as a critic than as a brother.

Our shortcomings are usually evident to everyone but ourselves. That is true not only for us who are elders but also for those who are young. And so, whether we are priests or religious, parents or teachers, students or public officials, we can all learn from the other members of our communities and families. God brings these others into our lives not as critics but as gifts because their constructive criticisms and helpful suggestions reveal how we can grow. Nevertheless, when someone points out a fault to me, I may still feel pain. But if I let go of my hurt, I can see that in fact I have been blessed. I have been given a chance to change, a chance to become a different person—a better person.

Ultimately we grow when we change. It simply requires that we remain open to the gift God is offering us when someone suggests a way to improve our behavior. Then what might seem like a loss and truly be painful will prove to be heaven's way of preparing us for our final home in God.

Bill Blum, C.S.C.

August 2

This does not mean that our Lord forbids foresight and human initiative. He recommends elsewhere work, order and economy in the use of temporal things, but He forbids all anxiety, because this is a reflection on his paternal providence.

—Basil Moreau

To BE SURE, I have anxious moments as we all do. These are the times in life when a given task may seem too large or impossible. As a result, I might feel alone, perhaps even abandoned. But at such times I have only to pause and to reflect on the reality of love that surrounds me—the care and support I know from family, friends, brothers in community, and others who share my life and work. This love is wonderful. It is a sign of God's love for me. It is the way in which God guides me to his end. This is Divine Providence.

So much has been said about God's loving care for each one of us. St. Paul recalls that, "In Him we live and we move and we have our being" (Acts 17:28). God is the source and sustainer of our lives. All that we are and hope to become is from God. And so we can begin each new day in that sure and confident hope that God provides for us. We are all parts of the marvelous plan that our good and gracious God has for all of creation. To live in Divine Providence, though, means that we can never be passive, simply waiting for God's will to unfold. We are each uniquely gifted with wits, abilities, virtues, and zeal. The more that we come to know that we are loved, the more we will live to return that love to God and to others. For what we lack, the good Lord will provide.

John Conley, C.S.C.

August 3

Our vows not only bind us in community; they are to mark our life as community. Open and generous and hospitable love is to characterize our houses and our service. As a congregation and in each of our local communities we are committed to the use of few belongings and to simple living.

—Holy Cross Constitutions

WE IN HOLY Cross are a family. Our vows of poverty, chastity, and obedience unite us—despite all our differences in temperament, personalities, and backgrounds—into one family walking side by side in our following of the Lord. At the same time, these vows challenge us to open ourselves in generous service to others.

It might seem paradoxical, however, that we profess a vow of poverty, yet work to alleviate poverty in the world. I myself have passed a great deal of my life in Holy Cross living and working with the economically destitute. It has almost always seemed that I have had more material things than the poor whom I've served. In these moments of tension, the theology of our vow provides me guidance as to how I might serve authentically—by possessing few belongings, living simply, sharing goods in common, and entrusting myself fully to God and the generosity of his people. This calls for an act of faith. It demands that we open our lives and our homes through the generous love with which Christ binds together the human family.

In striving to live this openness and generosity, I have been inspired by the example of the poor families to whom I minister in Monterrey, Mexico. Time and time again they invite me into their homes—reminding me always that their home is also my home. The hospitality that these families so powerfully display is a virtue that helps all of us, both in the Holy Cross family and in the human family, to put into practice the love that unites us together as one.

Leonard J. Collins, C.S.C.

August 4

If the tree of the Cross has been planted in the vast field which is ours to cultivate; even if, more often than not, its fruits have seemed bitter; we must recognize that it has become a tree of life and that we are now reaping from it fruit which is as "pleasing to the eye as it is good to the taste."

—Basil Moreau

A YOUNG SAILOR greeted me and asked to speak privately. I was his chaplain aboard an aircraft carrier. He began, "I have been aboard the *Midway* for three years and have been awarded for my performance. We have accomplished so much, and I am proud to have been part of this crew. We have visited so many exciting places, ports of call in Asia, Africa, Australia, and others along the way." Tears then welled up as he continued, "But you know, chaplain, all of life, the whole world looks the same from a bar stool." A profound grief gripped the young man. A deep longing had stirred within him.

He was not alone. Sometimes referred to as "souls," five thousand men inhabited the aircraft carrier. From chipping paint to keep rust at bay to piloting fighter jets to patrol the skies, every member of the crew had a job to do in support of the overall mission. While attending to duty in support of that common purpose, each soul also engaged in his own personal quest for truth, peace, and ultimately, for life.

In this quest, we find the Cross planted in our lives. As suffering takes root, willfulness and the desire to control may intoxicate us. Wounded, trust may escape us. Frightened, doubt may consume us. Deep within, however, the Spirit cultivates fresh hope. Uplifted, the Cross carries us. Forgiven, we are awakened to a new day.

William D. Dorwart, C.S.C.

August 5

*Prayer and devotedness to duty are universally accepted
as essential to Community life.*

—Edward Sorin

I DO NOT like house cleaning. The dust makes me sneeze,
and I always seem to have something better to do, making
the chore a real inconvenience. Yet I live in a community with
my brothers in Holy Cross. And, whether I like it or not, I
have the responsibility, or duty, of taking care of the part of
our house assigned to me. If I don't do the cleaning, not only
will the house remain dirty, but the order and the peace of the
community ultimately might begin to unravel. We have to
perform with devotedness the little duties of our lives, lest we
also neglect our bigger responsibilities to one another. In Holy
Cross such neglect threatens the very witness that our religious
life has to offer to the world and the Church.

The gift of religious life, and of any Christian community
for that matter—whether it is a school, parish, or family—is
to show that the promise of Jesus Christ is true: People can
live, pray, and serve together in peace and love. This is the
essence of our calling as Christians. In doing the little things
like cleaning the house, being faithful to prayer, and helping
in the yard we are living out our baptismal call to witness to
the kingdom of God. Cleaning toilets, sweeping floors, and
other thankless chores are not glamorous, but they are necessary for the life and witness of our Christian communities.
Only when we have fulfilled these smallest of tasks might our

lives together cause people to exclaim: "See how they love one another!" Then we will have proclaimed Christ more effectively to the world.

Matthew McKenna, C.S.C.

August 6

It is not merely we who pray, but his Spirit who prays in us. And we who busy ourselves in announcing the Lord's kingdom need to come back often enough and sit at his feet and listen still more closely.

—Holy Cross Constitutions

VOCATUS ATQUE NON vocatus, Deus aderit. I give this inscription on a laminated card to every novice who enters the Holy Cross novitiate. It is also inscribed on a bronze plaque in my office. It means: "Bidden or not bidden, God is present." At the same time that I present this card to the novices, I ask them to go through a kind of detox, giving up their cell phones, the Internet, and all of their electronic toys for the year. It is not an easy task for anyone. Can we imagine our lives without all of these props? Without all the noise? Without all the busyness? To discover joy, renewal, and refreshment in the silent presence of the One who is always present to each of us is what we learn at the novitiate. Once we have experienced this gift of sacred time, sacred space, and intimate relationship with the Lord, then the line from Psalm 46, "Be still and know that I am God," becomes real.

All of us grow anxious and busy with many good things, especially the mission of Jesus Christ in the world today. We all need to maintain an awareness of Jesus' presence with us whether we are active and busy or not. We all need to carve out some sacred time and sacred space to sit at the feet of Jesus, to be still, and to listen to the voice of God. Then our relationship with the Lord will deepen and we will be conformed all the more to Christ, who will send us back out into the world of our busy lives refreshed and renewed.

Tom Lemos, C.S.C.

August 7

It is consoling, it is encouraging, it is wonderfully rejoicing, to breathe a prayer for a friend, for a child whose welfare is as dear as that of oneself.

—Edward Sorin

"HOW ARE DON Clemente and Doña Rita?" This is the type of question the students at Our Lady of the Lake University in San Antonio, Texas, ask whenever I return from a trip to Mexico. In my work as a campus minister there I lead students on week-long immersion trips to La Luz, our Holy Cross parish across the border in Monterrey. In a single week, in spite of language barriers, I am blessed to witness the friendships that form between our young people and the parishioners of La Luz.

While we are at the parish, we spend time with the children, youth, and elderly. We assist with after-school programs for students. We eat lunch with the older members of the community. We take communion to and visit with the sick. But mostly, we simply spend time getting to know the people in the neighborhoods of the parish. When we return to the United States, the students talk about their desire to work with the poor and to live more simply. Even more, however, they talk about their friends in Mexico, whether those friends are newly adopted grandparents or children they met in the very poor area of the parish. They speak sincerely of keeping them in prayer. Likewise when I return to the parish, the people there always ask about their friends in San Antonio and tell me that their young American friends are remembered in prayer.

These prayers, as much as they are petitions for the other, are expressions of joy and thanksgiving for the good that God has brought through these relationships. In turn, these prayers keep ever new the grace of these encounters—with Don Clemente, with Doña Rita, and ultimately with our Lord.

Mike Winslow, C.S.C.

August 8

Those who care for us and for the Kingdom will expect our way of life to be modest and simple. However, our local communities should be generous in continuing our tradition of hospitality to confreres, *to those who labor with us, to our relatives and neighbors, and to the poor, especially those who have no one to have them in. The measure of our generosity will be the sincerity, the simplicity and the sensitivity of our welcome.*

—Holy Cross Constitutions

As a COMMUNITY, Holy Cross has grappled with trying to define our particular charism, or gift to the Church. While we may haggle over some characteristics, we are in agreement that the virtue of hospitality stands at the heart of who we are and how we minister.

Our *Constitutions* speak of modesty and simplicity in the way we live our lives together, but we don't hesitate to pull out all the stops on occasions when we host family and friends in celebrating the milestones that mark our religious life. Some of the most significant moments that we in Holy Cross share with others happen when we celebrate the deepening commitment that each of us makes to God and to one another in our progression toward final vows and, for some of us, the priesthood. These events turn into festivals of praying and partying such that it's difficult to appreciate when one has ended and the other begun. They appear not to be mutually exclusive.

Our hospitality is and should be evident, too, in our efforts to minister to the poor. The work that Holy Cross does through our parishes and universities, and particularly through Andre House in Phoenix, Arizona, and the Downtown Chapel in Portland, Oregon, speaks to our desire to include those whom we might otherwise overlook in the practice of our hospitality. Indeed, for all Christians, the measure of our generosity will be rooted in the sincerity of our welcome.

Jim Lies, C.S.C.

*The Lord Jesus loved us and gave up his life for us. Few
of us will be called to die the way he died. Yet all of us
must lay down our lives with him and for him. If we
would be faithful to the Gospel we must take up our
cross daily and follow him.*

—Holy Cross Constitutions

BR. ANDRÉ BESSETTE, C.S.C., was a man who knew the Cross
well. He encountered it when he was orphaned as a child. He
knew it in the frail health that he endured throughout life. He
felt it in the skepticism and ridicule he received from people
who questioned the healings attributed to him. Most of all, he
experienced the Cross in the crowds of people who lined up
to see him day after day, people who often came to him sick,
desperate, and looking for nothing less than a miracle.

Br. André did not choose the crosses he bore. His ministry
of healing was not something that he sought. But when he
encountered profound human suffering, he did not shy away
from it. He embraced this cross willingly because he trusted
that this suffering could be redemptive when united to the
sufferings of Christ. And God blessed his ministry abundantly,
using this simple man as a powerful instrument of healing and
evangelization.

None of us gets to choose where we find the Cross. We
are rarely prepared for the suffering we encounter in our own
lives or in the lives of others. But if we can trust in the presence of God even in the midst of human suffering, we might

learn to recognize that grace, like suffering, can be found in unexpected places.

Steve Lacroix, C.S.C.

☩

August 10

Sweet, indeed, and most consoling must be to a dying Religious the assurance that as soon as he shall have breathed his last, hundreds of fervent friends will fall on their knees and approach the Holy Tabernacle, entreating the Divine Master to grant His faithful servant the reward He has promised to those who, for His sake, have left father and mother, brothers and sisters, lands and all, and denied themselves, to take up His Cross and follow Him!

—Edward Sorin

IN THE *CONFESSIONS*, St. Augustine tells of his mother's death as they were traveling back to their home in North Africa. They had reached Ostia, the port of Rome, when Monica fell ill. As her conditioned worsened, Augustine expressed deep distress that she would die and be buried in a foreign land. Monica's response was to trust in God and the prayers of her friends. She said she was confident that when the dead are raised God would know where to find her. She asked simply that her friends remember her when they gathered at God's altar, and she took comfort in knowing she would be joined to them in their prayers.

Fr. Sorin finds the same consolation in the prayers offered for deceased members of Holy Cross. Death would not separate them from their brothers. They hoped to be together at the final resurrection, but in the meantime they would be joined in prayer. Those who had worked, worshipped, and sacrificed together had created an everlasting bond.

This Christian solidarity extends to the whole Church. Our baptism brings us into a community of mutual prayer and faith. We work out our salvation together and continue to be members of Christ's body after death. While we wait for the final resurrection, we pray for our deceased brothers and sisters and know that those we leave behind will pray for us.

Louis Manzo, C.S.C.

August 11

Here begins the sacred task to make of the new-comer a Christian and a scholar, for both of which God's grace must be solicited, and suitable attention secured from teachers.

—Edward Sorin

WE IN HOLY Cross, as Fr. Sorin attests, have always considered education a sacred task. From the beginning, cultivating students' hearts and minds, nurturing their faith as well as their reason, has been one of the major ministries of our community. Generations of Holy Cross priests and brothers have given their lives to the education of the students entrusted to their care. Education is indeed a sacred task because teaching involves us in the mediation of God's grace to young people as they develop and grow into adults. We who teach do not make students what they become; instead, we are privileged to have some influence on them as their minds and hearts develop and they determine what ideals will guide their living. At our best we are conduits of God's grace, as God seeks to touch each student.

True concern for the student is essential to this ministry. Students need to be challenged, nurtured, and empowered to become who God calls them to be. But teaching and learning do not occur only in the classroom or in other formal educational settings. We all teach and learn from each other in daily life. The attention good teachers must devote to their students is the sort of attention and concern we ought to devote to all the people we encounter. Attention to this sacred task of teaching and learning opens us to the very presence and call of God's grace.

Thomas E. Hosinski, C.S.C.

August 12

A pilgrimage is no pleasure party; it is essentially a praying movement, an earnest search after Divine assistance and protection.

—Edward Sorin

WHILE STUDYING ABROAD as an undergraduate in London, I visited some fellow Notre Dame students who were taking classes that year in Rome. We had a wonderful time, sharing delicious pasta, gelato, and vino. Of course, we also visited the important landmarks in the Eternal City.

While at the Roman Coliseum, I saw an elderly woman holding a little prayer book and touching the walls of that ancient edifice. I was stopped dead in my tracks. In the middle of tour groups yelling and cameras clicking, she was praying. How right, I thought. The Coliseum was indeed more than an archaeological treasure or an architectural marvel. It was a holy site. Here, hundreds of Christians were tortured and martyred for their faith in Jesus, and their blood had hallowed the very ground on which we were standing. How right this woman was to treat her visit as a pilgrimage and not merely as sightseeing.

As important as a good vacation can be for our mental and physical health, a pilgrimage changes a mere "pleasure party" into a movement, both physical and interior, toward deeper intimacy with God. When we are on pilgrimage, like that woman at the Coliseum who touched the stone wall and prayed for the intercession of the martyrs, we touch the presence of God in our world and ask our brothers and sisters in Christ, living and dead, to pray with and for us for God's protection. And how much more refreshing that Divine assistance is than any vacation or sightseeing.

Stephen Koeth, C.S.C.

August 13

*Far from complaining of these trials, we must learn to
love them, for if we bear them as we should they are
worth their weight in gold. These nails and thorns will
be changed later into the many precious stones which
will make up the crown of glory reserved for those who
have been faithful to the duties of their vocation and
have worn lovingly, even to the end, their Savior's crown
of thorns.*

—Basil Moreau

WHILE I HAVE never really learned to love suffering, I must
admit that what I have truly learned in my life has usually
been at difficult moments. The maturity I have gained and
the wisdom I have garnered through these situations are
as precious to me as gold tested by fire. Even knowing this
about myself, I am also aware of my continued resistance and
reluctance when confronted with new challenges.

If anything, however, I have learned that our vocation as
Christians is fundamentally a call to hope. And yet we often
get caught up in hopes for specific things and particular
outcomes, only to see those hopes dashed. True hope, real
hope, however, is malleable. It is not merely the belief that
this or that will occur or even that all will be well. Rather, it
is the belief that no matter what happens, in God the result
will make sense. This truth can only be learned through
suffering and loss. For it is only when our hopes for things
have been dashed that we experience the meaning of our lives

that endures come what may. Having experienced that truth, our hope bounces back, finding rest in faith's abiding trust in Divine Providence, a trust that can transform even the sharpest nails and thorns into the most precious of stones. It is then that hope, indeed, springs eternal, flooding our hearts and teaching us even to embrace our sufferings, difficult though that may be.

Stephen Walsh, C.S.C.

August 14

Ours should be a perfect chastity that purifies all our thoughts and affections, words and actions, in a word, our bodies and our souls.

—Basil Moreau

DUE TO IT coming as the result of some well-intentioned trickery, our only photograph of Fr. Moreau—and every subsequent portrait—depicts him with a stern and dour expression. Yet I wonder if this expression does not reveal a truth about our founder's rigorous discipline in the spiritual life. Whatever the case may be, it is clear that Fr. Moreau worked very hard to develop a "perfect chastity" that allowed him to focus all of his energy and attention on the mission of Holy Cross and on the kingdom of God.

When I first explored a vocation in Holy Cross the one thing that most impressed me was the fun-loving joy that seemed to radiate from the religious I met. We spent our first days as seminarians each new academic year at our summer camp in Deep Creek, Maryland. There we would discuss the upcoming year, get to know one another, and learn to play and relax as brothers. I can remember pondering at camp how proud the founder would be to see his children relating to one another with such uncomplicated joy.

I believe that both Fr. Moreau's legacy of self-discipline and the community's fun-loving joy are two sides of the chastity not only that we seek in Holy Cross, but that the Christian tradition teaches all Christians are called to live. On the one hand, our vow of celibacy commits us to the sort of purification which makes room for God alone. Our entire person, body and soul, is called to surrender to the project of growing into the likeness of Jesus. And yet such perfect chastity cannot be lived without an openness to love that makes our joy apparent and our commitment true.

Steve Wilbricht, C.S.C.

August 15

The congregation began and developed in a manner so mysterious that I can claim for myself neither credit for its foundation nor merit for its progress. Therein lies the indubitable proof that God alone is the Founder of this congregation.

—Basil Moreau

THE INSIGHT SURPRISED me during prayer while on retreat. I was giving thanks to God for the joy and fulfillment I felt in parish ministry. I was grateful for the success of everything I had done to get to the parish in southern New Mexico—researching the needs of the community and writing a proposal for ministry that won the approval of my superiors. It was all working out very well. Yet in the midst of my rejoicing came the words, "You're there because I want you to be there."

I took this staggering revelation to heart. I was there only because God so desired. Despite my self-congratulatory prayer, nothing depended on me. God matched my gifts to the needs of his people. This graced insight into the mystery of my place in God's larger plan made me less possessive and more available to serve as needed. I could entrust my life to God because God knew me, loved me, and desired my happiness. I could be confident that I was where God wanted me to be.

Fr. Moreau, a man of surpassing vision, talent, and zeal, claimed no credit for founding the Congregation of Holy Cross. With faith, humility, and a profound sense of Divine Providence, he accepted his role in God's unfolding plan, knowing that it was ultimately the Lord who was working through him. Each of us, too, has an essential vocation, a unique way in which we are called to let God bring forth the kingdom through us. And, it is our confidence in God's great love that frees us to be instruments of that mysterious, divine plan.

Richard Critz, C.S.C.

August 16

There is in our eyes of faith nothing that merits our respect and our adoration more than the Sacred Heart. If we contemplate it as it is, it is a part of the flesh of our Lord, the center of a life that was consecrated wholly to the salvation of the world, and the source of the precious blood that purchased us for God.

—Basil Moreau

To REALIZE THAT a human heart contained the fullness of God's love is a truly astounding thing. This beauty of the Sacred Heart of Jesus is not manifested solely in the intensity of the love that it contained—this one Heart so full of love that it is literally aflame with passion. The wonder includes the reality that humanity and divinity were united in it—in the Heart itself and as a result of it being pierced and poured out for us all. The mystery of this Heart also encompasses the reality that it did not cease to be at the Crucifixion. Rather, through Jesus' bodily resurrection and ascension, he continues to carry this Heart still beating and burning with love for all.

Contemplation of this wondrous Heart leads to the realization that we are invited to enter into it. To enter into this love involves not only the sheer joy of knowing that we are loved, but also the potential of being set ablaze. Truly letting go and being consumed by this love is daunting, for who knows where it will take us? It is intimidating to step forward into that vast love, yet how can we not? That we may live in that love is the very reason that fleshly Heart was formed and pierced. To be enveloped in that love is the end for which we were created. It is meant for us, and we are meant for it.

James Gallagher, C.S.C.

August 17

Are not the same opportunities offered to all? Is not each one supplied with the same means of becoming a saint? Most undoubtedly; but in religion as in the world, we must confess, some are more in earnest than others. Some live for God, others for themselves.

—Edward Sorin

I WAS ABOUT to board a bus leaving a small Mexican village on my way back to the United States when a grizzled, dirty, ragged, smelly, nearly toothless middle-aged man ran up and pushed a small, torn piece of paper into my hands. On it was handwritten an offering of ten thousand prayers to the Sacred Heart of Jesus. At first glance, I thought he was the village idiot, but watching him recede into the distance as the bus pulled away, I realized he was the village's saint. His face shone with a joy that made him rich and lordly. He will forever symbolize for me what it means to belong wholly to Christ. I kept that scrap until I got pickpocketed in, of all places, Rome. It was the most valuable thing in my wallet. I hope the thief realized it, too. I had been graced with more than eleven years of prayers.

Charity does good, but it is more important in God's eyes that we be good. Blessed indeed are the poor. When they are not absorbed by possessions or ambitions, they are free to extend love and prayers to strangers. When they have nothing but prayers in their wallets, they are liberated to spend their energies struggling to empty their hearts. That is the life's work of every Christian—to realize that what dwells within is more valuable than anything we have. And the less we keep, the easier it is to give.

James B. King, C.S.C.

August 18

Above all, let us work with that strength, unity, and clear understanding which come from mutual cooperation and the possession of all things in common. We must never lose sight of the fact that strength of numbers, joined with unity of aim and action, is the greatest of all strengths and is limited only by the bounds of the possible.

—Basil Moreau

BEFORE I ANNOUNCED a new capital campaign for our parish grade school, rumors circulated like wildfire in the pews and in the parking lot. "There is no way we can raise that much money. The pastor must be out of his mind!" More than $2.1 million in donations later, we had achieved our goal and broken ground on the new gym.

Fr. Moreau was a man who met many skeptics along the way as he worked to found the Congregation of Holy Cross. More than one hundred fifty years later, his fledgling French congregation has taken root in five continents, providing valuable service to the universal Church in each diverse location around the globe. Fr. Moreau never faltered in the face of criticism or failure. He believed that God would send him collaborators, fellow workers in the Lord's vineyard, who would embrace his bold vision for religious life. With prayer and complete trust in Divine Providence, Moreau's tiny band of followers grew into a group of dedicated disciples who live the evangelical counsels of poverty, chastity, and obedience.

When it comes to discipleship, we all need friends and companions who will journey with us. The road we walk is sometimes treacherous, uncertain, and beyond comprehension, but the gentle voice of Christ will lead us beyond our doubts, fears, and anxieties until together we reach the fulfillment of our hope—divine union with our God. As followers of Jesus, we believe, even in the face of adversity and failure, that, united with each other in Christ, all things are possible with God.

Michael C. Mathews, C.S.C.

August 19

May you have but one heart and one soul. May you show complete disregard for whatever differences of talent or occupation could prevent or weaken this perfect union. Let us all strive after the same goal by constantly using the means which our rules point out to us for its attainment.

—Basil Moreau

ALL THAT MARKS the graves of the men in Holy Cross who have laid down their lives in service of the Lord are silent rows of crosses. If these simple crosses could speak, we would hear an interesting and colorful accounting of saints and sinners, of master builders and humble servants. Yet, beyond personal talents, abilities, or occupations, these crosses would speak of men whose ultimate goal was to know, love, and serve God and, in turn, to make God known, loved, and served. In seeking to conform their lives to Christ, these men were of one heart and one mind.

Like those who have gone before us, there will be some among us recognized for their great talents and accomplishments. But that will not be the case for the vast majority of us. Most of us lead lives of steady faithfulness. For each of us, whatever our journey in life, our road to greatness is to walk the path of holiness that is set before us each day. It is to accept and live each moment mindful of God's presence. It is to trust in God's grace, generous in our love for others. It is to remain faithful to who we are and what we are called to be. Through this fidelity we are drawn ever more fully into the mystery of God's love at work within us, opening us to God's transforming grace wherein we, too, are then able to say that it is no longer we who live, but Christ who lives in us.

Ken Molinaro, C.S.C.

Let us then renew our generosity in His service, and if our work seems hard and difficult, let us remember that, after all, it will last only a short time, whereas its reward will remain forever.

—Basil Moreau

"LIFE IS NOT a dress rehearsal." A priest once gave me a t-shirt with this slogan on it when I told him I was considering the seminary. It was inspiring to me because, like similar mottos—*"Carpe Diem,"* "No pain, no gain," or "Just do it"—it reminded me that I have to face the present challenges of my life with strength and courage. Holding back, giving less than our best effort, is never the better option.

Some challenges in life—often the most important ones— are both difficult to do and slow to show any results. But we are called to do them anyway, even when they're difficult. A life dedicated to teaching, preaching, or working among the needy means using our abilities and talents for others, not because we're going to get instant gratification, but because it's our vocation. We feel called by God; we feel compelled to reach out and do what we can with the gifts that we've been given.

Fr. Moreau felt compelled to found the Congregation of Holy Cross, and some of us have felt called to follow him. Yet each Christian has his or her own unique calling in life as well, filled with its own challenges; the fruits of which might not always be very obvious. The truth is that God may never show us the real impact we've had on others in our lifetime. But holding back is not an option. Our lives are not just rehearsals for the next life; we are called to action right here, right now, so that we may be blessed with the rewards of the life to come.

Randy Rentner, C.S.C.

August 21

A grand, a noble task has been assigned to us as educators of Christian youth; a task, the importance of which none of us can duly appreciate and for which we shall never be able here below to return proper thanks to God.

—Edward Sorin

NOT A DAY passes during which I fail to recall and reflect on the thousands of students—from grade school to graduate school—I have been privileged to educate in my more than four decades of teaching. Fr. Sorin's words to our young community more than one hundred years ago are still a sobering reminder for all who are helping young people to grow to be conscious of our role as educators of Christian youth. Teaching, and indeed, parenting, coaching, and mentoring are all tasks of great importance. Ultimately, beyond all of our efforts, only God knows the totality of our successes as well as our failures. I pray daily that what I do to educate those entrusted to our care furthers his plan for these souls, and I ask that what I fail to do does not harm them.

More important than crediting our own efforts, though, is realizing that what we accomplish is first and foremost the work of God. Whatever we have been able to do to instruct young men and women is certainly important, but we are effective because education in the faith makes the difference in our students' lives, and we willingly share in that wonderful mission.

Fr. Sorin understood well that all of us engaged in forming youth are unable to thank God properly for the graces we have been given to serve as educators. That, however, does not excuse us from thanking him daily for having given us the privilege of forming men and women in the faith.

Donald J. Stabrowski, C.S.C.

August 22

Through Mary salvation came to this world: such was, and forever will be, the channel through which the Divine grace is to flow to us.

—Edward Sorin

I REMEMBER THE first time, as a wide-eyed freshman, that I saw the Grotto at the University of Notre Dame, as well as Mary's statue atop the Golden Dome. Those images of her made me feel right at home because I had grown up valuing devotion to the Mother of God. Yet it was only in the Congregation of Holy Cross that I encountered Mary as Our Lady of Sorrows.

And at first I failed to resonate with this image of Mary. But, through my ministry in Holy Cross, I have developed a growing appreciation for her under this title. The more I have worked among those who suffer—whether with recent immigrants, people with AIDS, and struggling families in suburbia, or with those in soup kitchens, hospices, nursing homes, and homeless shelters—the more kinship I have felt with Jesus, who suffered and died for us, and with his Mother Mary, who stood with her Son at his Cross.

In God's wisdom and goodness, Mary bore much sadness that she could not understand—she heard the prophecy of Simeon, escaped from Herod's jealous rage, lost her Son for three days and found him in the temple, met him on the way to Calvary, watched him die on the Cross, held his lifeless body, and ultimately witnessed his burial. And so, in her, our Lord's first and truest believer, we can find a channel of faith and hope in the midst of the crosses of our lives. For through Mary, Our Lady of Sorrows, Christ continually offers his saving grace to all God's children.

Michael Belinsky, C.S.C.

August 23

Come into solitude to re-enkindle your faith, your fervor and your zeal. Imagine you hear our Divine Lord inviting you as His apostles of old: "Come apart with me to rest for a while." It is a rest which your soul needs, a period of quiet during which it can become more attentive to the inspirations of grace.

—Basil Moreau

FR. MOREAU WAS a man committed to ministry while grounded in prayer and solitude. His practice of solitude was born from his intimate love of God. By reminding us of Jesus' invitation to "come apart with me to rest for a while," Fr. Moreau reinforces our own desires for intimacy with God, which are purified only in the solitude of our own hearts.

Solitude is resting in God. Even when my prayer often gets tangled up in myself and my preoccupations, time alone with the Lord continually teaches me to let go and simply to rest in God. Yet, I never have as much quiet time with God as I need. I struggle to make time for solitude. This is especially true when I am caught up in my deepest fears and the seductions of doubt. I need actively to pursue moments of quiet where I rest in God and set aside everything else. As a result, I seek solitude in a number of ways. There are spectacular places, like the top of the Rockies, where my awareness of God is so acute I could burst. There are special times, like during a long run, where I find myself one with the God of all creation. There are ordinary spaces, like my prayer space, where I can rest in my hunger for God and God's hunger for me.

Union of heart with God is essential for Christian discipleship. Ultimately, our universal call to holiness is grounded and renewed in this union that can only be cultivated by prayer and solitude.

Richard S. Wilkinson, C.S.C.

August 24

In order to be a foreign missionary, one must know the mystery of the Cross. From the mystery of the Cross, the missionary must draw the apostolic strength of those generous imitators of Jesus Christ, whose life below was but a continuous martyrdom.

—Basil Moreau

THE PEOPLE OF Holy Cross Parish Dandora in Nairobi, Kenya, know suffering up close. Persistent poverty, job scarcity, hunger, violence, and disease threaten the dreams of every family there. And so it didn't surprise me that they wanted the roof of their new church to feature the Cross prominently.

The original design had a large, heavy cross at the top of the church, held up at a 30-degree angle by iron supports fashioned to look like the arms of people. It was to represent our parishioners' everyday struggle to carry their crosses together. But it was not to be. "The proposed design makes it appear that the Cross is defeating us, is too heavy for us," the parishioners said. "But that is not true. With Jesus, we can lift it high. The Cross is not just a sign of struggle with suffering. It is our sign of victory, even in the midst of suffering. It should stand tall!" And so it does today, stretching upward from the peak of the new church, straight and tall into the African sky.

Victory even in the midst of suffering, the very mystery of the Cross, is so often taught to the missionary, and to all of us, by the faithful poor. And it is this mystery, fully embraced, that keeps us from fleeing suffering and enables us to sacrifice willingly on behalf of those who suffer most. Yes, like the first disciples, we are tempted to run from the Cross. But in the end there is no other place in which salvation might be found.

Tom Smith, C.S.C.

August 25

Our rules certainly ensure the necessary training for the mind, but their first and foremost concern is with the formation of the heart through the development of those religious dispositions which alone can make a good person and a Christian.

—Basil Moreau

As a young child, I remember the excitement I had getting ready for my first day of school. How thrilled I was with new clothes, books, and school supplies. I had new pencils and pens, notebooks, and even a ruler. As the years progressed, life became more complicated. Braces on my teeth made me afraid to smile. Eyeglasses for reading made me look silly, but saved me from headaches. All sorts of new, unwritten rules of conduct had to be learned, like how to get along with the "in-crowd" or how to act around members of the opposite sex. Sometimes I thought I was the only clueless one.

When Fr. Moreau offered the first rules, or *Constitutions*, for his young congregation, he was offering a pattern for living, loving, and growing as Christians, as children of God formed into a holy community. At the heart of the definition of "rule" is "pattern." For all Christians, Jesus Christ is our pattern for discovering the way to the Father and communion with all people. Just as the Word was made flesh, the rule is a pattern en-fleshed in us through a relationship with Jesus, whose heart burns with love for all of his children. He is unyielding until our hearts are set on fire, too. Fr. Moreau gave to both his community and the Church the transforming pattern of the Cross as our only hope. To embrace this pattern forms our hearts to receive the One who is the way, the truth, and the life. For indeed, God loves truth in the heart. And in the secret of each heart he will teach us wisdom.

John Donato, C.S.C.

August 26

We can scarcely realize how much is at stake for us when we begin to study. But we may be easily convinced that one of the surest means to obtain such an enviable result as an exceptional success in our studies is to place them, as so many wonderfully learned men have done, under the special protection of Mary.

—Edward Sorin

WHEN I TEACH, I always begin with a prayer—first, the Our Father, the prayer that Jesus taught us, followed by "Mary, Seat of Wisdom," to which the students dutifully respond,

"Pray for us." It is fitting in whatever we study, whether theology or politics or science or business, that we turn to the woman who "kept all these things, reflecting on them in her heart" (Lk 2:19). Reflection is the fruit of learning, and analysis and application can happen only when we have taken the basic ideas to heart. Mary, then, is the model for the scholar, whether student or teacher.

For the student, Mary shows us how learning is related to love. Her openness to new and surprising realities, like bearing the Word in her womb and her questioning how this could be, reflect a thirst for the truth that is never so much satisfied as eternally whetted. For the teacher, Mary shows us the desire to share the truth with others, as she generously displayed her newborn to the shepherds and the Magi. She also shows us the possibilities for knowledge to change a situation, as when she approaches Jesus at the wedding feast to tell him, "They have no wine." Her direction to the servants at Cana is, no doubt, what catechists throughout the ages have taught to those who wish to follow Jesus: "Do whatever he tells you" (Jn 2:5).

Mary knows that all knowledge and all wisdom lead to her Son, and it is for this reason that she is our special patroness in learning.

Brent Krueger, C.S.C.

August 27

Grace is a participation in divine nature, a created gift, a divine principle which gives us the life of God, divine childhood, and the right to a heavenly inheritance, so that the Holy Spirit really lives in us with the Father and Son to whom He is united always. He produces godlike actions in us.

—Basil Moreau

ONE OF THE greatest gifts God gives to creation is a participation in his life. The very human lives we live are a gift from God; this very world is a gift from God and is filled with his holy presence. Throughout history God has called people to be his very own, to live lives in relationship with him. The spectacular culmination of that call came through the Son. Through his Incarnation, ministry, passion, death, resurrection, and sending of the Holy Spirit, the Son filled the world with the invitation to participate in God's life.

The world has been filled with grace—allowing us to participate in the life of God and giving us the help we need to live in the divine presence. To help us remember this call and this grace, Christ founded the Church and gave us the sacraments—real, tangible, and reliable encounters with that grace. The very first sacrament we receive, baptism, makes us God's sons and daughters; it draws us into the divine life. The remaining sacraments enrich that life and, when we fail in that life, repair it.

Most of us live grace-filled lives. In a sense we cannot help it because we live in a grace-filled world. The challenge for followers of Christ is to be conscious of living that life. God has given us the gift, God has given us the grace. But as with all gifts, it must be accepted. It must be remembered. It must be lived in grateful response to God's action in our lives.

Jeffrey Allison, C.S.C.

August 28

Go on, my brave little band, with your noble work of gratitude; be just and honest; make good returns; give in proportion to what you receive.

—Edward Sorin

WHILE IN THE desert of Arizona, near the place where many immigrants die attempting to cross into the United States, I met a woman named Maria who had crossed the border without papers. She had come north from Guatemala, looking for work so she could provide food and medicine for her family. After stowing away on a freight train for a week, she tried to cross the border three times. The first time, her *coyote*-guide attempted to rape her. The second time, gangs mugged her and took everything she had. The third time, she walked across the treacherous desert in 120-degree heat, ran out of food and water, suffered heat exhaustion, and began to vomit. Ultimately, border patrol agents detained her and sent her back over the border.

After listening to her story, I asked her what she would say if she had fifteen minutes to talk with God. She said, "First of all, I do not have fifteen minutes to talk with God. In my journey I have felt that God is always with me, and I am always talking with him. But if I could see him face to face, the first thing I would do is thank him for having given me so much and for having been so good to me." In Maria's eyes, her difficult life, from leaving home in Guatemala to attempting repeatedly to find work in the United States, was all an act of gratitude. To praise God amidst such adversity is a source of continual inspiration to give in proportion to what we have received.

Daniel G. Groody, C.S.C.

August 29

When we do serve him faithfully, it is our work that rouses us to prayer. The abundance of his gifts, dismay over our ingratitude, and the crying needs of our neighbors—all this is brought home to us in our ministry and draws us into prayer.

—Holy Cross Constitutions

IT SADDENS ME to hear someone say, "My work is my prayer." I fear that the work will soon become less of a prayer and more of a disillusioned drudgery followed by a diagnosis of burnout or low-grade depression. To be sure, work can be prayer, but when it becomes our only form of prayer, the emphasis tends to be on our own talents, resources, and ego.

Those of us engaged in the work of the Lord—in the office, on the street, over the counter, at the altar, or around the dining room table—sooner or later find situations overwhelming and beyond our puny abilities. In short, it becomes too easy for us to lose confidence, give up hope, and change our mantra to, "I did all I could."

There comes a time in every endeavor when we conclude we have done everything possible. For example, Fr. Moreau's

darkest hour came when he was tested by Satan: "All is lost."
It is then that we must join with the psalmist in humbly saying, "My help comes from the Lord." It is then that we must
ask for the guidance of the Holy Spirit. And it will be then
that the embers of burnout will be reignited with the fire of
hope and debilitating low-grade depression will be elevated to
confidence in the Lord. It is then that we will be able to say,
"Our work is sustained by our prayer." Indeed, our work is
transformed by our prayer.

John F. Tryon, C.S.C.

August 30

*Christ was anointed to bring good news to the poor,
release for prisoners, sight for the blind, restoration for
every broken victim. Our efforts, which are his, reach
out to the afflicted and in a preferential way to the poor
and the oppressed. We come not just as servants but as
their neighbors, to be with them and of them.*

—Holy Cross Constitutions

As PEOPLE BROUGHT near to God through Christ, our primary preoccupation must be to stand with the poor and the
afflicted as neighbors. This is a countercultural and difficult
charge, but it is only from this position that our message of
life will have enough appeal to convert and deliver the world.
"Solidarity," in a local language in Ghana, translates into
"being a part of the life of another." It goes beyond empathy.

It means that we identify with the poor and share their lot. It means we come not just as servants but as their neighbors, to be with them and of them.

To do this, we have to make Christ our model. He identified with the poor in his birth, ministry, and death. He was born in poor circumstances and the first message of his birth went to shepherds, people considered poor and simple. In his ministry, Christ began by announcing, "The Spirit of the Lord is upon me because He has anointed me to bring glad tidings to the poor. He has sent me to proclaim liberty to captives and recovery of sight to the blind, to let the oppressed go free, and to proclaim a year acceptable to the Lord" (Lk 4:18–19). Even in his death, Christ hung on a cross as a common criminal between two thieves. Thus, as far as solidarity with the poor and the afflicted is concerned, Jesus clearly remains unsurpassed. As we follow his model, Christ is able, through our lives, to bring conversion and deliverance to many.

Michael Amakyi, C.S.C.

August 31

Adore, praise and bless the God of generosity who dispenses His graces so abundantly. Lose not a moment that God has given you to work out your salvation.

—Jacques Dujarie

I VISITED EAST Africa one summer with a group of Holy Cross priests and several of our lay collaborators. After Sunday

Mass at the parish in Bugembe, Uganda, we were led on a walking tour of the neighborhood. Several families welcomed us into their homes, gave us food, cool drinks, and a place to sit for a while. We made whatever conversation we could muster in their broken English or through an interpreter. One elderly gentleman, who lived alone, had only the shade from a single banana tree to offer us. But his wide, toothless smile and gracious manner made us feel like royal dignitaries.

The generosity of the poor is one of the most humbling things I have experienced. Time and again, in spite of our limitations and failures, people who know the God of generosity open their hearts and homes to us. When I was a new seminarian for Holy Cross our class went on a retreat led by the late Sr. Kathy Reichert, C.S.C. The frame for the retreat was Jesus' comment on the Widow's Mite. Sr. Kathy spoke of the call all of us receive in the shade of the Cross to give not from our surplus, but from our want.

Frs. Dujarie and Moreau began an ambitious work with very little at hand. Something impelled them to forsake comfortable lives and take up the urgent needs around them. The flip side of Fr. Moreau's confidence in Divine Providence was a deep, sustaining gratitude to the God who provides. Gratitude is the foundational disposition of Jews and Christians, the fountain from which all virtue and all authentic progress in the spiritual life springs. All depends upon God's generosity. All is gift.

Mike Connors, C.S.C.

SEPTEMBER

September 1

The Lord's Supper is the church's foremost gathering for prayer. It is our duty and need to break that bread and share that cup every day unless prevented by serious cause. We are fortified for the journey on which he has sent us. We find ourselves especially close as a brotherhood when we share this greatest of all table fellowships.

—Holy Cross Constitutions

WHEN I FIRST came to know Holy Cross as an undergraduate at the University of Portland two things struck me: these are men who work hard, and they are men who pray. It wasn't until later, as a member of the community, that I learned the vital connection between the two: work only becomes ministry when it is nourished by prayer. In every Holy Cross house I have lived in or visited, the Eucharist is the center of our daily life. Sure, it's nice to have a thirty-minute retreat every day when we come together for some peace and inspiration at Mass, but the Eucharist is so much more for us—it reminds us who we are as Christians and as religious, and strengthens us to serve our Lord well.

Every time I come to the altar, I remember the words of St. Augustine, who taught that we actually mean two things when we hold up the consecrated host and say, "The body of Christ." We are saying both that this host in my hand is the body of Christ, and that those who receive it are the Body of Christ. Thus, when we gather as the Church, and partake of the Eucharist together, we become evermore who Christ created us to be—his Body here on earth. If we are to continue Jesus' mission, we must fortify ourselves by receiving his body and blood. It is only then, nourished and bound together at this greatest of all table fellowships, that we become bread broken and wine poured out for the life of the world.

Dan Parrish, C.S.C.

September 2

We must become ever more and more people of prayer and mortification. These, with vigilance, are the two conditions on which our Savior has promised victory. Without these dispositions, on the contrary, we shall lose ourselves even while striving to save others, or at the very least we shall deaden the spirit of God among us.

—Basil Moreau

FOR PRIESTS, THE central prayer every day is the Mass, which, in a sense, recapitulates the suffering of Christ for our salvation. We priests pray the Mass not merely as a pious prayer, but as a prayer for the whole world, for everyone. We try to promote the kingdom of God in all we do, and that activity itself is a prayer. It can be a prayer that involves suffering at times. It can include hard tasks and difficult things. And it certainly necessitates the mortification that is a part of daily life for anyone who follows Christ if we truly submerge our human desires and tastes to the will of God. We will find plenty of mortification doing the tasks assigned to us. On some days, even just getting up can be enough.

The Christian life, though, is not simply a matter of mortification, but also a matter of giving of ourselves and our talent and our energy to promote the kingdom of God. This complete giving of ourselves is easy to do if we are truly doing it for God. And so the first prayer I say every morning and the last one I say at night is: "Come Holy Spirit—*Veni Sancte Spiritus*." I say it over and over again during the day, dozens, maybe even hundreds of times. It has been the one prayer that has carried me through life because it has always given me the two things I needed: the light to see and the strength to do.

Ted Hesburgh, C.S.C.

☧

September 3

We form a community as did those who first believed in Christ's resurrection and were possessed by his Spirit. The whole group of believers was united, heart and soul. No one claimed as private any possession as everything they owned was held in common. With one mind they shared the same teaching, a common life, the breaking of the bread, and prayer.

—Holy Cross Constitutions

THE *CONSTITUTIONS* OF our congregation articulate an ideal of community living rooted in the example of the earliest Christians, who "devoted themselves to the teaching of the apostles and to the communal life, to the breaking of the bread and to the prayers" (Acts 2:42). The touchstone of this vision is the unity made possible by the workings of the Spirit. We serve others because the same Spirit motivates and encourages us all. Though we are "many minds," as we say at Stonehill College where I teach, we gather for "one purpose," that is, to educate our students' minds and hearts for lives that will make a positive difference in the world. To declare a single purpose is not to say that we are automatons, but that we place our gifts at the service of one another, our ministry, and the world in order to allow the Spirit to do the work of transforming our lives and the lives of those to whom we minister.

We can pursue this mission only if we are inspired by the same word and strengthened by each other's sustaining presence, especially during gatherings for prayer, meals, and celebration. We must come to know and trust each other if we are to continue to strive for an authentic union that is both emotional and spiritual. This is the goal of all Christian communities, as it was the vision of Fr. Moreau, inspired by the prayer of Jesus for his friends: "That they may be one" (Jn 17:11).

George Piggford, C.S.C.

☩

September 4

"I have chosen," says the Lord, "and have sanctified this place, that my Name may be there forever, and my eyes and my heart may remain there perpetually." Oh, how

fervently each of us should wish these words should ap-
ply to our own hearts.

—Edward Sorin

ONE DAY WHILE I was flipping quickly through the local paper at lunch a name in the obituary section caught my startled eye. "It cannot be," I thought. But it was. There before me lay the condensed life story of a man I had thought long dead. He had been my father's one-time employer and he had passed away at age ninety-five.

More than fifty years before, when I was a Holy Cross novice, my young father suffered a fatal heart attack, leaving my mother with nine children still at home. She was without a job or money, without insurance, and with mortgage payments due. Quietly, my father's boss took over the mortgage payments and arranged for the firm to continue sending my father's salary checks to my mother for years afterward. His heroic action rescued my mother and saved my family. "He was my friend. What else could I do?" the man explained.

This man's goodness had a permanent effect on my life in so many ways, providing material care and comfort that could be felt and tasted. It takes a lot of reflection for me, or for any of us, to understand even a small measure of the gifts that God has given to us because many are not tangible. We need a great deal of prayer to ask for the strength in order to bring those gifts to others, to be a continuous source of nourishment, and to act with the same selfless love that has been etched in our hearts.

James Kane, C.S.C.

September 5

Prayer is the key of heaven. With it, the just person opens up all the treasures of heaven where the soul may draw its ease.

—Basil Moreau

PROFESSOR LINEHAN ENTERED the classroom on the first day of college Latin and overturned a box of buttons. "Choose one," she commanded us. I grabbed the green one because it was my favorite color. Examining my unexpected gift, I read, "*Ubi est tesaurus tuus, ibi est cor tuum.*" I happily clipped the pin to my backpack. Professor Linehan's first homework assignment was to translate the quotation. I was surprised to learn it was a scripture verse from the Gospel of Matthew, "For where your treasure is, there also will your heart be" (Mt 6:21). These were profound words for a college freshman. A few years later, in a crowded New York subway, the button fell off my bag and tumbled onto the tracks below. The pin was lost forever, but the gift of those words had already become a part of my personal prayer and meditation.

Prayer opens us up to the mystery of God in our lives. While here on earth, preoccupied with all of the tasks of living in the modern world, we can only but glimpse what lies ahead for those of us who believe. Nevertheless, that brief encounter with the Divine gives us the strength and the courage to live out our Christian commitment in our daily lives. What might start out as mere words on the page of a prayer book, or even on a button, through the process of reflection becomes a part of us, our treasure, to nurture and sustain us on the long journey home to heaven.

Jonathan Beebe, C.S.C.

☩

September 6

Everyone must show his gratitude by ever-increasing generosity. Let us then renew our zeal; and the better to ensure success in our efforts, let us sanctify ourselves constantly by fidelity to chastity, poverty and obedience.

—Basil Moreau

THE *CONSTITUTIONS OF the Congregation of Holy Cross*, the rule of life for those of us in Holy Cross, speak of our vows as an act of love for the God who first loved us. For all of the many mysteries that may surround living the vows of poverty, chastity, and obedience, that simple phrase has always answered for me the question of why men and women would seemingly forsake so much of the world to live the religious life. In the depths of our own hearts we hear a voice that recalls for us the abundance of grace and love that each of us has known in our lives.

Although now an ancient way of life, the vows are renewed in every age by men and women who hear that specific call to religious life as a way of giving back to God for all that we have been given. The surest sign of a true vocation to the vows we profess is the freedom and joy present in our lives because we give ourselves back to God in gratitude. While my vocation may be to live out this gratitude as a professed religious in Holy Cross, are not all men and women of faith called to make of their lives an offering of thanksgiving to God? The life of any faithful Christian, well lived, is a free and generous act of love for the God who first loved us.

Walter E. Jenkins, C.S.C.

September 7

We wished to abandon all to follow Christ. We learned in time that we still had it within ourselves to hold back. We wish to be wholehearted yet we are hesitant. Still, like the first disciples we know that he will draw us along and reinforce our loyalties if we yield to him.

—Holy Cross Constitutions

HOW EASY IT is for us to create for ourselves a God we want, a God who, instead of being the ground of our existence and the center of our life, sanctions our life's choices after we have already made them. All who grow into the holiness God envisions for them, as priests, consecrated religious, or lay people of God, learn this truth in their strivings to remain faithful to their callings. Our sinfulness has a stubbornness not easily overcome, a clinging resilience not dissolved by even the most earnest choices made in the fullness of all the freedom possible in a given moment. In the face of sin's intractable nature, vows can be necessary, but insufficient—pledges and promises desirable, but fleeting. Instead, grace has to make and remake us, over and over again. In this divine refashioning, we learn just how dependent we are and how seductive are the ways in which we claim our independence from God and not through God.

Here the wisdom of the Church—the wisdom of truths proclaimed and lived, of generosity practiced and preached—becomes the indispensable plank of our salvation. For in the Church, all who seek to follow Christ are drawn together in his body. Then, from one another's strivings after faithfulness, from our regular, heartfelt worship and prayer, the body of Christ draws us along and teaches us how to follow him from whom we receive the fullness of our identity.

Paul Kollman, C.S.C.

September 8

In our attempts to love others, Jesus Christ is our model. Notice what great charity He practiced in His public life. This charity was evident everywhere, especially in His bearing, His reserve and His constant patience with others. There was no distinction; He cared for everyone.
—Basil Moreau

NOTICING TWENTY OR so bodies of children—infants, really—piled limp and doll-like, three and four deep on metal racks in a sweltering hospital morgue in Haiti, my students stood in stunned silence. When they asked about the horror before us, I did not have a particularly good response. I muttered something and suggested a quick prayer to remember these kids whose lives had obviously ended prematurely and who were probably now saints. Most died for no good reason—hunger and its illnesses, a minor accident left untreated for lack of a physician, the absence of life-saving vaccines due to a corrupt official looking for a bribe, or a simple infection grown fatal because of filth. As a priest and biologist working in Haiti, I have witnessed all these stories. Destitute poverty and early death evoke a reaction in us of shock—then empathy. Yet the reaction of these children's parents is even more surprising. They often speak of the hope they find in Jesus Christ and his sacraments.

The degree to which the sacraments nourish the soul is vividly apparent in a place like Haiti. Our Lord was correct. Blessed are the poor. They can find comfort and grace where we see tragedy. Everywhere we followers of Christ serve the poor, we can help to make the charity of Jesus more evident through word and sacrament. We manifest his charity when we work to heal. We do this not because we will solve poverty or because any particular person deserves our charity. Our actions come from our following Christ because, yes, we try to model his love for others.

Tom Streit, C.S.C.

September 9

The Apostles knew the prophecies and yet, "They understood none of these things." From such wonderful ignorance, let us learn, ourselves, how little we know, naturally, of the deep and elevated doctrine or science of the Cross. God alone can reveal its rich treasure and beauty.

—Edward Sorin

WONDERFUL IGNORANCE SAYS it all. I may be a priest of Holy Cross, yet along with those apostles, I must confess that when the Cross shows up, I need an act of God in order to understand its rich treasure and beauty. For sure I am in awe of Jesus' great act of love for us on the Cross. For sure I can say profound words and sing great songs about the Cross. For sure I am quick to celebrate the patronal feast of Holy Cross, Our Lady of Sorrows, which is a precious reminder that Mary suffered much in the unjust Crucifixion of her Son.

Yet these sentiments have a way of disappearing when the Cross finds me in my day-to-day life. I forget the words, the beautiful music, and the model Mary provides. In particular when I feel that I am being treated unjustly, I'm more than aware of how easily I can fall back on the old saying, "Don't get angry, get even." Several years ago a parishioner spat in my face. Albeit "a small cross to bear," it was still an ugly experience. Getting even, I punched him in return. To this day, I continue to be embarrassed by my response, especially when I read how Jesus endured the spit of soldiers in his passion.

We in Holy Cross, however, profess that even the Cross can be borne as a gift. Hostility, hatred, misunderstanding, and betrayal are gifts? Disease, cancer, suffering, and death are gifts? The Cross as a gift? How does one take in such a mystery? That God reveals the beauty of each cross is a wonderful consolation when we come face to face with our own wonderful ignorance. That is, if only we can see it.

Tom Zurcher, C.S.C.

September 10

Since we form with Christ but one Body and draw life from the same Spirit, He urges us to remain united with Him, like the vine and the branches, borne by the same root and nourished by the same sap and forming together but one plant. Just as the branch cannot bear fruit of itself unless it be united to the vine, so neither can we unless we are united in Christ Jesus, the Vine of which we are the branches.

—Basil Moreau

THE TREE OF the Cross is planted in the soil of Canto Grande in Lima, Peru. The *barrio* is located in a valley surrounded by the Andes where dirt fills the air and covers everything. Small houses, some with three walls, half walls, or no roofs, cover the sides of the mountains in no apparent pattern. Holy Cross is in the middle of it all, staffing a large parish of two hundred fifty thousand souls, a large school with two thousand children, and a formation house for young Holy Cross.

As I look out, the houses that meander up the mountains look like the twisted branches and tendrils of a vine. They seem to branch out from the house Holy Cross has built. Holy Cross is far from numerous here, a mere twenty or so men united in Christ Jesus, working together to be the love of Jesus to the Peruvian people.

This vine is planted in other places around the world, some exotic, some ordinary, some beautiful, some plain, but all with the same strong branches and tendrils. This is the Body of Christ made visible. United in Christ and giving glory to him, all of his members across the world work together to make this body alive in the Spirit. Wherever we are, each of us is called to help draw others into his body, by extending the love and knowledge of Jesus to them. For with that love and knowledge, we root them in Christ, the precious gift of hope.

Thomas A. Dziekan, C.S.C.

September 11

It is God who up until the present has directed all those events which appeared most contrary to the execution of His holy will. If we seek only God's glory and are ready to make every sacrifice for the love of so good a Master, then the more trials we will have to face, the better everything will succeed.

—Basil Moreau

"**WHY?**" **IT'S A** question I'm frequently asked as pastor of a parish. "Why couldn't things have turned out differently?" "Why would God allow such a thing?" "Why do bad things happen to good people?" These questions challenge me, as they challenge all of us who bear the name Christian, to give an account of our faith amidst the trials and sufferings of our world.

For Fr. Moreau, who endured many trials in his life's work of founding and governing Holy Cross, the unfailing response to the question of suffering was to trust—to trust in Divine Providence, to trust that God is in control. Fr. Moreau exhorted his sons and daughters to love God and abandon themselves to his holy will because he had experienced in his own life and the life of the Congregation how the Lord brings fruit from every trial. He let faith be his strength and guide, trusting always that God would provide for the future.

Sometimes it's hard to trust, especially when events appear to be contrary to God's will, like the death of a loved one or the affliction of a debilitating illness. Yet, when the darkness overshadows us, we can let faith be our guide. When moved to ask "why?" we can respond as Fr. Moreau did, trusting in Divine Providence and abandoning ourselves to the holy will of God out of the desire to sacrifice for the love of so good a Master. God did not let Fr. Moreau down; nor will he let us down in our time of need.

John DeRiso, C.S.C.

*We should find our greatest consolation and even our
delight in spending ourselves in the glorious task of
training up young and childlike souls for heaven. Let,
then, God's holy remembrance permeate all our efforts
and their efforts.*

—Edward Sorin

AS A RECTOR of a residence hall, I receive students at my door
daily for tape, recommendation letters, screwdrivers, confession, even needle and thread. I have given ironing lessons and
knotted bow ties. I cook a five-gallon pot of chili every week.
I have learned to tune out stereos that can be heard halfway
to Ohio. I tell them not to wear brown shoes with blue suits
to job interviews—then suggest a haircut. I have been asked,
"Do you know how to boil water?" I tell freshmen parents,
"I'm just a stay-at-home priest!"

Our more humdrum tasks test our patience while cumula-
tively nurturing our devotion to our students. If they emerge
from our universities as mature, thoughtful, and prayerful
adults, it is because their personal and spiritual growth outside
the classroom outpaces even the expansion of their intellects.
The constant friction of aspirations butting up against failure
and frustration teaches them patience, wisdom, self-discipline,
and perseverance.

So it is, too, for all who spend themselves in service of
youth. We are predictably pleased when they return transformed from a summer experience in Africa, receive their

diplomas as seniors, or later join hands with their life's love at the altar, but it also is our delight simply to journey with them as their lives and ours intersect. We mark the milestone moments joyfully, but we know that our embrace of unsought knocks and mundane routines is what grounds our service in Christ and demonstrates the depth of our obedience to God's call.

James B. King, C.S.C.

September 13

Sustained by grace, we shall be able to work for our neighbor's salvation without endangering our own, and to devote ourselves to works of apostolic zeal without forgetting that task which should be our constant care and without which the others cannot succeed or at least will be of no avail—the work of our spiritual sanctification.

—Basil Moreau

IN PRAYER EVERY night, I examine the actions of my day. One such night, I recalled how that day I, as a pastor, dealt with some personnel conflicts, wrote a memo about the placement of the dumpster, and talked with maintenance about the condition of the pavement on our parish grounds. The only priestly thing that I did during the day was to bless a rosary. No confessions. No anointing of the sick. Another priest celebrated the Mass that I attended.

Was it good work for my neighbors' salvation that I did? Did I devote myself to works of apostolic zeal? I hope so. I am zealous for the apostolate. I love my ministry. The mundane and day-to-day can drive me crazy. The attention to detail can be, for me, excruciating. But, when things progress more slowly than I expect, I remind myself that the vision is bigger than the reality.

Each one of us can identify those things in our work or ministry that drive us the most crazy. If we cannot, perhaps we are not sufficiently committed to or engaged in what we are doing. Experiences of conflict between people and worries about dumpsters, roofs, and boilers are as important for spiritual sanctification as preaching a good homily, offering sage advice in a confessional, and visiting the sick. Sometimes a healthy dose of our own limitations and failings serves as a good reminder of our task to work and to pray to become holier disciples in Christ.

Christopher Cox, C.S.C.

September 14

Jesus entered into the pain and death that sin inflicts. He accepted the torment but gave us joy in return. We whom he has sent to minister amid the same sin and pain must know that we too shall find the cross and the hope it promises.

—Holy Cross Constitutions

"YEAH, CHAPLAIN. HAVE you got a cigarette on ya?" That was not the response that I had been expecting when I told the inmate in the maximum security prison what I thought would be the saddest of news—the untimely death of his mother. His face, however, remained unchanged. There was simply no mourning in his heart for the woman who had abandoned her infant child to pursue her drug habit. Even his bitterness toward her had faded. She had fought her own demons and lost. What was that to him now?

The prisoner calmly explained that it was his grandmother who had compassionately stepped in and raised him. Her death would have broken him up, as hers was the only mother's love he had ever known. And now he lived tormented with the dark thought that his own sinful, angry acts had disappointed her in her old age. It hurt to be away from her and from his own children who were being raised without a dad's encouragement, just as he had been.

The chain of sin and suffering visits every generation. We who are sent by God to minister know this very sin and pain, but we also know the hope and joy that rise from the devastation of the Cross. Only a relationship to the Crucified can help us bear the crosses of sin and suffering so that the new generation might come to know encouragement, joy, compassion, and hope. It is only when we are anchored in the hope of the Cross that we have the strength and the courage to enter into the darkness of life.

John Phalen, C.S.C.

September 15—Our Lady of Sorrows

When Jesus Christ wished to express the great love of His Father for us, He said that God the Father loved us so much that He had delivered His only Son up to death. This is what Saint Paul referred to as the excess of divine love for human beings. Now, the heart of Mary was capable of this same excess because she gave her only Son, the adorable child of her womb, for the redemption of the world. The suffering of Jesus caused deep and bitter suffering to the Virgin, such that we will never be able to find suitable expression to give an accurate idea of the martyrdom she suffered. This martyrdom did not begin on Calvary, but at the very moment when she was visited by the archangel. That we may better understand this, let us remember that Mary's heart was the tenderest and most loving heart imaginable, after the heart of the Savior Himself.

—Basil Moreau

A MOTHER'S LOVE is foundational to the human experience of love. A mother carries her child in her womb, almost as if mother and child were one being. A mother gives birth in suffering, but forgets her pain in the joy of giving birth. A mother watches and encourages the many steps of transformation from infancy into maturity, but no matter how old her child becomes, a mother's love never ends.

We need to remember this basic human reality whenever we contemplate the role of Mary in the story of our salvation in Christ. Mary was the first to believe in Jesus and the first to receive him into her life. Born of her womb, his face most closely resembled hers. At Cana, Jesus worked his first miracle, revealing his identity as the Son of God, at her confident request. Yet on Good Friday, both her faith and her *fiat* were tested beyond measure when the prophecies of Simeon were at last fulfilled—this child is destined for the fall and rise of many in Israel, a sign that will be rejected. Then speaking directly to her, he had predicted—a sword of sorrow will pierce your heart.

What terrible anxiety Mary must have known when she heard that her Son had been arrested, beaten, and judged by the priesthood of her people and then scourged, mocked, and condemned by the pagans. How immense her suffering must have been when her eyes met his as he carried his Cross. What indescribable agony she felt when she heard the nails being hammered into his hands and feet. She watched the soldiers gamble for the clothing that with such love and care she had woven for her Son. She heard her Son's words of forgiveness, his words to her and to the beloved disciple, his prayer of desolation, his cry of thirst, and his final words "It is finished." When they took him down from the Cross, his few faithful friends laid his tortured body into the same embrace that once had comforted him as a child. How inconsolably she cried out. How deeply she prayed. How many her tears. No human ever loved Jesus as much as Mary or shared more in his suffering. In the beginning of his life, Mary held in her heart all those things that she did not understand. Now at the end, a sword of sorrow pierced that same loving and immaculate heart.

In the religious family named for the Cross of Christ, our saintly founder Fr. Moreau chose as our patroness the same Mother of Sorrows. From its very inception, our congregation was inspired to see Jesus and his holy Cross through the luminous eyes of Mary. Taught by Fr. Moreau, the religious of Holy Cross strive to imitate Mary's unshakable fidelity and find strength in her maternal love. It is in imitation of Mary, Mother of Sorrows, that all of us who follow her Son might come to know the Cross as our only hope. Then it may be said of us, as has been sung of Mary—by the Cross her station keeping, stood the mournful mother weeping, close to Jesus to the last.

Daniel R. Jenky, C.S.C.

September 16

There is no looseness or indifference about a devoted Religious; you see in his very countenance, in his bearing, in his every step that he is in earnest; that he means to be a doer and not a talker; that he feels an interest in the cause; that he feels happy in proportion as he devoted his energy to that cause.

—Edward Sorin

AS AN UNDERGRADUATE in the 1940s, I did not personally know Fr. Peter Forrestal, C.S.C. To me, he was simply another old Holy Cross priest on the University of Notre Dame campus. I recognized him as rector of Sorin Hall and as a

Spanish professor, but as far as I knew, those were his only duties.

How wrong I was. I learned later that this self-effacing Irish immigrant had been a man of boundless energy and pastoral zeal, the kind of man who spots a problem and then does something about it. As one of his brothers once said, "Pete does more ministry before breakfast than a lot of people do all day." Years before, Fr. Pete had discovered the large, Mexican-American migrant camps around South Bend. As if he didn't have enough to do on campus, he established a ministry to the Spanish-speaking peoples in the local area, administering the sacraments and becoming their friend and confidant.

Revered as a saint, Fr. Pete lived up to Fr. Sorin's description of someone who was earnest about what he believed, someone who was a doer and not a talker. In my life in Holy Cross, I've met many whose unwavering commitment and zeal were a lot like Fr. Pete's. These men and women devoted themselves to helping the poor and the marginalized. And, as Fr. Sorin said, they were happy and fulfilled because they knew that they were doing the Lord's work. Their example has provided inspiration for me, and it shows the way for the rest of us to be doers, not just talkers, for Christ.

Thomas McNally, C.S.C.

�

September 17

Let us then love poverty, because it is indispensable to our vocation; let us love it because it makes us share in

the first of the evangelical beatitudes. Let us love it be-
cause it enriches us with spiritual gifts without depriving
us of those of earth. On the contrary, it multiplies those
earthly goods by freeing us from the dangers of riches.
—Basil Moreau

IT IS DIFFICULT to understand how love for poverty is desirable, because economic destitution seems to offer no enjoyment. Yet we in Holy Cross profess the vow of poverty, and our *Constitutions* call us to share the lot of the poor and unite in their cause, trusting in the Lord as provider.

Poverty, when practiced and embraced as this trusting dependence upon God, radically shifts our personal and spiritual focus. It forces us to concentrate our energies on things other than material acquisition. Although acquiring personal wealth is not an evil in itself, the true danger lies in attributing importance to the material things we acquire, becoming attached or accustomed to them in our lives. As a result we can even come to perceive those without the same possessions as somehow deprived.

As Christians, we are to view material goods as tools to achieve God's ends and not as beacons of our own prominence and accomplishment. Detaching ourselves from the pursuit of material accruement makes us heralds of Jesus' vision of poverty in the Beatitudes. Hence, poverty does not entail depravation. Instead, it is our commitment to be completely vulnerable to God and dedicated to the wellbeing of God's people. Faith beckons us to place all of our talents at the Lord's disposal. Only then do we become full participants in Jesus' mission to love our neighbor. For we practice poverty not to feel good about ourselves, but to help us view all people equally and to focus our energies on our most privileged endeavor—a life in God.

Jesus Alonso, C.S.C.

☩

September 18

When our expressions of thanks are offered together, they will more fully satisfy the debt of the family of Holy Cross. Our homage, rendered in this way more agreeable to our Lord, will be the source of new blessings, because, as St. Bernard says, ingratitude is like a burning wind which dries up the channels of the waters of grace.
—Basil Moreau

AT THE VERY core of the Christian faith is the attitude of thanksgiving. Indeed, followers of Jesus might well be defined by their desire to render thanks unto God at every moment of every day. To celebrate the Eucharist, the communal prayer that the Church calls the source and summit of our faith life, is to give thanks through the perfect offering of Jesus' self-sacrifice on the Cross. This is not just what we do but who we are.

The daily struggle for each of us is how to live a life of thanksgiving. How do we continue in our everyday actions and words the thanksgiving that we celebrate together in the Eucharist? We may, in fact, be tempted to dismiss the need to maintain a thankful heart in our daily routines since the fruit might seem inconsequential and the results unnoticeable. Whether or not anyone notices, our thankfulness truly matters.

Fr. Moreau founded Holy Cross as a family united in heart. The first seal of the congregation was an anchor with three hearts for Jesus, Mary, and Joseph—depicting the intimate relationship of Holy Cross priests, sisters, and brothers. Fr. Moreau trusted deeply in the power of prayer generated by hearts united in faith and love. He knew that all of our expressions of thanks are most powerfully offered together. If the grace of thanksgiving fills our individual hearts and links us closer to the thanksgiving of our sisters and brothers, then surely the waters of grace will flow from our lives and will help to revitalize the world we touch. Such thanksgiving makes a difference.

Steve Wilbricht, C.S.C.

September 19

My great and ever-growing ambition is now to finish the work I have commenced or continued, that, when I disappear, it may remain and go on increasing and developing for the glory of God and the salvation of souls.
—Edward Sorin

As ONE WHO has never lived or ministered at the University of Notre Dame, I always stand in awe when I arrive on campus. I visit the Log Chapel, pray at the Grotto, and imagine Fr. Sorin and the first Holy Cross religious arriving in 1842 and deciding that this place would be the site of their mission. I then wander around campus and take in the sights and sounds of students and faculty engaging one another in the wisdom of the ages and the search for new knowledge. I also visit the retired religious who live at Holy Cross House, the Community medical facility, and share their stories and memories.

Fr. Sorin came to America as a young priest to found a place where the young could learn. In his wildest dreams, he never could have imagined the university that stands today. Yet he believed in a dream and allowed it to sustain him through many trials and tribulations. And that dream was taken up by successive generations of Holy Cross religious and their lay collaborators who have helped to build a place where literally hundreds of thousands of young people receive an outstanding education and become the next generation of Catholic leaders in our society.

We, too, must dream and imagine a world different from our own. Our efforts must look toward a reality beyond ourselves and our own time. And we must do so recognizing that it is God who is both the source and the goal of our service. When we do this, we truly participate in the story of salvation, a story that continues with each generation and has as its end the proclamation of the kingdom.

Mark Cregan, C.S.C.

Union is a powerful lever with which we could move, direct, and sanctify the whole world. We who are disciples of a God who died for the salvation of souls who are perishing, we do not realize all the good we could do for others through union with Jesus Christ.

—Basil Moreau

AS I WATCH the television news, I feel a deep connection to places I have never been and to people I have never actually met—typhoon flooding and political unrest in Bangladesh; civil war in northern Uganda; attacks on Christians in India. These seemingly distant places and events are made close and personal by the fact that I have brothers and sisters in Holy Cross living and working there. From its very earliest days, the Congregation of Holy Cross has been an international congregation. From France, Fr. Moreau sent his spiritual sons and daughters to Algeria and America, Canada and Bangladesh. And so, put simply, I have family around the world.

As Catholics we are all members of an international community. Even though we are spread across the globe, in every nation of the world, speaking hundreds of different languages, we are all still united as one in Christ. Indeed, the plant of which we are all branches is in fact the Cross of Christ—the tree of life. And so the sap that nourishes us is the blood of Christ poured out for the world. After all, we are disciples of the One who died for our salvation. And it is his salvific death that continues to draw us together into himself. We have Christ's assurance that if we remain rooted in him, and thus deeply connected to each other across distant places and different cultures, we together will draw from his life, grow, and bear abundant fruit in God's kingdom.

Stephen Koeth, C.S.C.

September 21

Try, then, to become perfect copies of the Divine Model, and nothing will ever shake your vocation. Not only will you carry whatever crosses you encounter in accomplishing the duties of your holy state, but you will love these crosses. Yes, you will even desire them and, after the example of the Lord, will choose them in preference to anything else.

—Basil Moreau

THE VOCATION OF every Christian is to give one's life as a loving sanctuary for the Word of God to become flesh. From time to time, however, the foundations of this self-giving will be shaken by trials and crosses. How do we stay secure in what matters and learn to bear and even love the questions and doubt? For Fr. Moreau, living this tension produces something Christ-like in us. It positions us to seek the Cross of salvation above all things.

One of the first things a novice in Holy Cross learns is common prayer. I still remember my first lessons during our orientation to the community—not the instruction really, but the encounter with the harmonized song of brothers who sang from memory and of love in the soft-lit camp chapel. I wanted to be like them. By the time I prayed at the Moreau Seminary chapel a week later, with its rich acoustics and its moving stained glass window of the heavenly angels, I was well on my way to becoming a perfect copy of the Holy Cross religious at prayer—in love with psalmody and, later, with Jesus Christ.

Fr. Moreau exhorted the religious of his time to become perfect copies of the Divine Model. We become like the "Original Copy" by finding our place in the Church at prayer. We Christians find our "originality" as the Cross produces in us a love for God, unparalleled, except by Jesus.

Daniel J. Issing, C.S.C.

September 22

May we learn how to rise above the joys of a day and secure everlasting enjoyments.

—Edward Sorin

WHEN I FIRST entered the seminary, I had no clear idea of what I preferred to do as a priest. So many possibilities held attractions for me—parish assistance, retreat preaching, hospital ministry, and so on. But I gradually enrolled in several classes at the University of Notre Dame taught by outstanding Holy Cross priests. Following their example became especially attractive to me, and eventually my superiors sent me on to graduate studies and assigned me to university teaching.

For more than forty years I have thoroughly enjoyed helping young men and women grow intellectually, researching and writing on my own, and being a small part of such an outstanding Catholic institution as that of Notre Dame.

This also poses an exciting challenge. Should not any occupation—teaching, growing crops, working in industry, managing a business, caring for a home—be more than a satisfying and enjoyable career? It can and should be if we view it with the eyes of faith. The classroom teacher is assisting young men and women to perfect their intellects, created in the image and likeness of God. The farmer and gardener are cooperating with God in renewing his creation year after year. Industrial workers can be making life happier and more comfortable for their brothers and sisters in the Lord. Parents and homemakers are assisting the young to grow and become ever more the persons God created them to be. This list could go on, but one goal of life is to choose a worthwhile career, to experience genuine joy and satisfaction in it, and to discover its true worth in the eyes of God.

Thomas Blantz, C.S.C.

☩

September 23

All the members must cultivate the spirit of mutual love and cooperation and have at heart the welfare and success of the association as a whole. Joys and sorrows will be mutual. If anyone fails in health or is incapacitated before his time, the others will support him and provide

for his needs. Then it is that we shall taste the happiness
of a life of poverty, chastity, and obedience in the midst
of the fathers, brothers, and sisters in Jesus Christ.

—Basil Moreau

A WISE ELDER brother once excused the discontent of two young religious, saying, "Perhaps they haven't needed the community yet." Experience gained through ministry, prayer, and community deepens our realization that we need each other in order to live our vowed life and accomplish our mission. Similarly, another brother in community often reminds me, "We are in this together." Through my brothers' acceptance of me as I am and their encouragement of my ministry, through their sympathy when loved ones have died and their support when I have failed, I have been well instructed in the bonds and responsibilities of community.

Times in which we truly have to depend upon each other underscore our need for community. I learned this as one of four brothers initiating a collaborative project in rural southern Georgia. As pioneers and as members of a Catholic minority, we faced many obstacles in responding to the needs of the local church. But together we found our way.

We in Holy Cross are strengthened and energized by our diversity and by the dynamics of sharing resources in service of our common mission. Like Holy Cross, all members of the universal Church share the task of cultivating the spirit of mutual love and cooperation in service to the mission Christ entrusted to his followers. We all need each other. We are in this together.

Richard Critz, C.S.C.

September 24

*You will prove to the world that there flows in your veins
the same blood that coursed in those of the early martyrs of zeal and Christian charity. You will also show that
people who are in the habit of dying daily to the world
and themselves in the spirit of evangelical renunciation
do not fear death when their lives can be useful to their
neighbors.*

—Basil Moreau

SEVERAL MONTHS AFTER the main killings of the Rwandan
genocide, I visited our Holy Cross parish there and our
Canadian priest who was pastor. He had worked in Rwanda
for several decades, but on that day he was still reeling from
the recent bloodbath. We listened to a tape he had made of
machine gun fire and anguished screams as the mobs attacked
the Tutsi refugees he had tried to shelter at the parish. "I made
this tape," he said, "because I was afraid no one would believe
the terrible story we would tell." Now he was worried about
revenge as the new army had arrived and new scores were
being settled. He had already given an interview to the foreign
press, and the authorities were angered by the unhappy pub-
licity. A certain colonel had told me clearly, "You tell him he
better be careful and keep quiet."

On that day he was just glad to talk and to laugh about
Holy Cross. We ate and drank and said a few prayers. He said
he was pleased that the people were returning some of the
furniture that had been looted from the clinic. He seemed

somehow to have a glimmer of hope. Four nights later they came to his house during dinner—his dessert plate was still on the table. The soldiers led him into his bedroom and let him kneel in front of the crucifix for a while. Then they broke his skull open with a hammer and left him in a pool of martyr's blood.

Our passion is to be his servant. Our peace is in his will.

Thomas McDermott, C.S.C.

September 25

"He alone searches the heart," and from His scrutiny nothing is hidden. What a source of consolation and encouragement for the exemplary Religious! And what a cause of fear for the lukewarm and "wicked servant," as the Evangelist terms him!

—Edward Sorin

IN TROUBLING TIMES, we long for a god who vindicates the righteous and inflicts justice on the wicked. When the innocent suffer and their tormentors prosper, we find it comforting to turn to a god who makes all things right in the end. Such a god, however, may not exist, if the Father of Jesus is indeed God of all the earth. For Jesus teaches that his Father causes the sun to rise upon good and bad alike, and sends rain for the unjust as well as the just.

The Searcher of hearts, it seems, is not gathering up evidence to use against us in a court of law, to ensure that each receives as his or her conduct deserves. A parent does not keep score of the failings of a beloved child. If we who are evil know how to express tender care for those we have loved into existence, would our Eternal Father do less?

A sure comfort is to be found less in the conviction that the upright will ultimately be rewarded and evildoers punished, than in the awareness that nothing can separate us from the eternal love of God. Such awareness is consoling, however, only for those who know themselves as deeply flawed. The righteous do not need a physician or forgiveness. More genuinely to be feared, by contrast, is the possibility of dwelling everlastingly in the presence of such love, even as we know ourselves to be frauds, in the certainty that the Eternal sees right and utterly through us.

Russ McDougall, C.S.C.

September 26

We must lay down deep in our hearts the foundation of a new spiritual structure; in other words, we must humble ourselves before God, for "He gives His grace only to the humble."

—Edward Sorin

I STILL REMEMBER vividly the ordination Mass of a new priest in Uganda, where I lived and worked. Hundreds were present. At the time of the offertory, everyone came forward with their donation clasped between their two hands, as is the custom in that culture. As they reached the large woven basket set on a table each in turn placed his or her two hands over the basket and released an offering. Typically most of the offerings were a fifty shilling coin, the smallest minted currency, not because of the poverty of the people so much, but because, as in so many cultures of the world, the Church often gets the smallest coin of the realm. As the line was ending, an old woman of perhaps eighty years came shuffling barefooted with her donation in her clasped hand. When she reached the offertory table, she carefully left her offering, a fresh egg, on the table. The market value of an egg at that time was one hundred shillings.

Immediately the gospel passage of the widow giving her last coin came to me. I realized again that what matters in our offering is not the amount that we give to the collection, but rather the sincerity of our motivation at the time of our giving. Ultimately, it is a reflection of the sincerity and generosity with which we live out our daily lives. Simply put, being poor will not guarantee the graces of God. Instead, living humbly, no matter what our economic situation may be, is what will be blessed.

James Nichols, C.S.C.

September 27

You can appreciate the beauty and glory of your calling if you but know how to make yourselves worthy of it by faithfully imitating the hidden and public life of our Lord.
—Basil Moreau

IN THE SIXTH century, St. Benedict wrote his timeless rule with its motto *Ora et Labora*—Pray and Work. This phrase sums up the totality of the life of Jesus. We know from the gospels that he spent long periods in prayer from which he emerged to be about his Father's work of teaching, healing, and sharing the good news of God's unconditional love.

It is rather easy to imitate the public life of Jesus, at least in the working aspect. No matter what our vocational calling, there will always be ample work to be done. The problem is that the work can be grueling and demanding, and it can get in the way of our appreciating the beauty and the glory of our vocations. It's only when we step back like Jesus did and enter into conversation with our loving God that we can gain the true perspective of our callings.

The true beauty and glory of our callings is that they come from God. Therefore, we can look upon our quiet, hidden time with him as an opportunity to report back on what we are doing during our public works. This quiet time of reporting back is very important for our spiritual growth. In the quiet of prayer we will find God waiting with joy and with love to hear of our best and most successful undertakings. In the quiet of prayer, we will also find God with his hands open to receive all of the burdens of our most challenging and discouraging endeavors.

George Schmitz, C.S.C.

September 28

Let us not forget that the development of the work entrusted to us depends upon our acceptance of the inspirations of grace and our fidelity in seconding the designs of Divine Providence. We should not count on individual talents to assure the successful cultivation of the portion of His vineyard to which He has visibly called us, but rather on the religious spirit.

—Basil Moreau

AS A PARISH priest, I have my fair share of duties filling my calendar. But I have found that my busiest days tend to be when I have the fewest things scheduled. For example, one day I was hoping to reorganize a program and to get an early start on my Sunday homily. But Providence had other ideas. First, a woman dropped by whose marriage was falling apart. Then a call came to anoint someone in the emergency room. After that a parishioner arrived, scared that she might be evicted from her home. I truly felt God calling me to accept his plans and to work with his designs for me that day.

Other days I am delayed as I try to do something "important," only to find myself bumping into a person at the door of the Church or coming out of a school classroom whose first words are, "Thank God you're here, I really needed to see you!" Often they do not need to see me, just someone who represents that God is here with us, by our side. Whenever this happens, I find myself saying, "So, God, this is why you delayed me," and praying that I can be the instrument of his grace.

Such experiences teach us about the need to accept the designs of Providence more than depend on our individual talents and plans. They challenge us to see that interruption, delay, and "coincidence" can sometimes truly be "God incidents," that is, events in which Divine Providence is guiding us in cultivating his vineyard.

Eric Schimmel, C.S.C.

September 29

We heard a summons to give over our lives in a more explicit way. It was a call to serve all people, believers and unbelievers alike. We would serve them out of our own faith that the Lord had loved us and died for us and risen for us and that he offers us a share in his life, a life more powerful and enduring than any sin or death.

—Holy Cross Constitutions

HEARING IS THE hard part. God's call comes in soft and quiet ways. We live with the incessant rumble of our selfish desires and the world's steady call to material success. These can drown out the still, small voice telling us that there is something better, that the heart's desire is not satisfied except in serving, that there is a spiritual reality more enduring than the stuff we acquire.

Christian faith proclaims that our existence is about receiving and giving, getting life from God and spending it in service. It is about responding to his love for us by loving others. In a world in which everything rusts and rots, we are offered the chance for something eternal by accepting a share in the divine life and expressing our thanks by doing to others as God has done for us. Once someone has heard this good news, worldly pleasures no longer seem so comfortable.

Listening for God's summons is a lifelong task because other calls maintain their appeal; and so we must remain alert to hear the sound of the gentle breeze in which God speaks. Religious gather in community in the hope that a common life of prayer and service will amplify the divine voice above the distracting din. Yet religious life is but one way to live the Christian faith. The truth is the same for all. Our Church is a community in which we all try to listen to the divine summons and say to one another, "Did you hear that?"

Louis Manzo, C.S.C.

September 30

Since, however, our sad experience with the inconstancy of our hearts prevents us from trusting in even our better resolutions, let us go to Him who holds in His hands the will of humanity. Let us ask Him to establish and confirm us in well-doing, to proportion His grace to our needs and weaknesses.

—Basil Moreau

As young religious and priests, my brothers and I accepted the call of Jesus to follow him, professing our vows to live publicly and perpetually as members of the Congregation of Holy Cross. We were filled with an idealistic desire to search for God's will and to be prophetic signs of his great love and mercy. We saw all of the wonderful things we could do in the name of Jesus by following in his footsteps right to the Cross.

We zealously set out to fulfill our ministries of teaching the young, assisting and preaching in parishes, and working as missionaries abroad. But then reality struck. We quickly discovered that we had not truly understood or appreciated the rigors of discipleship. We had overestimated our own resources to remain constant to our calling to live and work among God's chosen faithful. Our resolve to follow Jesus even to the Cross was constantly stymied by our own needs and weaknesses.

As all of us Christians come to realize in our own lives that our work is not ours but God's, we must turn to the Lord, asking for the help we need to do his work. Our constant challenge is to be linked to Jesus in such a powerful way that he fills us with the grace that we require to overcome our own needs and weaknesses. For then, and only then, can we fulfill God's will for us and for those we serve each day.

Charlie Kohlerman, C.S.C.

OCTOBER

October 1

Even in this life God blesses human efforts surprisingly, when the cause of His holy Mother is interested in them. Whoever neglects her deprives himself of something essential to success.

—Edward Sorin

IN MY FIRST few days as a new provincial, I received from a predecessor a storied rosary that was well-used, old, and fragile. According to him the rosary first belonged to Fr. Edward Sorin, C.S.C. Fr. Sorin had given it to Notre Dame faculty member Fr. Cornelius Hagerty, C.S.C. Fr. Hagerty had mentored the young Patrick Peyton at Notre Dame and had given this precious rosary to him. More than fifty years later, as he lay dying, Fr. Peyton, the American Apostle of the Family Rosary, passed the rosary on to his provincial superior at the time. And, in turn, it was given to me.

Two years before ordination to the priesthood, Patrick Peyton had been diagnosed with terminal tuberculosis and advised by doctors that he should try prayer since they had exhausted all of their remedies. He returned to Notre Dame from Washington, D.C., to die at the community infirmary. Fr. Hagerty, his favorite professor, visited him at the infirmary and told him, "Mary is alive. She will be as good to you as you think she can be. It all depends on you and your faith." He told Patrick to pray to the Mother of God that he might be healed through her intercession if it be God's will. He and his friends in Holy Cross prayed the rosary for that intention.

Later, perplexed doctors examined him carefully and confessed their bafflement. He was going to live. He was ordained Fr. Patrick Peyton, C.S.C., two years later and spent fifty-one years as a priest enriching and strengthening the lives of families all around the world. God, indeed, will bless our efforts if we seek the help of his Holy Mother.

Willy Raymond, C.S.C.

October 2

Here is what I want you all to be—the guardian angels of the dear young souls Divine Providence entrusts you with.

—Edward Sorin

GOING TO SCHOOL in first grade was initially not a happy time for me. I missed my familiar surroundings, my toys, my family, and my friends. Yet one of the earliest catechism lessons that our teacher, Sr. Agnes Angela, C.S.C., taught us was about guardian angels. She explained that God gave each one of us our own special angel. Her kind words reassured me. I even tried to make a little extra room on the seat of my desk so my angel could sit beside me.

The priests in our parish have the custom of helping the younger children out of their cars in the morning when they come to school. We greet them and help them get their backpacks and lunches out of the car. One day, early in the school year, a little kindergartner had tears in her eyes as she got out of the back seat. I sensed she was scared, like I was so long ago, about coming to school. I told her what Sr. Agnes Angela had told us: "Don't be afraid. God has given you a special friend called your guardian angel. You can't see him, but it's like having your mom with you when you are away from home."

As she walked off to class, I suddenly realized the deeper truth of what I said to the little girl. We, too, are those special friends sent by God to be there for someone in need. Often, it is just a small gesture—a word of encouragement, a helping hand, or a smile. Sometimes we feel overwhelmed: "Why doesn't God take care of this problem?" But indeed God has. He made you and me.

Tom Jones, C.S.C.

October 3

In our common life we give an immediate and tangible expression to what we profess through our vows: in the local community we share the companionship, the goods and the united efforts of our celibacy, poverty and obedience.

—Holy Cross Constitutions

ONE SUNDAY MORNING when I was very young, sitting in a not-so-angelic state in the pews of our church, one of my older sisters and I were sharing a brief moment of "sibling rivalry." This undoubtedly involved some elbowing and pinching. There were no harsh words from my mom, no furrowed brow, and no scolding. She simply leaned close and, pointing toward the altar, asked if I could see the lamb carved there. She whispered to me that that lamb was Jesus. I was intrigued, but I wouldn't really understand for some time the depth of her comment. In that instant, however, my mom had patiently redirected my attention and literally pointed me toward Jesus when I was the most distracted.

As with our own families, we in religious life often learn from and are guided wisely by others in community. The vowed life helps us to stay focused, but it also requires patience, trust, commitment, and, undoubtedly, guidance. It is in the process of learning and living the vows of celibacy, poverty, and obedience well that we are pointed toward, and can point one another toward, Jesus.

No matter what our calling in life, it is easy at times on our journeys of faith to lose focus of what is most important to us. Sometimes, to stay on the path, we will need to be guided, but we, too, will need to be guides for others. And, inasmuch as we are good companions both in word and in action, we must always help to point one another toward Christ.

Tom Eckert, C.S.C.

October 4

The perfection of this life stands out particularly in that purity of intention which seeks not self, but God alone; aims only at heaven and not at anything earthly; strives for nothing but the happiness of possessing Jesus and belonging to Him and to His beloved mother; and directs all interests, goods and rights to the sole honor of the Divine Master and the salvation of souls.

—Basil Moreau

SURROUNDED BY THE enticements of secular culture, we do not readily recognize that deep down in our hearts we want, both for ourselves and for others, to love God above all else. Only people live forever. All of our constructions of stone and steel will someday be worn away by erosion. God gave us this earth in order for us to learn how to be human, to learn how to be compassionate, to learn how to love one another as Jesus loved us.

We call God our Father, Jesus our Brother, and Mary our Mother. And so I try to see in everyone a baby, born innocent, a miracle both of human development and Divine Providence. I try to see in all growing people those inevitably crucified by life's wear and tear, by their own mistakes and sins, and by what has unjustly been done to them. And I see the Father's love for his crucified Son, Jesus, in each one of us because we are all temples of the Holy Spirit, whether we know it or not.

We love God best when we love our neighbor; we love our neighbor best when we love God in the creation we see and the person we befriend. Only people live forever. And if we love God, we shall lack nothing.

Nicholas Ayo, C.S.C.

October 5

We asked how we might follow, and we found many footprints on the road. A great band of men had passed this way, men who had made and lived by their vows, men who had walked side by side in their following of the Lord. They beckoned us to fall in step with them. We wanted to be part of the family they formed in order to share in their life and work.

—Holy Cross Constitutions

THERE WERE MANY things that impressed me about Holy Cross when I first met them while I lived in Phoenix, Arizona. They performed great apostolic work, they lived their charism faithfully, and they dedicated themselves to the common life. But as much as I admired all of these things, what finally compelled me to cast my lot with these men and join their community was pretty subjective. The parish priests I knew were joyful men, and their joy seemed to be directly connected to their priesthood. The religious I encountered at Andre House exuded this same type of joy even though they worked among the poor and homeless in seemingly hopeless circumstances. I saw the peace that their religious consecration had given them, and I longed to have that same peace in my own life. This is a large part of the reason that I joined Holy Cross, and it has continued to be a source of strength in my own vowed life.

There are countless ways in which all of us show each other how to follow the Lord. Sometimes this happens through the work we do, but often it has just as much to do with how deeply we love. We are attracted to Christ through the lives of those who have found their greatest joy by offering their lives to him. Our hope must be that our lives will demonstrate that same level of Christian witness to all those who encounter us.

Steve Lacroix, C.S.C.

October 6

Every time a sad report reaches our ears, let us remember the waves threatening the boat in which the Savior slept, and we will, as often, turn to Him and cry out, from the depths of our hearts: "Lord, save us lest we perish"; and He will awake and still once more the winds and the sea.

—Edward Sorin

As HOLY CROSS District Superior in East Africa, I received three times the phone call that I never wanted to hear—that one of our young men in formation had died or was near death.

One such call concerned a candidate who had developed signs of Ebola. The news was horrific. Not only would he most likely die, but his fever might take out the whole formation house—staff and students alike. Could this be God's will for us who were trying to plant Holy Cross in East Africa? Had God forsaken us? "Lord, save us lest we perish." Hours slowly turned into days. Our formation house was quarantined, but the students and staff did not lose heart. Any one of them could be next. Still they gathered each evening to keep vigil around a blazing fire, praying, singing, and sharing memories of our brother who lay near death in a hospital isolated from all human contact. Death followed soon for Aliseni, and his suffering was over. Eventually Ebola was ruled out and the others were out of danger.

Fr. Sorin knew the pain of news that threatened his plans for the future of Holy Cross. But the life of Holy Cross, like all of our lives, is and must always be God's. When we live our lives as God's and not our own, we, too, can cry out to the Lord from the depths of our hearts, and he will awake and still once more the winds and the sea in our lives.

George J. Lucas, C.S.C.

October 7

Prayer should be the beginning and end of your studies. It should awake with you and take its place at your bedside. It should accompany you even in your recreations and perfume all your occupations as with a divine balm.
—Basil Moreau

I STILL REMEMBER distinctly my own first encounter of prayer with Holy Cross on the Notre Dame campus. I was a new student and Holy Cross's undergraduate seminarians had invited me to Mass in the Log Chapel. Not sure what to expect, I ventured across campus with some slight trepidation. Yet people met me at the door and I quickly felt at home. As we began to pray, a sense of peace came over me. I have come to realize that the prayerful hint of God's abiding presence and the lively spirit of friendship that I experienced that evening are both fundamental to Holy Cross.

As I entered religious formation and continued toward profession of vows and ordination, my experiences of prayer developed. Along the way, I discovered prayer in community and prayer in solitude; prayer as an inspiration and impetus for ministry and prayer as a means of recollection and reflection; prayer as a consolation and prayer as a challenge for new growth.

All who follow Christ are called to find daily hope and encouragement in the same spirit of prayer I first encountered in the Log Chapel. We draw inspiration and fortitude for our journeys through the lives of prayer we cultivate both individually and communally. Through this, we hold the same hope in our God who stands by us in our need, who walks with us in solitude, and who calls us each day to a life of community and of family that refreshes us, strengthens us, and helps us on our way together.

Charles A. Witschorik, C.S.C.

As virtues are greater, the occasion of practicing them becomes rare. So, giving up all one's goods, sacrificing self for an enemy, or confessing Jesus Christ before tyrants are virtues we rarely get to practice. But doing everything out of the motive of divine love, putting up with the failings of our neighbors and adjusting to their moods, never speaking evil of others nor in praise of self—these demand a constant self-denial.

—Basil Moreau

IMMEDIATELY AFTER MY ordination to the priesthood, I spied Fr. Jerry Wilson, C.S.C., a mentor and hero of mine in Holy Cross. I ran up to him and said, "Isn't this awesome? Now all I need to do is to die a martyr's death!" The smile left his face, and he said, "No, that would be too easy. Your martyrdom will be giving over your life day after day as a priest, putting up with the difficulties, trials, and tragedies in your life and in the lives of the people whom you will serve."

Many years later I am beginning to understand the wisdom behind those words. While I still from time to time imagine being a great martyr like St. Stephen, St. Lucy, or St. Maximillian Kolbe, I have found it much more realistic to see in my daily tasks and responsibilities a communion with Christ's self-sacrifice on the Cross. For all of us, there will be dying to do on our way to the Father.

The gift that most of us are called to give is not something that happens in a single dramatic moment; it is a life dedicated to God amid all of the uncertainties and challenges of this world. These challenges can be momentous, like the death of a loved one, or they can be simple—even mundane—like being misunderstood or experiencing loneliness or discouragement. No matter what we face in our daily lives we can all certainly pray for the grace to imitate the martyrs and saints who had their eyes constantly fixed on Christ above all things.

Bill Wack, C.S.C.

October 9

Jesus Christ speaks to us in the Holy Scriptures where we can find His teachings. He speaks by the voice of His ministers, by books of piety. He speaks by the good thoughts He inspires in us, by remorse of conscience and the interior consolations He has us experience. His voice is refreshing, persuasive, and touching.

—Basil Moreau

WORDS AND THOUGHTS are intimately related. We could not even think to ourselves if we had never learned a language. Language is central to our very identity as human beings and to our personal development. It also points to the communal nature of our existence. Significantly, we are taught a language by others. We learn our first words from our parents and teachers. We listen to others, and learn from their words as well. We are fed and nourished with words. Words shape and form us.

The most formative word for us is the Word of God. God spoke his Word in the beginning, and all of creation came into being. The Word became flesh through the Virgin Mary and dwelt among us. As one of us, the Incarnate Word touched and healed us; he taught us about the kingdom and how to love the Father and one another in the Holy Spirit.

As followers of Christ, we are formed principally by listening to the Word speaking to our hearts. So above all, we must be men and women of prayer, attentive to the Word spoken to us in scripture, in the liturgy, in quiet solitude at the foot of the Master, and in our consciences. Then, formed by this Word, we go forth as educators in the faith to help God's people re-Word their lives. We speak Christ's language so that our very lives allow others to hear the Voice that is so refreshing, persuasive, and touching to their souls. And thus we make God known, loved, and served.

Terrence Ehrman, C.S.C.

October 10

Imagine hearing that Divine Babe saying to you, with an accent that cannot be described, while turning His eyes from you to the Blessed Virgin: "Here is thy Mother"; and then, looking to His Mother: "Here is thy Son."
—Edward Sorin

I HAD A conversation with my mother in which I made the mistake of telling her that I had made it safely home from a trip. She quickly reminded me that home is where your mother is. After a lively debate about what defines "home," I received a coffee mug from her with the gentle reminder on it: "Home is where your mother is."

Like so many in our increasingly shrinking world, I have already lived in many places and realized that part of life, especially as a religious priest, requires the freedom to move wherever one is called to serve. In such a world, what does it mean to call one place home? One of the essential things I have learned from my mom is that home is not so much a place as it is a relationship. Even more so, my parents have taught me that a true loving relationship is one that both gives a sense of stability, love, and support, and also sets us free to do the same for others.

In John's Gospel, when the disciples ask Jesus where his home is, he never shows them a place. Instead, he invites them into a relationship with him as he says, "Come and see" (1:46). This relationship with Christ becomes their true home. Even until his last moment on the Cross, Jesus continues to teach that it is through relationships—relationships rooted in him that we find meaning and grace in our lives. As Jesus invites the beloved disciple and his faithful Mother into this relationship, he offers a way for God's home to endure among us.

Sean McGraw, C.S.C.

October 11

Let us ask this good Savior for a humble heart which knows its origin in nothing, a gentle heart which knows how to contain itself, a loving heart which is compassionate to the sorrows of others and eager to relieve them. May we have a pure and faithful heart which will be faithful to its work and generous in fulfilling its obligations, obedient to the counsels of faith and the inspirations of grace.

—Basil Moreau

A STUDENT ONCE asked me if hearing confessions was not depressing, hearing of the worst of people's deeds. His idea was far from the reality. The penitent, in naming sins, confesses the faith and the desire for holiness against which those sins are measured. Many moving tales of the quest for holiness can never be told because they were heard in confession. There we see the truly humble heart. There we also see the heart full of hope. It is the hope that the quest for goodness will succeed, that sin may be left behind. And it is the hope, the sure and certain hope, that the Lord from whom we ask forgiveness will grant forgiveness. In this simple act of asking forgiveness we experience our nothingness, our utter dependence on God, our dependence on a love which we do not deserve. We experience, too, the absolute dependability of that love.

The humility and faith expressed and experienced in confession are models for our way of life. In knowing the compassion of our Lord, we are all are moved to compassion.

In seeing our need for forgiveness answered, we are moved to forgive. In the reawakened hope that our lives may become holy, we embrace our lives, our work, our obligations. We seek the counsels of faith and the inspirations of grace, hoping that our lives may be schools of humility and hope.

Richard Bullene, C.S.C.

October 12

We shall always place education side by side with instruction; the mind will not be cultivated at the expense of the heart. While we prepare useful citizens for society, we shall likewise do our utmost to prepare citizens for heaven.

—Basil Moreau

TO BE A Holy Cross educator means to wrestle with two competing realities. On the one hand, in the person of Jesus Christ, we worship the Divine Craftsman, through whom and for whom our world was created. As Gerard Manley Hopkins put it, "The world is charged with the grandeur of God." And so by delving into its depths—through natural and social sciences, theology and philosophy, art and literature—we come to know and even love God. This is the fundamental justification of Catholic education, and the ultimate reason that Basil Moreau and we, his successors, have poured our life's gifts and energies into sustaining education in the faith at every level.

On the other hand, by our very same faith, we must contend with the reality that, as St. Paul points out, the wisdom of God is foolishness to the wise. As Pascal said, "There are reasons of the heart of which reason is unaware." In Holy Cross, we consciously seek to form the heart as well as the mind, and to have the heart and mind mutually form and inform one another. Even more, as we seek to uncover the fingerprints of our Creator throughout creation, we never lose sight of the way revealed to us by the Son in which creation is turned upside down. Christ and his Cross reveal to us that the poor are rich, those who mourn laugh, and the leader must become a servant.

Like we in Holy Cross, all who seek to pass on our Christian faith must teach these competing realities simultaneously and boldly. In doing so, we, as educators in the faith, invite others into the depth of God's creation, fully aware that both the journey and the destination are infinitely richer than what we can conceive.

Timothy Scully, C.S.C.

October 13

To learn our duties is one thing. To obtain grace to fulfill them is another; and more importance is attached to the latter.

—Edward Sorin

IN THE GOSPEL story of Martha and Mary, Jesus praises Mary for sitting at his feet to listen to his words. Martha is preparing a meal, and she is upset with her not-so-dutiful sister. In the parable of the Good Samaritan, which Luke places right before this dispute of the two sisters whom Jesus loved, the Samaritan rescues an injured man with a charity that goes beyond the call of duty. Doing our duty, however it sustains the life of those around us, becomes the charity of Christ himself when we also listen to his words and sit at his feet in prayer and discipleship as Mary shows Martha how to do. Then our duty becomes more fully a work of God's grace, whose initiative in us always precedes our activity and our willingness to do it.

I used to think that I brought myself to prayer, and that I brought myself to help someone in distress. It was my decision. I have come to believe that whatever good we do is a response to a prior prompt by the grace of God. And thanks be to God, we are from the very outset always invited by him. Unless we heed that invitation, we will not notice the wounded man in the ditch, or we will not do our duty for the right reasons and in the right manner. Only when so immersed in God's grace can we hope to bring a love in our dutiful day that is the love of Jesus Christ.

Nicholas Ayo, C.S.C.

October 14

It ought to be clearly understood among us that in everything we should be governed, not by private views or self-interest, but by principles.

—Edward Sorin

ONE OF MY wiser brothers in Holy Cross often reminds me, "Religious life is for the weak." For the weak religious, there is strength in community. It is not simply the strength from trusted brothers who will pick us up when we fall—or when we arrive at the airport late at night—but more importantly it is the collective wisdom that the community offers. The worst of our individual weaknesses can be redeemed by opening ourselves to the best of this collective wisdom. The principles of obedience, prayerfulness, and poverty that organize our lives demand that we tether our personal futures to the community's. They also enable us to do so. To be healthy as religious, we must beg the Lord for the humility, transparency, and simplicity that permit us to embrace our common way of life.

Of course, even if religious are the weakest of Christians, we know that all of us, being human, are weak. Fortunately, the principled life of Christian community offers strength. Principles calling us past selfishness begin at home—obedience to our parents, fidelity to marriage vows, hospitality to guests. These are the beginnings of living for others. Extending outward from the home, we bind ourselves to a parish and the rules of the larger Church—committing ourselves to a discipline not of our individual choosing. Within these strictures, we find ourselves able more deeply to comprehend and embrace our Lord's twofold commandment to love God and others. Indeed, the precepts of scripture and tradition are the true principles giving shape, meaning, and vitality to the principles of our common life. To neglect that reality is to risk that our devotion to common disciplines will become a stifling legalism and an obstacle to the very new life it is meant to foster.

William R. Dailey, C.S.C.

October 15

Let us bear in mind that, as it is written, we are temples of God, that His Spirit dwells in us, and that this temple is sacred. These temples of ours are much more sacred than the material edifice where we gather to pray.

—Basil Moreau

A TEMPLE IS a place where we worship God, a place where God dwells. Our bodies are places of worship. We stand to pray, holding up our empty hands in the ancient sign of dependence, in the universal sign of surrender, in the street beggar's gesture of request. We sit to read, to follow with our eyes the words of revelation, the prayers of the ancients, the petitions of the universal Church. Even in meditation without words, we hold our bodies in a posture of waiting, of expectation. The rhythm of our breathing and the beating of our hearts speak their own prayer, speak to us as well as to God.

No matter where we are, the actions of our bodies and the attitudes that we manifest are holy beyond the holiness of consecrated stones and beams. Our churches themselves are made holy by the bodies of the believers who kneel, bow, and walk in the rituals of the Church.

And when our prayer moves us into service of others, we sanctify our bodies even more. For the same Spirit who gives us the desire and utterance for prayer also provides us with the energy and impetus to love our neighbors. At those times when we tire, when we relent, when we are no longer able or willing to press our bodies into service, is it then that we recognize most clearly the indwelling of the God whose creative power holds us in existence and draws us to himself. Our bodies are places where God dwells; indeed, they are temples of God.

David Sherrer, C.S.C.

October 16

Our teaching leaves behind us all the aspirations of the world and fits our pupils for eternal life.

—Edward Sorin

SPIRITUAL DIRECTION IS the graced accompaniment of one soul with another on the journey to God. In monthly, one-on-one meetings as a spiritual director, I have been blessed to listen to the faith journeys of many inspiring men and women as we together discover their God-given gifts.

Of all the graces I have witnessed, one example stands out. I directed a Hispanic woman who, by participating in an Old Testament course, indicated her interest in going deeper into her spiritual life. She did not at first understand the purpose of spiritual direction. But as we talked, she began to discover her own gifts and her calling from God. The call she uncovered through spiritual direction led her to leave her job at a jewelry store and become a director of religious education in a parish. This call continued to unfold as she sought further training, accepted a diocesan position as a faith educator, and completed a master's degree in theology. Now God works through her to train others at catechesis conferences across the country.

At the heart of her story, however, is her dedicated development of a life of daily prayer and meditation. It is this deep prayer life, refreshed and renewed by on going direction, that has sustained and guided her. And this is the end of spiritual direction, indeed, of all forms of faith sharing and education in the faith—that people see God as their deepest longing and are able to see their worldly responsibilities in the light of their commitment to him.

John Connor, C.S.C.

October 17

Our experience in Holy Cross is demanding. It is joyful as well. And so it should give us a life to which we would happily invite others. The Lord's call will be heard in our steadfast witness to the gospel, the companionship we offer one another, the cheerfulness with which we serve in our mission without counting the cost, and the sincere welcome we openly offer men who join us. If we delight in our vocation, we will share it with others.

—Holy Cross Constitutions

WHEN I WAS a seminarian, my superior liked to say, "You should go about your daily tasks as if you enjoyed them." Although we used to chuckle when he said that, there was truth in what he said. For how do any of us experience delight in our vocations? The answer simply cannot be that things are running smoothly, although that helps. Neither is the answer that we enjoy success in all we do, since we learn more from our failures than our triumphs. Nor is it that we are in control, since much of our lives is beyond our immediate control. No, delight in our vocations comes when we realize that, "the Mighty One has done great things for me, and holy is His name" (Lk 1:46). In realizing how much God is doing for us, with us, and through us, our hearts are filled with gratitude. And it is gratitude that makes us delight in our callings, come what may.

When I do find myself in a grumpy mood, I try to get over to the parish school and visit the children in the primary grades. They can't wait to share what's going on in school, or where their family went last weekend, or show off something they did that makes them feel proud. Their delight is contagious. These young ones remind me, indeed all of us, that delight in our vocations comes with the decision to be grateful for what we have.

Tom Jones, C.S.C.

October 18

Sorrows and afflictions are never separated from our joys here below.

—Edward Sorin

AS AN ADVISOR at the University of Notre Dame to students interested in pursuing medicine and the healing professions, I find my attention can focus on the grades, MCAT scores, and résumés of the students approaching the application process. But all of these are thin criteria by which professional schools evaluate applicants. While they tell us something of the applicant's knowledge and motivation, they don't get to the heart of the healing encounter and the qualities required by physicians and embodied by the "good doctor."

Abraham Heschel once wrote that, "to heal a person, one must first be a person." To know how to respond to the sufferings of others, to be able to walk with them as they confront the most difficult moments in life, healers must have faced these moments in their own lives or grappled with questions of their own vulnerability and finitude. How do I cope with my own suffering? Is there anything of value in me that will last as my abilities decrease? How have I learned to face the reality of death of loved ones? My own death?

Fr. Sorin knew the presence of pain in this life, not just physical pain, but spiritual, emotional, psychological, and relational pain. But he also knew that, to be a minister of God's healing, he had to be open to the healing power of God in his own life, bringing his suffering to the foot of the Cross and allowing Christ to take it up and transform it. Only then is the mystery of human healing revealed—the power of the Great Physician to whom belongs the glory.

James Foster, C.S.C.

October 19

Even should persecution redouble rather than diminish, as is the case now, there would be no reason to fear for God's work. All the malice of the world and hell cannot change the will of the Lord, nullify His sovereign rights, render useless the work of His power, or make foolish the designs of His wisdom.

—Basil Moreau

As a history professor, each time I teach a class on the Holocaust a student inevitably asks, "Where was God?" I cannot count the number of times I have asked myself this same question. If God is all-sovereign, how could he allow such chaos and human destruction? We may pose similar questions in reference to the many challenging and horrifying events in our world today. Through this process of questioning and struggle, however, we hopefully will come to see that God never neglects us in his own time. That is, evil never triumphs completely in history, only partially. But even when evil does succeed partially, God is there with us in the midst of the evil, on the Cross, behind the barbed wire of some moral catastrophe, underlying our need for a change of heart and for grace. Ultimately, of course, God's sovereignty will show forth in people and events, in the Lord's own time, especially in the freedom that God offers each person and generation to walk the path of Christ or reject it.

At the heart of Fr. Moreau's spirituality was his desire to collaborate with all men and women to bring forth the kingdom of God. It is a vision that emphasized respect for the dignity of every human person. If we truly embrace such an outlook, then we will find it impossible in our own freedom not to respect the gifts which God has bestowed upon us. In turn, we will become signs of God in our world, reminding all whom we encounter of the Lord's eternal love and support for us.

Kevin P. Spicer, C.S.C.

October 20

Mary's praise went up to heaven like incense because her heart was humble and filled with gratitude and love. What love in Mary, who became the mediator of the grace of her divine Son.

—Basil Moreau

To go to Jesus through Mary—*ad Jesum per Mariam*—is what so many students at the University of Notre Dame do when they visit the Grotto. Modeled on the Grotto at Lourdes, this quiet place for prayer is never without students lighting candles and asking for Our Lady's intercession. There, in spring blossoms and autumn leaves, in winter snow and summer heat, during the day and into the late hours of night, they are asking her to help them to follow Christ and to be good Christians. I myself have often prayed at the Grotto. And each night I say the Litany of the Blessed Virgin before I go to bed. In that prayer we have a long list of what Mary means to us and how she can help us to grow more like her and her Son in all those qualities.

Mary is the mediator between her Son and all men and women. The safest and best way for all of us to approach her divine Son, to live our lives in imitation of him, is to receive advice from her. The imitation of Christ is the Christian life. And who knows Christ better than his mother? Who was more loyal to Christ than his mother, standing there at the foot of the Cross and, in a sense, undergoing the tortures he suffered for our salvation? She is also our Mother, and she leads all of her beloved children to a deeper understanding of her Son. That is the role she fulfills in all of our lives. She wants all people to take her Son as their Lord and Savior, to come close to him.

Ted Hesburgh, C.S.C.

October 21

The spirit of faith fills the just in all the details of their conduct, as the soul is the principle of all the movement of the body. Their thoughts and judgments are always according to the Gospel. Their conversation is in heaven.

They see God always and everywhere. It is the Holy Spirit which enlivens them. Jesus Christ lives in them.

—Basil Moreau

AS CHRISTIANS WE strive to live as Christ did, devoted to the service of God and enlivened by the presence of the Holy Spirit within us. St. Paul spoke of the Christian community as the body of Christ. In a sense this is not merely metaphorical. It is Christ who is our soul, the life force within, directing the movement of our lives and service. Whether as priests, religious, or lay men and women, we seek to establish Christ as the source of all of our actions and interactions in our families, communities, Church, and world. This is our ideal aim as Christians.

But day-to-day we often are not conscious of this deep grounding of our lives. We are all too human, it seems, to be the living body of Christ. The grind of daily life can seem quite ordinary, nothing like the high ideals we hope to achieve. The ambiguities of our human society and of the physical universe can make it difficult to see God always and everywhere.

But if we ponder the implications of Christ living in us, we come to understand that the Divine dwells in the ordinary—in flawed humans, in our common life, and in our uncertain world. The infinite God became one of us and embraced our world; and in redeeming it, God filled the ordinary world with extraordinary value and beauty and love. To see God always and everywhere despite the ambiguities of life is one of the deepest blessings of the spiritual life.

Thomas E. Hosinski, C.S.C.

October 22

We shall accomplish very imperfectly the designs of Providence on each of us, if to the love of retreat and prayer, we do not apply ourselves at the same time, as did St. Basil, to cultivating our intellects and enriching our minds with the knowledge proper to our state.

—Basil Moreau

OUR CULTURE VERY much values the intellect. Yet the dominance of reason in our secular as well as religious discourse has led to a crisis of faith for many. In looking at the tradition of our great Church, however, we find that while we frequently need to remind ourselves to develop our hearts, we must never neglect our minds. We desire to develop both fully so that they may work in harmony for the greater glory of God. Perhaps the disharmony in our culture's relationship to reason is not our use of reason, but our overuse. Ideally, our reason, our intellect properly oriented, gives us greater faith and brings us closer to God.

The grace of Providence speaks silently without the ear of reason to hear it. How can we know God's will if our senses, working with our intellects, are not tuned enough to experience it? How do we know where God draws us if we cannot feel the movement of his gentle, guiding hand? We develop our intellect not as an end in itself but as a means to a greater understanding of how God, especially as Providence, is present in our lives and in the lives of others. Whether it be through culture, language, history, science, or even through our everyday experiences, God speaks to us and through us as his human children. The beauty of our intellects fulfills Providence and allows us to participate in the conversation God so desperately desires to have with us.

Gregory Haake, C.S.C.

October 23

The first means of perseverance in our vocation is prayer. Without it, our soul will soon become lazy and will quickly die. We are made of body and soul, and each part needs its food. The food of the soul is grace, and God does not ordinarily give grace except through prayer.

—Basil Moreau

AFTER ALL THESE years I still feel like a beginner at prayer. And yet a high school student requests, "Bless my hands, Father, so that I'll catch a pass during our football game tonight." I want to bless the hands of this hopeful youth, hands that some day may be extended to consecrate bread and wine at Mass. We've talked about a vocation to the priesthood, he and I. A colleague at work e-mails a plea to pray for her soldier son in Iraq. I hit "reply" with a promise to pray each morning until he returns home. I want to pray for his courageous heart ready to give all for a peaceful world. In sunrise solitude, I pray for this young man, his mom, and me, that we may courageously seek the peace that only God gives. Our superior general sends the obituary card of my brother in Holy Cross, requesting prayers for the repose of his soul. With gratitude for his life and ministry in Holy Cross I am happy to offer Mass and pray for this man who has gone before me in religious life—grant him eternal life for his labors in this passing world, O Lord.

Fr. Moreau understood that God's grace is food for the soul, food that sustains each of us in our vocation to do his will. This nourishing banquet is provided for us in prayer. To this conversation with God, who loves us more than we will ever know, we bring our hopes and fears, our weaknesses and strengths, our living and our dead. We bring ourselves. As a beginner or as one who is well seasoned, let us pray.

Tom Zurcher, C.S.C.

October 24

Our commitment is an invitation for our fellow Christians to fulfill their vocation, and for ourselves it is a concrete way of working with them for the spread of the gospel and with all for the development of a more just and human society.

—Holy Cross Constitutions

So MUCH OF our modern society rejects the idea that the human person does in fact have a vocation—something to which God calls him or her. Intent on defending a secular and individualistic view of freedom, our culture teaches that we determine our own path in life and make our own choices.

Our beloved Pope John Paul II knew better. When he told the story of his own vocation to the priesthood, he entitled the work *Gift and Mystery*. These two words perfectly capture not only the reality of God's call, but also our experiences of vocation. God's call is sometimes mysterious, difficult to discern, and we often feel unworthy of it. But this does not make it any less real. In fact, it is precisely because it is mysterious, and because we are unworthy of it, that God's invitation to share in his life and mission can be experienced as true freedom, indeed, as a joy-filled gift.

As priests, brothers, and sisters, we in Holy Cross consecrate our lives in witness to the reality of God's call. In attempting to answer faithfully his call to us, we hope to convince all people that they, too, are called by God. Whether it be as a husband or wife, father or mother, doctor, teacher, civil servant, businessperson, or any number of other callings, God invites all of his faithful people to holiness and to a share in his life and mission. This universal vocation beckons all to work together in joyful hope for the coming of God's kingdom.

Stephen Koeth, C.S.C.

October 25

Look not to the number, but to the quality. Twelve men sufficed, in God's own mind, to convert the world.

—Edward Sorin

NEAR THE CREST of the hill that rises above Saint Mary's Lake at Notre Dame there is a small monument of stones resembling a cairn. Rather than a burial marker, this cairn marks the birth of the mission of Holy Cross in the United States. At this spot, a small group of seven Holy Cross religious first beheld the abandoned Potawatami mission that would become their home and the site of their life's work.

Often on a football weekend, visitors to campus, clad in sweatshirts and green plaid slacks, stand at the monument and read off the names. Next, they follow the path to Old College, where they read the plaque for the "cradle of the university" in a loud, inspired voice. Over the years, countless undergraduate seminarians in Old College have had their Saturday mornings—the one morning they are allowed to be college students and sleep late—interrupted by the repetition of the these names and by some variation on the refrain, "Imagine Mildred, so much grew out of so little!"

I can think of no better introduction into the mystery of the kingdom, as preached by Christ, which rises from the tiniest seed. Like the twelve sent out by the risen Christ, like the small band of immigrant missionaries by a snow-covered lake, like these countercultural few in Old College who choose religious life in our own day, we can feel overwhelmed by the wideness of the work before us when compared with the scarcity of our numbers. When venturing out, we can be too cold in our assessment of our own qualities, not to mention those of others. What is the quality of which Fr. Sorin speaks but the zeal that arises in us when we believe that what we find lacking, God proves sufficient to his end?

Peter J. Walsh, C.S.C.

October 26

On Calvary we see how much Mary loved us. She was standing even at the foot of the Cross, among the executioners and soldiers, so close to her dying Son that not a single detail of His death escaped her. What was in her heart at this sorrowful time? While Jesus Christ offered Himself to the Father for our salvation, Mary offered Him herself for the same end.

—Basil Moreau

IT WAS NOT easy for Mary, to stay there, to stand there, watching her Son die a brutal death. But she did stay. Because of her love for Jesus, she could be no place other than the foot of the Cross. Yet, as powerful as a mother's love for a child is, Fr. Moreau indicates that God's love for all of humanity was at work in Mary. For her, the events of Good Friday were not merely the result of Jewish and Roman political machinations. Her Son was completing God's will for the good of others, for us. Mary chose to be a part of that, and so she stayed.

Mary could not have known that her assent to God's will, years before, would lead to this day. And so, too, it is with us. If we decide to follow God's will for our lives, we cannot know the pathways down which it will lead us. But wherever it may lead, Mary's example is a challenging reminder that our lives, struggles, experiences, and gifts are for the good of others. That is their true nature; and yet, we must decide to live for others.

Our everyday activities, the way we greet others, the care we take in completing tasks, the help we extend, the inconveniences we accept—these and so many other little things, all within our reach, provide us with ample opportunities to live for others. Such a life is the way for us to stay, like Mary, and deal with whatever we confront. Such a life is the way for us to take up the graced adventure of completing God's will.

Joel Giallanza, C.S.C.

October 27

Divine Providence has blessed us with a spirit of devotedness and energy that will remain, I trust, as the characteristic feature of all the children of Holy Cross.

—Edward Sorin

MORE THAN FORTY years of my life in Holy Cross have been devoted to working with youth. Yet from time to time I have wondered what good, if any, I was accomplishing. I suspect this is true of most of us regardless of our vocations in life. "Why do you expect so much from me?" "Come on, Brother, give me a break." Similar questions or pleas were common reactions when I tried to bring out the best in my students. Believing they had much more talent and potential than they could see in themselves, I would find the energy and wherewithal to challenge and stretch them beyond what they could imagine for themselves. Such single-hearted devotion to educating the mind and the heart is essential for the success of our mission as educators in the faith.

In my current role as provincial superior, I visit with many of our alumni and hear their stories about brothers who taught them. So many say in different ways that the Holy Cross brothers, or one brother in particular, made them who they are today. Others recount how the brothers believed in them, giving them the confidence to make something of themselves. These inspiring and life-changing stories are repeated by all those whom Divine Providence has blessed with a Holy Cross education.

We all want to make a difference in the lives of others. Believing in Divine Providence gives us the assurance that God puts us in the right place, at the right time, and with the right people. We will make a difference if we have the devotion, the generosity, and the faith to respond to God's grace at those moments in our lives.

Robert Fillmore, C.S.C.

October 28

Only a religious spirit which understands the power of His Cross can sustain our courage in the midst of all these trials. Happy indeed are we if we know how to profit by them and to understand the unspeakable advantage of becoming more and more conformed to the image of the divine Christ crucified.

—Basil Moreau

IT'S ALL IN the spin. We are too familiar with this line from politicians, publicists, and marketers trying to spin the truth to reflect their own self-interests. In our culture we have often bought into the various spins that misrepresent truth. Take, for instance, the common notion of the pursuit of pleasure and the avoidance of pain. Whether it is a migraine or a failed relationship, we are told to make the pain go away quickly so that we can move on to something more pleasing and satisfying.

For a Christian, however, this spin just doesn't work. If we are to model our lives after Jesus Christ, we will soon discover the truth that a life free of pain and suffering is a life free of courage and hope. To shun the crosses we encounter in our daily lives is to miss an opportunity to identify with the Cross of Christ. And without the Cross, we can have little hope for the resurrection.

In the face of our personal trials, therefore, Christ challenges us to see suffering differently. Instead of accepting our suffering only as hardship, we can accept the invitation repeated by Fr. Moreau to embrace it as a privileged moment of conformity to the divine Christ crucified. After all, isn't it all about the spin? It remains only for us to find how even the Cross can be borne as a gift.

Paul Bednarczyk, C.S.C.

Never did we need, as much as now, to live by faith, so as to make of our life an incessant prayer.

—Edward Sorin

I NEVER CONSIDERED myself pastor material, nor did I envision parochial ministry as the primary focus of my priesthood. My talents, I felt, were better suited to education or Catholic communications, but God's ways are not always our ways. When the request to serve as a pastor came my way, the divine sense of humor was made manifest with a call to minister to not one, but two parishes. Faced with this awesome responsibility, I find that Fr. Sorin's exhortation to live by faith speaks powerfully to me. For God does work in strange ways and we can find ourselves faced with responsibilities, and the crosses that come with them, that are not always of our choosing.

Success in any ministry is not the success of the individual, but rather it is the grace of God and the work of the Holy Spirit. For me this is especially true in the shepherding ministry of a parish pastor. I am simply an instrument. If there is success, it is the work of the Spirit; if there is failure or inadequacy it must be because I asserted myself over the Spirit's movement.

To be a worthy instrument of God's grace requires a life of faith rooted in prayer. I have never prayed as much or as ardently as I do now. Indeed, the first responsibility of the pastor is to pray for the people entrusted to his care. Every decision, whether pertaining to the care of souls or the repair of a leaky church roof, is for me a prayer decision. Good pastoring, good teaching, good parenting, and good living are all fruits of a rich life of prayer and a deep life of faith. Incessant prayer feeds the life of faith and is the driving force of any Christian worth his or her weight in holy water.

Ed Kaminski, C.S.C.

October 30

Where then shall we find intelligent, zealous, and devoted teachers for the poor? Only in the inspiration of religion. For religion not only promises that those who have taught justice to their brothers and sisters shall shine as stars in the firmament, but likewise ranks among the proofs of the divinity of Christ's mission the fact that "the poor have the Gospel preached to them."

—Basil Moreau

THERE IS A poverty that crosses all cultures, social levels, and areas of society. It is a poverty more subtle than what we're accustomed to handle. It has to do with the loneliness and affective emptiness with which all young people wrestle. After many years working with young people from different levels of society in both parishes and schools, I am struck by how this affective need is common among economically and culturally wealthy youth as well as among those from poorer backgrounds. There is no distinction.

All young people have a need to find someone who might pay attention to them. They are immersed in a society that renders them so needy and fragile that it's not surprising that they would so easily join groups and adopt fads and lifestyles that allow them to forget their loneliness and make them feel that they are somebody or part of something that confirms their identity. It is not just their affective lives that are hurt, but also their spiritual lives, to the extent that often the only place where they've heard talk about God is in school.

In this context, the role of all Christians as educators in the faith is vitally important. All of us have a part in helping our young people to discover God as the One who gives meaning to our lives and as the Father who welcomes us, listens to us, and reveals our deepest identity.

Jorge Urtubia, C.S.C.

October 31

The tears that blind my eyes bear witness that I say the truth when I declare that I had never known before what love God has infused into my heart for all He has entrusted to my care.

—Edward Sorin

ST. PAUL USES the image of an earthen vessel to describe how he—and all disciples of the Lord—carry within themselves a treasure that derives its transcendent power from God alone. All of us who are called to Christian service quickly become aware of our own human limitations. Yet, despite our self-doubts and our misgivings about our natural abilities, hopefully we answer God's call like Isaiah the prophet, "O Lord, send me."

In this spirit, Fr. Edward Sorin left his home and native country to help catechize, pastor, and educate in a priest-poor region of northern Indiana. He was a man of vision, deeply spiritual, with a ready confidence in the plan of Divine Providence. Despite tragic fires, financial exigencies, disputes with neighbors, and insufficient personnel, his dream to establish a great Catholic university named after Our Lady has, through the decades, born much fruit.

When I became Fr. Sorin's fifteenth successor as president of the University of Notre Dame in 1987, I was both humbled and honored. I was given the privilege, as a Holy Cross religious, of carrying on a work that had been so nobly begun. All the while, I was fully aware that a great institution of higher learning and thousands of people around the world had been entrusted to my care. I was comforted, like St. Paul and Fr. Sorin, with the knowledge that I shared this responsibility with my fellow Holy Cross religious and with a whole host of dedicated women and men. Together, we could give one another greater confidence that God's holy purposes would be fulfilled.

Edward A. Malloy, C.S.C.

NOVEMBER

November 1

Above all, let our Religious, to a man, strive to preserve in our Congregation a feature which has always been characteristic of the children of Holy Cross—I mean the spirit of devotedness.

—Edward Sorin

WE'VE ALL HEARD it said that the devil is in the details. This old saying implies that any great idea will have a countless number of details to which we must attend if our idea is to succeed. Indeed, these little details somehow seem to take up the bulk of our days. Despite our best intentions, most plans will fail if we don't do the little things well.

This attention to detail is a huge part of the Christian life. Our average days are filled with routine things that we do for our families, our co-workers, and our Church. And yet these day-to-day activities are the primary ways that we show our love for these people. Occasionally we might be able to express grand gestures of love, but more often than not we have to show our love in the ordinary things of our day.

The holiest people I know are the ones who can transform simple activities—cooking a meal, making a phone call, saying a prayer—into acts of charity by performing them with love. When we make a conscious effort to do this, we don't just show our love for the people we serve—we show our love for God by serving those around us. Infusing the routine actions of our days with love turns simple jobs into encounters with the Lord. And that is exactly where we can expect to find him—in the details.

Steve Lacroix, C.S.C.

November 2

The footsteps of those men who called us to walk in their company left deep prints, as of men carrying heavy burdens. But they did not trudge; they strode. For they had the hope.

—Holy Cross Constitutions

ON THE ROAD connecting Notre Dame and Saint Mary's College lies a cemetery that is the final resting place for hundreds of Holy Cross priests and brothers. This hallowed ground is lined neatly with limestone crosses. The inscriptions on each cross bear witness to the brevity or longevity of their lives, and taken together, they tell pieces of the story of those who have gone before us.

My introduction to the power of this holy place came when I was full of doubt about my own abilities as a religious. I confided my struggle to a Holy Cross priest who invited me on a walk. As he listened and questioned, he slowly and steadily guided our journey to the middle of the cemetery. We both grew silent for a moment, and then he spoke to me words I have never forgotten. "All these men here," he said, his arm sweeping the rows of crosses, "they are praying for you right now."

I know that my ministry in Holy Cross is not my own. It belongs to God. But my ministry also belongs to those who have gone before me, for all who follow the Lord water the seeds planted and reap the love sown by generations of the faithful departed. We are never alone, for we walk in the footsteps of those whose hope and fidelity sustain us still. They had their share of burdens and struggles, joys and sorrows, and from their place in heaven they call out to us, reminding us that it is indeed the Cross that is our only hope. And so, all of us can return often to the graves of our family and friends, to stand in their midst and to ask for their prayers, that we might follow faithfully in their footsteps.

Peter Jarret, C.S.C.

November 3

Who do you suppose are the most valuable members of our little religious family? Undoubtedly those who pray best. Then each one may say, "Why not I?"

—Edward Sorin

WHEN I WAS in the seminary, someone introduced me to *The Practice of the Presence of God*, a holy little book written by Br. Lawrence, a seventeenth-century Carmelite monk. The preface describes him as an ordinary kitchen worker who, "learned to live in God's presence so consistently that whether amidst the clanging of the pots and pans, or at the Lord's table, he sensed God just the same."

When I read of Br. Lawrence, I was reminded of Br. James Edwin, C.S.C. Br. James was a shy, quiet, and gentle soul who always seemed to be praying, though not always in a conventional way. He had a smoking niche in our seminary garage where he had a couple of boxes stacked up in a corner. Every time he smoked a cigarette there, he prayed the names of each seminarian written on a note card. While he smoked over the years, he managed to fill two notebooks with paraphrased scripture passages, which we later discovered in an old metal cabinet. Just as Br. Lawrence came to a continual awareness of God, whether in the chapel or in the kitchen, I believe Br. James came to the same continual awareness of God, whether serving at 6:40 a.m. Mass or shipping books at Ave Maria Press, where he worked for more than thirty years. Even smoking, his only visible vice, became an act of prayer.

The most valuable members of our Holy Cross family are those who pray best. Without realizing it, Br. James Edwin became a simple but genuine mystic through his daily faithfulness to prayer. His life is an invitation for all of us to find our own way toward a continual conversation with God throughout the day—no matter what we find ourselves doing.

Patrick Neary, C.S.C.

☩

November 4

Afflictions, reverses, loss of friends, privations of every kind, sickness, even death itself, "the evil of each day," and the sufferings of each hour—all these are but so

*many relics of the sacred wood of the true Cross which
we must love and venerate. We must enclose these precious souvenirs in a reliquary made of charity which is
patient, resigned, and generous and which, in union
with the Divine Master, suffers all things and supports
all things.*

—Basil Moreau

AS I LAY on my hospital bed in Uganda after my third attack
of malaria, I often looked at the crucifix hanging on the wall.
I was suffering, and I really wanted to die. My patience had
just about run out; my generosity was almost spent; indeed,
my resignation was complete: "Take me, Lord." Then, one
day as I received the Eucharist from the hands of our bishop,
I felt renewed as he said, "Body of Christ." It was as if God
had said, "Not yet." The crucifix on the wall gave me hope
just as the Eucharist within my body nourished me. I felt, for
a moment, at one with Christ on the Cross. I believe my real
recovery began at that very moment in union with Christ who
suffered for me·and supported me.

Our daily crosses in life are so many splinters from the
Cross of Christ. Fr. Moreau teaches all who would follow
Christ to see these crosses as gifts from God to assist us on
our journeys. Our lives are reliquaries made up of many
sorrows—loss of relatives and friends, sickness and privations,
sufferings and afflictions. All of these sorrows are splinters,
or relics, from the true Cross that we must hold on to and
encase in our very lives. Our love, our charity, becomes the
gold to make our reliquaries. Our patience, resignation, and
generosity become the gems that adorn it. Then our crosses

are made beautiful in our God, who suffers all things and supports all things.

Robert Nebus, C.S.C.

☩

November 5

When we die, one of the two following inscriptions shall be written on our tomb or in the minds of our survivors: "Here lies a brave soldier of the Cross. Honor to his memory! Though dead, he still speaks for the encouragement of the living." Or this other: "Here lies a poor nominal Religious, whose rule was his own will. Let his name be forgotten and his example remain without followers." Which of the two will best apply to us?
—Edward Sorin

WHEN I REFLECT honestly on which of these two starkly different descriptions fits me, I would have to answer that both of them have done so at different times—sometimes even on the same day. At times, I can be full of zeal—putting quality time and reflection into my homilies, being warm and available for the needs of parishioners, and remaining faithful to my prayer life. But I can also become wrapped up in my own interests and desires—displaying grouchiness when the phone or doorbell rings at an unexpected time, or being distracted needlessly in the midst of prayer or conversation with others.

I suspect this inner struggle between zeal and self-centeredness is true of everyone to some extent. Whether it be a question of the devotion we invest in marriage, parenting, church community, prayer, family, friendship, or work, there is always some kind of tug-of-war between our realization of the ideal and the temptation to be half-hearted and self-seeking.

By reminding us of the ultimate outcome of our lives, Fr. Sorin helps us to place this struggle in its proper context. We need to reflect frequently on how we want our lives to turn out and what kind of example we wish to leave behind. For, when we focus on our ultimate hopes for our lives, we will become more conscientious in asking God for the grace to live out our call fully and with generosity.

John P. Reardon, C.S.C.

November 6

If idleness leads to boredom and to the grossest of vices, study on the contrary is a course of pure delights. Let us then be men of study, but let us study the things we should know and in their proper order.

—Basil Moreau

FOR MOST PEOPLE, the world of academics and scholarship is a peculiar one. How many people find joy in sitting quietly hour upon hour mulling over old, yellowing documents and trying to make sense of them? Or in bringing together these discoveries for an article or book? Neither of these processes is easy. Both take time, inspiration, and patience. Similarly, both must be undertaken with rigorous discipline. And even though dialogue with those engaged in similar pursuits is essential and leads to further insights, it is often only through isolation and quiet that the truths of the past come to light.

In his writings, Fr. Moreau realizes his followers need to be people of study. He encourages us to step back from the busyness and distractions of our world to pray, to learn, and to discern. By offering such encouragement, Fr. Moreau follows the model of discipleship provided by Christ who, in the gospels, calls his disciples regularly to retreat to a quiet place to pray and reflect. Such introspective action, which is necessary for all of Christ's followers, allows us to center ourselves on the essentials of life in order to see the world with new insights. On the other hand, Fr. Moreau also realizes that we, too, live in a world that often challenges our Christian values. For this reason, he exhorts us to engage in and to learn from the world around us. This ongoing process of engagement and discernment enriches us and allows us to grow ever more aware of all the gifts with which God has blessed us.

Kevin P. Spicer, C.S.C.

November 7

Our concern for the dignity of every human being as God's cherished child directs our care to victims of every injury: prejudice, famine, warfare, ignorance, infidelity, abuse, natural calamity.

—Holy Cross Constitutions

"I'M A WORTHLESS, hurting, good-for-nothing," he mumbled to himself. Wounded in a knife fight, stitched up, and still bleeding, he claimed he was going to die of pain. A compassionate parishioner placed her arm around him and brought him in from the street to Mass. "I will ask Father to anoint you and that will help." Quite overcome by her kindness, the man received the sacrament of anointing and humbly thanked me as well as the parishioners who prayed for him. The next day his physician called to report that his wounds were healed; the doctor offered to send all his homeless patients to our chapel.

Called to express concern for the frail, needy, and those without voice, we are challenged to face up to the truth that all human life is sacred. Comprehending this truth is one thing; practicing it is quite another. Human misery and powerlessness are not welcome friends. Yet, Christ tells us, "When you welcome the stranger, however humble, you welcome me."

Allowing ourselves to get close to suffering and injustice can trigger pain, resistance, or anger in us. Christ up close is very human and sometimes uncomfortable. Yet, our care for all God's cherished children brings important blessings. We learn about our inner life, about our hesitations and exclusiveness, about our personal and institutional limitations, about the need for grace and healing within us, our Church, and our world. Those hurting among us could lead us to pray that God might give us eyes to see, ears to hear, and a heart to understand real dignity, that is, Christ among us all.

Richard Berg, C.S.C.

November 8

The rule forms our character; it softens our disposition and smoothes rough edges. It roots out faults of mind and heart and replaces them with virtues.

—Basil Moreau

HUMAN CIVILIZATIONS THROUGHOUT history have used a rule of law to govern themselves. Such systems, at their best, are liberating because they provide a framework in which citizens may live freely and work productively for the betterment of all. Without such laws society risks falling into chaos. In a similar way, religious life, since its beginnings in the fourth century, has structured itself within a framework that forms the character of the community and its members.

Fr. Moreau wanted his priests and brothers to flourish. Informed by the history of religious life, he knew this would happen best when rules were set and articulated. A religious rule of life requires a certain discipline and forces its adherents to reflect seriously upon their words and actions so as to conform to the higher order and good that the rule demands.

Beyond the confines of religious life, Christianity also is lived within the context of a rule as articulated by the message and mission of Jesus Christ. To follow the ways of the gospel is very challenging, especially in a contemporary society that often shows little value for Christian ideals. Those, however, who have the courage to follow the narrow path, the way that is often more difficult and filled with obstacles, will experience a sense of peace and manifest the virtue of love, the most fundamental and important of Christian virtues. For it is love that will free us from the bondage of this world. And it is the rule that allows love to permeate our lives and the society in which we live.

Richard Gribble, C.S.C.

November 9

I have a full list of all the Religious of Holy Cross. I carry it with me everywhere; and whenever I enter a celebrated church or chapel, I take the dear roll in my hands, and as soon as I make sure that I am listened to, I begin my litany and go through.

—Edward Sorin

TO CALL INDIVIDUALS by their name is to recognize them in their uniqueness. God calls each of us by name when he brings us into existence. He affirms us in our being with each breath that we draw. Each of us is unique in the eyes of God—a child of God, cherished and loved, affirmed in dignity.

We can imagine that as Fr. Sorin took the list of the religious of Holy Cross in his hands and read through the names, the faces of so many brothers and priests of Holy Cross would have come before his mind's eye. He would cherish each one in his uniqueness, for who he was and for what he contributed to the mission of Holy Cross. Then Fr. Sorin would lift each of them up in his prayer.

There is a "communion of the saints" at the deepest of levels that comes from faith. It binds us one to another with the bonds of love. It is a sharing in the love of God, the love of Christ. In our own prayer, each of us has a dear roll of those for whom we pray. As we recite their names, their faces come before us. We affirm them in their uniqueness, as objects of God's love and of our love. We lift them up through our prayer so that God will bless them with the gifts and the graces that they need. It is one powerful way that we share in the love of God, the love of Christ.

Arthur J. Colgan, C.S.C.

November 10

We are happy. We have the Lord with us. Only tonight we hung our sanctuary lamp where none had hung before. They tell us we won't be able to afford to keep it burning. But we have a little olive oil and will burn while it lasts. We can see it through the woods and it lights the humble home where Our Master dwells. We tell each other that we are not alone, that Jesus Christ lives among us. It gives us courage.

—Edward Sorin

FR. SORIN WROTE these words to Fr. Moreau upon the arrival of Holy Cross at Notre Dame, and they hang outside the entrance to the chapel in Siegfried Residence Hall as a reminder—what we do is God's work and we are never alone.

How bewildered, how busy those pioneer religious were in setting about to make their home, their daily work, their mission. We can only imagine the challenges, frustrations, disappointments and, yes, the successes they encountered. Life today is busy and has its challenges, too. There is always so much to do, so many choices, so many demands. Sometimes it seems as if the work will never get done—or at least be done the way we want it to be. And still there is no shortage of generosity as people give from their abundant blessings of talent and skill to help one another. Nevertheless, we all face moments of frustration, disappointment, and even failure. Sometimes we wonder if we are working alone and unappreciated.

It is then that we need to remind ourselves that it is God's work we do. It is God's will to which we seek to conform our desires, our will, and our plans. That's why we visit our churches often, to be reminded that we abide in the Lord and he with us. The sanctuary lamp reminds us of this reality. It is a light that from the earliest days has burned at Notre Dame, and it burns wherever Christ gathers his Church.

John Conley, C.S.C.

☧

November 11

Be eager to come and renew your zeal in the annual retreat which you will make whenever obedience calls. Let us cherish the silence which marks those on retreat and love the sacred walls of this solitude where we spend such quiet days and which now shelters us from the main attacks of the enemy.

—Basil Moreau

"A PASSION FOR ministry"—that was the phrase a friend once used to describe a zealous Holy Cross priest. Since then, this phrase has become an image for my understanding both of Holy Cross and of my own priesthood. No words could better capture our desire as priests, brothers, and sisters to make God known, loved, and served.

The question, however, is how we can sustain this passion for our apostolic ministry from day to day and year to year. How do we avoid a routine approach or attitude to the words, the people, and the events which constitute our lives as religious? How do we treat each person, every class, each sacramental moment we engage in as though it were the most important one ever?

It is for this reason that Fr. Moreau consistently underscored the importance of silence in our lives, not only on a daily basis, but for more extended periods of time as well. He urged this practice on his followers not only as a way to deepen their spiritual lives but also as a means of increasing their enthusiasm and passion for their work. In this way, all of us must imitate well our Lord who often went off by himself to pray. Maybe we don't have a week, or even weekend, but a few hours in silence with the Lord can be enough to remind us that God's love and grace surround us, always sustaining our zeal to live life to the fullest.

Richard V. Warner, C.S.C.

*If at times you show preference to any young people,
they should be the poor, those who have no one else to
show them preference, those who have the least knowledge, those who lack skills and talent, and those who
are not Catholic or Christian. If you show them greater
care and concern it must be because their needs are
greater and because it is only just to give more to those
who have received less.*

—Basil Moreau

A YOUNG MAN, a bit disheveled and hesitant in manner, comes
to the door. Just released from prison, he needs money to
get home to his wife and baby. There is still some innocence
left in his gaze, but not much. A family with young children
faithfully goes to church every Sunday. Mom and Dad work
hard, providing not only food, clothing, and shelter, but also
a secure and loving environment. The quiet student in the
back of the classroom shows little interest and looks terminally
bored. He doesn't smile and seemingly does not have any
friends. He seems very sad. A small Ugandan child, dressed in
her school uniform, exudes the sweetness of innocence. The
awe and wonder of the day's surprises light up her face. The
face I see in the mirror first thing in the morning has eyes not
quite opened and hair at odds with itself, sticking out in all
directions. It looks confused.

The image of God shines in all, no matter the person or
the circumstances, because it has been imprinted within us

like a sacred seal. We welcome, honor, and reverence this Divine Presence in each of us, especially in the person least welcomed, honored, and reverenced by society, for we share that same seal, the same divine spark, that marks us as created in the image and likeness of God. We can do nothing less. It is the Incarnation of God's love for us. We must preserve it all costs.

Thomas A. Dziekan, C.S.C.

November 13

On poverty, as I see it, depends the blessing of heaven on the Congregation of Holy Cross, the progress of its individual members in the love of God, and each one's perseverance in the spirit of our holy vocation. Poverty is a supernatural virtue which is born of faith, feeds on hope, and grows to maturity in the love of Him who said, "Blessed are the poor."

—Basil Moreau

WHAT DO WE own? What owns us? Frequently, the things we own, especially our most prized possessions, actually own us. If we have a fancy new car, we get mad if someone dings it up in a parking lot. If we own a nice sweater, a waiter's accidental spill of food becomes a much more heinous offense. After all, it is easy in life to acquire things. My sister and her husband entered their first home with little and left, according to the movers, with more than nine thousand pounds of things.

We grow accustomed to things, certain niceties. And even when we have little, we can cling to them with exceptional aggressiveness.

The inverse is also true. The less we own, the less those things will own us. For us in Holy Cross, poverty, like all of our vows, is to allow us to live with hands open, not grasping, not clutching, in this case, to things. And for all Christians, regardless of economic status, the clear call of the gospels is to give freely and generously of all of our blessings, even our material wealth, for those in need.

St. Luke tells us that Jesus said simply, "Blessed are the poor" (6:20). The blessing of heaven of which Fr. Moreau speaks is this vision of the Beatitudes. The more each of us can let go of things, the more God can take hold of us. In blessed poverty, may our hands be free from things to serve God and neighbor.

Christopher Cox, C.S.C.

November 14

Some of us may not see many another new year; neither age nor vigor will avail; but a holy life will enable us to look steadfastly upon death as a deliverer from temptation and misery, holding out the crown promised to those who shall have persevered to the end.

—Edward Sorin

No one knows how long we will be on this earth. Death will come to each person like a thief in the night. But for us children of God death is not something to be feared, as though it were a defeat or a total loss. No, death truly is our birth into eternal life with God. In faith each of us can say with St. Paul that, from now on, a "crown of glory awaits me."

I wonder if we spend enough time dreaming or fantasizing about heaven. St. Paul wrote that it hasn't so much as dawned on the human heart what God has waiting for those who love him. To me this sounds like a dare. It's as if he were saying, "Go on, dream big. Imagine the absolute best existence possible, and you won't even come close to the blessedness of heaven." The more we set our eyes on the kingdom of heaven, the better we will be able to live as true daughters and sons of God while here on earth.

Still, Jesus knew that we might become anxious, or even preoccupied, with our death. That is why he said, "Do not let your hearts be troubled" (Jn 14:1). He will come back for each one of us at an undetermined time. For our part we must live each day well in this joyful hope so that we will be ready for that great and glorious day.

Bill Wack, C.S.C.

☦

November 15

The tree of the Cross has been planted where our worthy Religious dwell. But these Religious have learned to savor its life-giving fruits, and if God in His goodness preserves them in the admirable dispositions which they

have chosen thus far, they will never taste death, for the
fruits of the Cross are the same as those of the tree of life
which was planted in the Garden of Paradise.

—Basil Moreau

THE SHADOW OF Christ's Cross enters every life, but it is not always recognized. Even less often is it welcomed. Yet in claiming and embracing the Cross as our only hope, we believe that a willing welcome of its shadow foretells a more life-giving light, welling up from within and without, protecting us from the despair that comes when a hope-filled horizon cannot be immediately perceived. To embrace the Cross thus means expecting hardship while counting on strength to bear it, anticipating agony, yet trusting untapped reservoirs of faith and peace. Such reservoirs lie in us, in our sisters and brothers whom we can see, and in God whom we cannot see.

Fr. Moreau believed that all who experience the Cross of Christ can trust God to be faithful. His connection between Calvary and Eden, an insight of the Church from its earliest days, reassured him that trees of life and death and knowledge, trees forbidden and enticing and torturing, rested on hills that needed to be climbed by all God's sons and daughters in their own way. The fruits of such trees can be thorns or berries, rough bark or supportive pews. Some fruits are immediately apparent, others—often the most fulfilling—take time to mature and make themselves known. The challenge for us lies in trusting that the trees of the Cross in our lives provide us with spiritual fruits that will nourish us, especially when inclinations tempt us to seek fruits that look more attractive in the short run.

Paul Kollman, C.S.C.

Whether it be unfair treatment, fatigue or frustration at work, a lapse of health, tasks beyond talents, seasons of loneliness, bleakness in prayer, the aloofness of friends; or whether it be the sadness of our having inflicted any of this on others . . . there will be dying to do on our way to the Father.

—Holy Cross Constitutions

IT IS COMMON enough for teachers or parents to become discouraged. A frustrated teacher may complain to me about students, saying that many do not hand in homework, that important projects are late or missing, and that others fail their quizzes in spite of constant review and extra help. It seems to the teacher, and to the parents of those students who may have similar issues at home, that all of their effort is wasted.

"You are the message," I tell them. From much experience I have found that students and associates of mine will not always remember what I said, but they will remember who I am, how I acted, how I treated others, and how I approached my responsibilities. Like tiny seeds, our behavior, which is the true message, takes root in others and undergoes a slow growth, a synthesis. "Your efforts do work," I explain. "It just takes time. Have faith."

I often wonder how exasperated at times Jesus must have become with his disciples. After all, he was the Master Teacher, but his students kept tripping over their own enthusiasm and self-interest. Nevertheless, Jesus remained consistent, patient, and unwavering in his love and in his faith. During prayer I realize that I am as dull as any of his disciples were. I pray that Jesus will show me the same endless patience. I pray that the message he has presented me will not be wasted, but will grow inside of me and bear fruit.

James Kane, C.S.C.

November 17

May we all, more than ever, find in each other's edifying example an efficient means of sanctification to the last.
—Edward Sorin

As a brother of Holy Cross for close to fifty years, I find that Fr. Sorin's words about edifying examples bring back memories of many people who, by the grace of God, helped me along the path to sanctification.

I have only to reflect back on my early assignments in houses with forty or more religious. As I think back now, it was the retired brothers who spent many days and years on the missions or in the classroom who gave us younger religious the greatest example—how they were devoted to personal and communal prayer, how they were faithful to our community life, and how thoughtful and kind they were with everyone living with them. These older religious were saints in our midst. I only wish that we would have taken the time then to look and follow their examples of living the vows a little bit more.

Then, through the years, there were so many lay men and women living with burdens often unknown to us religious. They labored in silence with children who were handicapped and parents who needed their care, while living with wages that barely covered their expenses. Many times these laypersons showed much greater dedication to our mission than we did. These people often saw the brothers and priests as examples to be followed, but if the truth be known, they were the examples we had to follow in reaching our own personal sanctification.

We just have to sit down and reflect for a while and we will all find a multitude of edifying examples, both in the past and present, to follow along our own roads to sanctification.

Charles P. McBride, C.S.C.

November 18

May our good God give us clearly to understand the sublimity of our vocation, to impart in us strength to fulfill, not in part, but entirely, the duties it imposes on every soul thus singularly chosen!

—Edward Sorin

FR. SORIN PRAYED that God would help those joining Holy Cross to understand the extraordinary value of their vocation so they would have the courage and perseverance to fulfill all the demands of religious life. The same wisdom that inspired this prayer applies to all vocations. Namely, the more we recognize the sublime beauty of our callings from God, the more we will find the strength to fulfill them.

This wisdom is particularly important now because examples of perpetual commitment of any sort are difficult for us to come by these days. Our culture no longer promotes or expects unfailing fidelity to one person, one family, one job, one location. Young folks are counseled to take time to investigate possibilities for themselves because if and when they make a life commitment, there will be few enough to support their decision and assure them they have chosen wisely.

When we sense God's call to the religious life or any other vocation, we must turn prayerfully toward the One who summons and listen intently. We must place before God the uncertainty we may feel, including the very uncertainty of what is implied in our saying yes. Going all out and arriving at a decision is essential, as is making a determined response. Yet, whatever the eventual outcome, we must be ready and willing to place ourselves in the hands of the unfailing love and support of the One who calls us by name, saying, "You are mine."

Phillip Armstrong, C.S.C.

November 19

The love with which the Sacred Heart of Jesus burned for us stripped Him of His glory, clothing Him in the form of a slave and making Him be born in a stable; this love made Him live among trials and sufferings; this

love made Him sad until death in the Garden of Ol-
ives and crucified Him on Calvary; this love holds Him
still among us veiled in the Eucharist and unites Him
so closely to our souls that we must therefore say with
Him: see how He loved!

—Basil Moreau

THE STARTLING REALITY of the Sacred Heart is often under-estimated because of our unwillingness to consider the depth of the emotion present. We hear homilies so often about the love of Jesus—about divine love—that we fail to consider the human aspect of what Jesus felt. In fact, I would go so far as to suggest that many of us are unimpressed when we hear that "Jesus loves you!" because we figure, well, that is his job, after all. Isn't he supposed to love us?

Jesus indeed came to fulfill the Father's will, but he did not live as if he were reluctantly accomplishing an onerous task. His desire and passion are told to us in gospels full of emotion. He was a man driven to share his love with others, a love that was undaunted by rejection, scoffing, disbelief, and even abandonment by his disciples.

Often in ministry I encounter people who cannot conceive of Jesus' love because of their own obstacles. So I tell them to think of Jesus liking them, having great affection for them, wanting to be their friend. The truth, though, is so much more—Jesus is just crazy about us. Having opened ourselves to being liked—being loved—by Jesus, we begin to have our own desires transformed into a genuine love for others. That is the secret of the Sacred Heart.

Brent Krueger, C.S.C.

November 20

The spirit of faith inspires and enlivens zeal, that is, the sacred fire that the divine Master came to bring upon the earth. So if one has faith and the zeal inspired by faith, that person can never think without heartbreak about the vast amounts of sin in the world. Such a person will be ready to go wherever obedience calls to save souls which are perishing and extend the rule of Jesus Christ on earth.

—Basil Moreau

AS A FIRST-YEAR teacher and coach at a Catholic high school, as well as a new pastoral associate at a parish, I met periodically with a ministry supervisor. He had spent many years in Latin America and was now the head of a Catholic secondary school. Needless to say, I was almost overwhelmingly busy. Yet, during the year, I was continually struck by my supervisor's tireless energy, compassion, joy, sense of humor, and willingness to do—as he liked to say—"whatever it took" to make people experience Christ's love and call. He had that twinkle in his eye that instantaneously called forth from others an almost impulsive desire to follow his example. Once I asked him for the secret to his boundless service to the gospel. He paused momentarily, smiled, and then said simply that God had given him three things—faith, a love of people, and a promise that there would be plenty of time to rest in the afterlife.

I often have reflected on these simple words. They reflect the deep relationship with Christ that has allowed my former supervisor to serve as a priest and religious in the poorest neighborhoods and schools from South America to inner-city Chicago. He had the energy to do this because he realized that this service was not his, but the Lord's. I pray often that I can have this same faith, this same love of others, and this same abiding trust that there will be time to rest in the afterlife.

Sean McGraw, C.S.C.

November 21

We propose, but God disposes as it may please His holy will. Happy those whose will is always ready to yield to the will of Heaven, without complaint or murmur, however eager and ardent the wishes of their hearts may be, even for what they consider purely aiming at God's own glory.

—Edward Sorin

THERE IS THE wise old saying, "If you want to make God laugh, tell him your plans." Yet, early each morning I review my commitments for that day to assure myself that I will not forget those I am to see and what I am to do. I try to do this preview in the context of prayer, so that each endeavor brings praise to God. And the purpose of all my planning is to serve God and his people as efficiently and effectively as I know how. For the most part, however, the bulk of the day and its most important moments are the interruptions. The events and people, the joys and sorrows that the Lord unexpectedly sends my way show God's power breaking through my stilted plans, filling each day with unforeseen graces.

Just as distractions in prayer can be God's way of getting our attention, so the many interruptions he sends let us know who is still in charge. Because of these interruptions, tasks I plan to get done never seem to be completed on time. I can grow anxious, worried, and curt with the people who disrupt my well-intentioned plans. I want it my way.

But then God reminds me as he reminds us all: "My thoughts are not your thoughts, nor your ways My ways. As high as the heavens are above the earth, so high are My ways above your ways and My thoughts above your thoughts" (Is 55:8–9). We can only bow before the awesome ways of the Lord, letting him guide us to a glory greater than our own.

Bob Epping, C.S.C.

☩

November 22

Let us learn how to put up with little sufferings for the sake of the community, without complaining at the slightest privation or contradiction. If we fail in this, we would not be good Religious or even good Christians, much less children of Our Lady of the Seven Sorrows and of the Cross.

—Basil Moreau

OUR DOWNTOWN CHAPEL community admits that no one on our street corner has enough money to hide suffering.

The stench from those carrying their only possessions fills our inner-city parish in Portland, Oregon. We see the behavior of mental illness clearly at our daily worship. We understand the addicts' cry to God for another day of sobriety as we witness their tears.

The parish's street corner teaches me about life and faith. No quick solutions and no easy answers fix the anguish here. As I plant my cross at this intersection and learn to trust people, I honor my own suffering that compels me into service. I rest in the heritage of others who have walked similar paths. Echoes of Bartimaeus calling out to Jesus along the roadside for new vision teach me about my own blindness. Crowds gathering to stone an adulterous woman and discovering their own sin teach me to honor the marginalized. The anonymous woman reaching out from the crowd to touch Jesus' garment shows me Christ within my reach.

We can all learn from Holy Cross's heritage to reverence suffering, not to run from it and not to judge others' pain or anxiety. Mary, the prophetic mother of Jesus, still shows us how to stand with people's inconsolable suffering even on days we want to flee from it all. She calls all believers to embrace our incomplete lives, with their many sorrows that lead to faith. Her example beckons us to be with those who cannot bear their burdens, those who carry crosses greater than our own.

Ronald Patrick Raab, C.S.C.

November 23

Time passes like a dream; eternity should fix our attention.

—Edward Sorin

PHILOSOPHERS AND THEOLOGIANS have speculated for centuries about the nature of time and have debated the question of how an eternal God might relate to creatures both temporal and mortal. Jesus embodies this paradox of the eternal-in-time, the incarnate Word that is both now and always. As St. John says in his Gospel, "the Word became flesh and made His dwelling among us, and we saw His glory" (1:14).

In our own lives we experience moments when eternity breaks through to us, when we seem to be, though briefly, in the company of our God. At those times the paradox makes itself present to us; we have the sensation that we, too, are both now and always. As Fr. Sorin puts it, eternity has fixed our attention. In other words it is the Eternal who acts, and we respond by focusing on its presence. For me these "God moments" have occurred while sitting on a hill beneath Pike's Peak at the Holy Cross Novitiate in Colorado; while meditating before the tabernacle and Holy Cross priest Fr. Tony Lauck's stunning stained glass windows at the Moreau Seminary chapel; and while lying prone on the floor of Sacred Heart Basilica at Notre Dame during the litany of the saints as part of the Mass of perpetual profession of religious vows. In instants like these, eternity fixes our attention, we become aware of a larger frame of reference, and time passes like a dream. It would be truly divine if only we could experience every moment of our lives this way, in the certain knowledge of God's eternal presence.

George Piggford, C.S.C.

☩

November 24

As to our ancestors, God has spoken to us in many and various ways; we hear His voice everywhere, we meet Him at every step. Since we conversed with Him in the stable of our novitiate, we never parted.

—Edward Sorin

IN RELIGIOUS VOWS and in the Nicene Creed we entrust ourselves to gifts already given—the gifts of faith and love handed on to us through the communion of the saints, those holy women and men to whom God has already spoken.

We religious, in our vows, give our hearts to the God who has first loved us. We profess poverty, chastity, and obedience in the midst of the Congregation of Holy Cross, for the community has handed on to us its experience of the provident embrace of God's love. We live in the power of what has been handed on to us, and so we turn to the stories of our ancestors in Holy Cross and know that if we but listen, we will hear his voice everywhere and meet him at every step.

We Christians, in the creed, give our hearts to God who is Father, Son, and Spirit in the midst of God's assembly, for that assembly handed on to us its experience of the creating, redeeming, and sanctifying love of God. We live in the power of what has been handed on to us, and so we turn to the scripture and to the tradition of the Church and know that if we but listen we will hear his voice everywhere and meet him at every step.

Both in religious vows and in the creed we pledge to become for others gifts given and handed on so that others might believe and love. Sealed in the covenant waters of baptism, we followers of Christ pray that our pledges of faith will bear fruit so that from him we might never be parted.

Thomas P. Looney, C.S.C.

November 25

Since God alone provides the means for the successful accomplishment of any task, it really seems evident that a person needs to be called by God to be a teacher if that person is going to be able to be effective.

—Basil Moreau

TEACHING IS A path to sainthood, or perhaps martyrdom. Either way, being an educator—especially a Catholic educator—is a vocation that demands devotion and humility if one is truly to educate both the heart and the mind.

During my first months of teaching high school, I had one particularly frustrating evening. As I was correcting papers, I came to the realization that several of my students had blown off an assignment that I had worked hard to create. Disheartened and drained by long and thankless days, I cried out to

God, "What am I doing wrong?" I walked down the hall and talked to Fr. Sean McGraw, C.S.C., and at his suggestion, I retreated to our chapel, bible and gradebook in hand.

There, before the Blessed Sacrament, I prayed the words of the parable of the sower and the seed. Christ told his followers that the seed they spread throughout the world would find many different kinds of soil, some rich and some rocky, but their charge was simply to spread the good news with reckless abandon. I realized that it would not be through my strength that these seeds would take root, but only through the power of the Holy Spirit. His was the mission, his would be the strength, and from him alone would come the grace to persevere in teaching each of the names staring at me in my gradebook. This, for me, is the divine call not only of teaching, but of all vocations—cooperating with God's grace, spreading the good news, and then getting out of the Holy Spirit's way.

Nate Wills, C.S.C.

November 26

For the kingdom to come in this world, disciples must have the competence to see and the courage to act.
—Holy Cross Constitutions

MINISTRY IN HOLY Cross begins with the transformative encounter with Jesus Christ, is nurtured by prayer and the sacraments, is sustained in community, and finds completion in zealous work for the kingdom. Because we love Christ, he tells us, as he told Peter, "Feed my lambs, feed my sheep."

The Cross is our only hope, and it teaches all of its disciples that service to God's kingdom in our world is often difficult, messy, frustrating, and discouraging. Comforted by assurances of God's love, we can sometimes be tempted to hold ourselves spiritually aloof, avoiding the hardships of practical achievement. We must never shy away from concrete engagement with the world for the sake of the kingdom.

Those seeking worldly riches and recognition make sure they are well prepared. They make sacrifices and show great ingenuity to win riches and acclaim. "The children of this age are more shrewd in dealing with their own generation than are the children of light" (Lk 16:8). If we fail to be equally prepared, equally committed, and show similar boldness and creativity, we can become a counter-witness, making it seem that worldly rewards and achievements are more to be valued than eternal ones.

Jesus proclaimed, "I came to bring fire to the earth, and how I wish it were already kindled!" (Lk 12:49). This same fire must burn in our hearts as we strive to serve the Church and the world. Our judgments and decisions must be well-informed and shrewd, and our endeavors bold. Then, rather than being discouraged by opposition, frustration, or failure, each setback becomes an opportunity to give ourselves more fully to the kingdom.

John Jenkins, C.S.C.

☩

November 27

It is God's own hand which has guided everything, and He it is whom we must thank above all. Hence I beg you to unite your thanks with ours in order that we may draw down more abundant blessings from heaven upon our work, and above all, not stop their flow by a want of gratitude.

—Basil Moreau

WHEN FR. MOREAU looked at the humble yet mysterious beginnings of the congregation he founded, the talented young people who began to join it, and the missions that were soon established, he felt a deep debt of gratitude to Divine Providence. He knew instinctively that gratitude to God was a sure way to receive even more abundant blessings.

As a nation, we put this spiritual principle into practice through the annual celebration of Thanksgiving. On this one day, we slow down and fuss less, enjoy the company of loved ones and friends, and realize during grace before a delicious meal just how blessed we are.

As a Church, the Eucharist is our privileged opportunity to express our gratitude to the Father for all that we have received in Christ Jesus. The word "eucharist" comes from the Greek word meaning "to give thanks," and for our weekly hour of praise and thanksgiving, untold graces are showered upon us.

In our families, grace before meals and bedtime prayers cultivate in parents and children alike an appreciation for the profound blessings of work, a home, food and clothing, friends, and the gift of one another. As awareness increases, so do blessings.

Forgetfulness is the only enemy of our blessings; for we may stop their flow by a want of gratitude. All of us, like Fr. Moreau, can help each other to appreciate our blessings and to realize that a little gratitude goes a long way. We can learn the power of gratitude, which unites us and opens up the floodgates of heavenly blessings for ourselves and those we are called upon to serve.

Patrick Neary, C.S.C.

November 28

In the Christian sense, the finding of the Cross is always that of a precious treasure. In the sense of the flesh, however, the sight of the Cross, in any view it may present itself, is ever frightful, painful, and unwelcome.

—Edward Sorin

ONE PURCHASE I never thought I would need to make as a priest was a crucifix. I had been surrounded by them for much of my life. I often carried the processional cross as an altar server, I continue to pray before the crucifix hanging on my bedroom wall during my daily prayers, and I marvel at the various crucifixes in our parishes, university chapels, and religious houses throughout the community. Yet I never really stopped to think about the specific details of the Cross until I needed to buy one.

The process of looking through more than a few catalogues for a crucifix—which was a bit odd in itself—led me to reflect on both the gruesomeness and the glory of the most recognizable symbol of our Christian faith. I had a difficult time selecting a crucifix that was neither too sentimental nor too bloody. Perhaps this is because trying to tone down a brutal and inhumane way to die is paradoxical. As much as we might try to sanitize the Crucifixion, there is no escaping the reality that Christ's death on the Cross was frightful, painful, and shameful. At the same time, we Christians know that the Cross is our glory for through the eyes of faith we can see beyond the nails and the blood to the One whom God raised from the dead three days later. Because of this, the Cross is our most precious treasure. And so we cast it in gold and silver, carve it out of wood and marble, and mold it in plaster and plastic ever to remind ourselves of the true hope and salvation born out of that frightful, painful, and unwelcome death.

Brad Metz, C.S.C.

November 29

Once entered into the house, having found the Child with Mary His Mother, and fallen down to adore Him, let us pause awhile in Their holy presence, forgetting the world with its vain noise and treachery. And opening our only treasure, our hearts, let us make Him our richest offering, our whole being, that He may dispose of it as He pleases.

—Edward Sorin

THOUGH I HAVEN'T experienced the joys and challenges of fatherhood, I am privileged to have eight nieces and nephews. Now a new generation is arriving—four great-nephews grace the family hearth, one from his place in heaven. I'm at a stage in life and ministry that I call "spiritual grandpahood"—baptizing the children of the children I baptized those many years ago.

How easy it is to give one's heart to an infant. Our attention is focused solely on that little child. Outside distractions fade away. We marvel at the tiny physical features, feel the clasp of small fingers, and lose ourselves in the depths of the little one's eyes. We get down on the floor and play with rattles and squeaky toys. We make silly faces. The "conversation" between ourselves and the infant is perfectly understandable to both of us. In other words, it's all right for us to let go of our adultness. An infant gives us permission to be a child ourselves.

So, too, it is with Jesus. True, we won't relate to him as though he were a baby, nor does he expect that. But how deeply Jesus desires the clasp of our hands, our gaze into his eyes. He longs for the language of our heart speaking to his heart. Playfulness is welcomed and cherished. We can let ourselves go with Jesus, just as we do with an infant. Yet one huge difference remains between Jesus and an infant. Sooner or later the infant's attention shifts to something different. Jesus never tires of us.

Herbert C. Yost, C.S.C.

God so loved the world that he sent his only Son that we might have life and have it abundantly.
—Holy Cross Constitutions

A PRIEST DINED, one winter evening, at the home of a sheep farmer. When the meal was over, the two men drew well-worn armchairs over to the fireplace and sat quietly gazing at the flaming hearth. The farmer's favorite border collie looked supremely comfortable stretched out on an old rug before the fire. The dog's head and one of its forepaws rested on the farmer's foot. After a while, the priest gestured to the collie and remarked, "I suppose for a dog it doesn't get any better than that." The farmer turned to the priest and replied, "You're wrong, you know. That's a working dog. He was bred to herd sheep. That's what he's for, and he's never happier than when he's doing it. It's much the same with any breed. A husky is happiest in harness, a pointer when it's hunting."

Something similar must be true of us. Christ came so that we might have life abundantly and live it to the fullest. We are fully alive not when we are resting comfortably, or being pleasurably entertained, but when we are doing what we're for—what we're intended by God to do. Created in the image of the God who is Love, we will be happiest when we are loving God and our neighbor, and giving our love active expression in the world. That's why it is fitting that the passage we reflect upon here appears where it does—at the beginning of the *Holy Cross Constitution* on Mission.

Charles B. Gordon, C.S.C.

December

December 1

As we grow in age, we grow in love for prayer. Oh! let us pray more than ever, and spread around us, by example and teaching, by constant and increasing efforts, the wholesome, the saving spirit of prayer.

—Edward Sorin

WHEN I WAS in Catholic grammar school we were taught during Advent to pray, "Divine Infant of Bethlehem, come and take birth in my heart." We were to say that prayer six thousand times because the world since its creation had waited six thousand years for the coming of Jesus. As a young boy, I actually accomplished that challenge, kept careful score, and even outdid the six thousand. Then, as I matured, I came to find the daily rosary as a way to pray always. In my growing affection for God, I discovered that I could pray day and night. Over the years, my familiarity with and love for the prayers freed me simply to finger the beads in a holy silence—a growing awareness of the presence of God in our world.

Prayer is the attention of the loving soul. We pay attention to the true, the beautiful, the good. Religion is not about what we are doing. Religion is about what God is doing in us and for us and all around us. Even our prayer of petition is a form of thanksgiving because we know in advance that God hears our prayers. Even our prayer of sorrow is a prayer of praise, because conversion of heart in the sinner is impossible by the sinner's own initiative. In the eucharistic prayer we proclaim, "It is right and just to give you thanks and praise always and everywhere." To recognize God's abundant and perennial Providence is to pray always. This love for God and love for prayer is a wisdom of our waning years that we would share.

Nicholas Ayo, C.S.C.

December 2

Before the Lord all of us are sinners and none is an enemy. We stand with the poor and the afflicted because only from there can we appeal as Jesus did for the conversion and deliverance of all.

—Holy Cross Constitutions

IN OUR RELIGIOUS houses, parishes, schools, and other apostolates we pray for the poor in our midst during communal prayers. When we ask God to raise the poor from their situation and to fulfill their needs, we pray not only for those who are materially poor, or who we think are poor, but also for ourselves. We are all poor. As the Akans of Ghana say, "*Nnipa hia mboa*"—"All human beings need help." Even if our material abundance blinds us to this reality, we are all bound together in and by our need. Beyond our material needs we share a hunger and thirst for human communion, a hunger and thirst for the Lord.

The deeper meaning of "*nnipa hia mboa*" is that all human beings deserve to be helped. The Akans of Ghana also say, "All human beings are children of God; no one is a child of the earth." Each of us bears a spark of the divine. That being the case, at the very least, none of us should be enemies. Rather, we should all be together as partners both in our need for food, clothing, and shelter, and in our need for each other and for the living God. It is impossible for us to fulfill this obligation to one another in our shared humanity as long as we live in isolation—spiritually or culturally. Instead, we must stand side by side as brothers and sisters before the Lord—saints and sinners, men and women, rich and poor. For it is there that we together can appeal, as Jesus did, for the conversion and deliverance of us all.

Michael Amakyi, C.S.C.

December 3

For many of us in Holy Cross, mission expresses itself in the education of youth in schools, colleges and universities. For others, our mission as educators takes place in parishes and other ministries. Wherever we work we assist others not only to recognize and develop their own gifts but also to discover the deepest longing of their lives.

—Holy Cross Constitutions

MY ENTIRE EDUCATION was through the good ministry of Holy Cross priests, brothers, sisters, and their dedicated lay colleagues. I attended St. Joseph Grade School, St. Joseph

High School, and have three degrees from the University of Notre Dame. I received an excellent education in everything from the ABCs to theology, but I could have learned those topics well in other schools. What made my Holy Cross education unique was that it taught me that education is more than just gaining knowledge. It is coming to know God's love in all things and learning to share that love, which is our deepest longing, with all people.

I definitely have come away from my education knowing that God loves me. It was evident in classroom discussions and in the way the Holy Cross religious cared for us. It was evident in the way that my classmates and I were formed as a community of disciples. It was even evident in the way that I was disciplined on the rare occasion that I misbehaved.

In my ministry as a priest, I strive to keep God's love as the center of my life. I try to keep myself grounded in good friendships, prayer, and the sacraments so that I might experience God's love in my own life and thus be able to share that love in all I say and do. It is God's love, freely given to all of us despite our sinfulness, that can inspire us when things are good and keep us going when times are rough. For, in the end, God has promised that we will be saved, and Love doesn't lie.

Anthony Szakaly, C.S.C.

December 4

Let us disregard the suggestions of self-love and forget ourselves to see only God and the Congregation. For the future, let us heed nothing but the spirit of obedience.

—Basil Moreau

WHEN I WAS a new seminarian, an elderly priest surprised me by claiming that obedience was the hardest of the vows to embrace. Chastity, he said, dulled in intensity over time, and poverty was easy since we all lived it together. Obedience, however, was always ready to jump up and bite you when you least expected it. I doubted that he could possibly be right.

Father was right. Now, more than twenty years later, I can affirm that it is obedience, the ongoing call to surrender the exercise of my own will, which proves to be a daily challenge. It is a radical leap of faith to trust that I hear God's will for my life through the voice of my superiors and the works of the congregation. Religious life militates against the spirit of individualism that drives the culture in which we live. Heeding the spirit of obedience is not only socially odd, but must, at times, be borne as a cross. The question is whether we accept that cross with hope.

Religious are not alone in heeding the call of obedience. Married couples also take vows in a moment and live them through a lifetime, subsuming their own wants and desires in the needs of the other. Embracing God's will, as found in our commitments and responsibilities, is a true dying to self. In seeking only God, living our commitments, and heeding the spirit of obedience, we come to know our true selves. In making this effort, we learn the profound depths of God's love.

Gary S. Chamberland, C.S.C.

☨

December 5

The face of every human being who suffers is for us the face of Jesus who mounted the cross to take the sting out of death. Ours must be the same cross and the same hope.

—Holy Cross Constitutions

WHILE PASSING THROUGH Grand Central Station in New York City, I noticed a woman sitting beside a wall near one of the trains. Like an empty, lifeless shell, she sat slumped with her head over her knees. After buying an extra cup of coffee, I sat down beside her and asked, "How are you doing?"

Guardedly, she said, "Fine."

"How has the day been?"

"Good," she quipped defensively.

"What's new?"

"Nothing!" she said. Then she turned away and shut me down, as if a wall had come between us.

We sat together in silence for about twenty minutes, and then she turned my way and said, "Who the hell are you anyways?"

I answered, "I'm a priest, and I just thought you needed a cup of coffee." Unexpectedly, she started to cry intensely. After a long period of silence, I asked, "What is your name?"

She said, "Sara." She then began to describe her cross—her life, its struggles and broken relationships.

Seeing Christ Jesus in her worn and weary face, I asked, "Sara, if you could change anything in the world today, what would it be?"

There was a long pause, but then she said, "I would change my mind. Only then might I find the way out of the prison of my own heart." As we sat together and drank our coffee, I experienced a glimmer of the hope born of the Cross of Christ. It was as if I could hear Jesus' words, "You are not far from the kingdom of God" (Mk 12:34).

Daniel G. Groody, C.S.C.

December 6

Jesus Christ Himself taught us what His life within us signifies when He told us that He is the vine and we are the branches. In a vine, the branches take their life from the sap which is brought to them by the trunk; the branches and trunk are united and form one vine. The life of the Christian comes only from his or her union with Jesus Christ.

—Basil Moreau

As I sit in the sanctuary of Holy Redeemer Church, a Holy Cross parish in Portland, Oregon, and look out at the students and families that comprise our community, the image of the vine and the branches takes on a whole new level of meaning. Like most Catholic parishes in this country, many of our members are the children and grandchildren of Irish, Italian, German, and Polish immigrants. Consistent with national trends, we have several hundred Mexican immigrants and their children. But our parish community also includes a dozen or so African American families and a similar number of families who escaped communist Vietnam on fishing boats and makeshift rafts. A handful of young men in our parish survived civil war and genocide in Africa.

Looking out at the congregation in our church, we might be tempted into thinking only of the differences. And indeed, each branch is unique in cultural custom, devotional life, and even at times language. But because we are all Catholic we are all members of the same family, branches of the same vine who is Christ Jesus. The same root of which we all are born is baptism. The same sap by which we all are nourished is the Eucharist. And so what I see as I look out at our parish family—and ultimately through this family to the universal Church—is a thriving plant with the most beautiful array of flowers imaginable.

Stephen Koeth, C.S.C.

Let us listen to the Good Shepherd, and pray that He will speak to our soul. Then, by means of us, He will speak to those we have been charged to teach and sanctify.

—Basil Moreau

GOD'S WORD IS a life-giving word. Genesis tells us that God spoke and all created life came into being. To take in God's word, to have God's word enter our being, is to allow God to change us, to reform us, and to make us into something new. In a very real sense, the word becomes alive in us, and so people begin to see God's word incarnate through us.

This is certainly an important part of what preachers are called to be and do. As proclaimers of God's word, they must let it into their very being. By praying the scripture, studying the scripture, and letting the scripture speak to their souls, preachers allow the word to change them so that by grace they might become the very word that they are preaching. In this way it is the Good Shepherd who speaks through the preacher. This is one of the great gifts and wonders of the ministry of preaching. As a preacher, I never cease to be amazed at how the Lord has used me to speak his word of healing, or forgiveness, or challenge, or direction through the vehicle of my preaching. It is an amazing grace and privilege.

Inner transformation by God's word is essential for preachers, but it is a grace and gift to all who are willing to let his word seep deeply into their being. So through our own personal prayer and study of scripture, we learn to heed the words of Fr. Moreau and listen deeply to the Good Shepherd in order that his words might change us into living witnesses for all the world to see.

Tom Gaughan, C.S.C.

December 8

Some of my best friends I may never meet again here below, however brief my absence; but thank God, the hope is laid deep in my bosom, I will meet them again and forever in heaven. God grant that we will all meet there where separation is unknown!

—Edward Sorin

DURING MY YEARS as superior of Holy Cross House, our community medical and retirement facility, I witnessed thirty-five of our priests and brothers leaving this world for eternal life. Many were comforted in their last moments by close friends with whom they had shared years of life and ministry together in community. They often sat in silence waiting for the Lord to come. The most common last words were, "Thank you, and I'll be seeing you." Sometimes these blessed reunions between classmates and friends were just a matter of weeks or months away.

The longer any of us lives on this earth, the more friends we have waiting for our arrival into eternal life. And as our longing for reunion with them grows, our longing for heaven itself grows as well. It is for this very reason that one of our elderly priests once told me how he had come to love Advent in his later years. He found comfort in the prayers of the liturgical season that voiced both his patient waiting and his growing desire for the Lord's coming to take him home.

Imagining the deepest human desire to return home, to be with loved ones, and to be in the very presence of God is not so difficult. No matter our age or state in life, this is our desire, too. Together, then, we can all look forward to the dawn of Christ's coming. Although we make the passage from this world into the next alone, we can give thanks, for we will see one another again.

André Léveillé, C.S.C.

December 9

To Him and to Him alone we must return our thanks, for He alone is the Author of all good gifts.

—Edward Sorin

MY PARENTS, EUSEBIO Antonio and Agapita Inés, were field workers in our village in Mexico. They served in our parish as catechists, preparing people for first communion, confirmation, and marriage. I was the eighth out of nine children. Only my younger brother and I survived. I almost died too, and my mother claims it was my baptism that saved me. My second-grade classes were held under a tree because our temporary school building had been hit by lightning and burned to the ground. A year later, when I was ten, my father fell ill, and I had to leave school to work. My father died the following year. I begged my mother to let me continue studying. She allowed me to finish primary school, but then I had to go back to work as we did not have the economic resources for me to continue.

For three years, I did not set foot in the church because I was embarrassed about being barefoot. My friend Gregorio kept inviting me to participate in activities at the church, and I kept saying no until one retreat. The word of God and the beautiful songs of praise captured my heart on that retreat. Now, more than two decades later, by the grace of God, I am a Holy Cross priest.

My vocation is my thanksgiving to God. I thank God for giving me life. I thank God for granting me the chance to praise him with guitar and song. I thank God for choosing me to follow in Fr. Moreau's footsteps in religious life in Holy Cross. I thank God for making me a gift to his Son, Jesus, in the ministry of priesthood. Only God, our Father, merits our love and thanksgiving for all the gifts we have received from his infinite love. We thank God.

Paulino Antonio Inés, C.S.C.

December 10

Wherever through its superiors the congregation sends us we go as educators in the faith to those whose lot we share, supporting men and women of grace and goodwill everywhere in their efforts to form communities of the coming kingdom.

—Holy Cross Constitutions

BEING EDUCATORS IN the faith might sound pretentious to some, yet the gospels call all Christians to take on this role. In my more than two decades serving as a priest and professor at the University of Notre Dame, I have learned that this task is the work of a community.

Since coming to campus, I have been a member of Corby Hall—the Holy Cross community at Notre Dame. Upon arriving, I was welcomed by many of my brothers in Holy Cross who have been models of faithfulness and holiness for me. Over the years, they have quietly lived Christ's call to educate students and colleagues in the faith. They are both generous and engaging, patient and giving. They challenge respectfully and multitask with grace. They educate best by their very example. Young religious bring vigor, energy, and hope to the apostolate. The elderly religious who are most faithful to prayer and to the common life of the community provide an important grounding to sustain the mission. Together we mold one community of educators, and we join with the rest of our colleagues at Notre Dame to form the university into a community of the coming kingdom.

And yet, as we strive to build this community, we know that we are all human. Along with professing faith in Jesus Christ, we also admit that we are sinful. As much as we have the ability to do good, we also have an equal or greater ability to do evil. And so reconciliation becomes an essential part of the work of education if we are truly to form communities that will educate the next generation in the faith. Shaped by community and renewed by reconciliation, we go as educators in the faith to those whose lot we share.

Austin I. Collins, C.S.C.

December 11

The perfect life will be an interior life, elevated to God by the habitual practice of acts of faith, hope and charity after the example of Jesus Christ, who is to be the particular model of our conduct. It is absolutely essential for us to lead with our Lord a life hidden in God.
—Basil Moreau

THE PERFECT LIFE will be an interior life. To be honest, I'm not really too sure about that. After all, we don't live only in the interior, we live in the world—a world of work and play, a world of struggle and joy, a marvelous world filled with the splendor of nature and the blessing of human relationships. And so, my practice of faith, hope, and charity must somehow or other express itself in this complex world. At the same time, this world expresses itself in my life. The secret of this interchange is Jesus himself, the creative Word made flesh.

In the midst of the daily hustle and bustle of everyday life, I have often thought of the restful consolation of a "hidden" life with our Lord. But then the doubts come. Can there ever be a life that is "hidden" in God? How could that be if God is indeed everywhere? As Jesus said, I have to go into my interior room, close the door, and there, in prayerful silence, converse with him.

I can't help thinking that the purpose of developing a deeper interior life, along with the practice of faith, hope, and charity, is to live out what we sing very often during communion in our school masses here at Saint George's College in Santiago, Chile: "To love, as you love; to feel, as you feel; to see things through your eyes, Jesus."

Robert Simon, C.S.C.

December 12

What shall we gain from knowing and believing that Jesus Christ died for us upon the Cross, unless we are willing to suffer upon it with Him?

—Edward Sorin

LIVING IN A comfortable world with warm clothing, plentiful food, central heat, and air conditioning, we might be pampered too much. The other morning, although I was warm under the blankets, it was cold in the room where I awoke.

Then the thought crossed my mind of the hundreds of thousands of people in Mexico and Central America who are unable to support their families, people whose relatives I would serve in ministry that day at our parish in Texas. As I struggled with the cold, they were struggling with the difficult decision of possibly needing to leave home and migrate north to the United States. In doing so, they would have to leave their loved ones and face all the dangers of the journey—robbers, extreme heat during the day, cold nights, and poisonous snakes. They had a hard decision. Then I thought of Christ and his passion—the agony in the Garden, the scourging and crowning with thorns, the carrying of the Cross, and finally the Crucifixion and death. My faith reminds me that his suffering and death led to his resurrection and the new life he offers all of us.

My first reaction was to be humbled. My few moments of discomfort would be nothing in comparison with those real sacrifices. And yet I hesitated, which made me question myself and how much I was willing to sacrifice for the good of others, willing to join Christ in his total gift of self. The only way to find out was to get out of bed and start trying.

John S. Korcsmar, C.S.C.

December 13

We are sojourners in this world, longing for the coming of the new creation as we seek to be stewards on this earth. The world is well provisioned with gifts from God's hand, but the gifts are often worshiped and the Giver is ignored.

—Holy Cross Constitutions

I CAN CLEARLY recall my initial encounters in Dhaka, Bangladesh. Everyone I met exhibited a palpable sense of the presence of God. Since I knew nothing of Islam when I first came to teach in this predominantly Muslim country, the experience was direct and fresh. Serving at the time as chair of the faculty of theology at the University of Notre Dame, I was learning how intimately our Christian faith is linked with the Hebrew scriptures as well as with living Jewish people. This interlude among Muslims led me to seek a similar understanding with the third "Abrahamic faith."

Subsequent study of Islam, both in Bangladesh and in the Holy Land, has shown me that Muslims have an acute sense of the gift of God's free creation. Whatever may happen, good or bad, is met with "*al-hamd-il-Allah*"—"God be praised." For Muslims, Islam can be seen as the "straight path" given to us to walk, so that we can learn how to return everything to the One from whom we have received everything. Yet does this not also describe how the revelation of God in Jesus, who asks us to "follow me," leads us to return everything to the Father from whom we have received everything? This total giving back is a lifelong process since we are ever prone to hold back something for a rainy day. My Muslim brothers and sisters have taught me that life is a path of discovering the gifts that we are and that we daily receive from a God who freely creates all that is and whom we are privileged to call Father.

David Burrell, C.S.C.

☩

December 14

Let us, at long last, be "children of the light"; let us turn our attention only to the conquest of the Kingdom of Heaven, by devoting ourselves unreservedly to the works of our vocation.

—Basil Moreau

SINCE 1910, HOLY Trinity High School has consistently served some of the poorest Polish, Hispanic, and African immigrants in Chicago, educating both their hearts and their minds in the Holy Cross tradition. I personally had the privilege of teaching and being an administrator at the high school for more than twenty years. It provided me a place where I could dedicate myself unreservedly to my vocation as an educator in the faith.

For me, fulfillment in this vocation has come in embracing Fr. Moreau's mandate to educate fully—to inform the mind, to form the heart, and to transform every young person, regardless of his or her talents or background, into a child of the light. This means, I believe, that all must be welcomed at the table, no matter the poverty of resources, the poverty of skills, or the poverty of power. As a result, we must come not just as servants, but as their neighbors, to be with them and of them. We strive not only to help them recognize and develop their own gifts, but also to guide them to discover the deepest longing in their lives.

It is my own longing to be a child of the light that has graced me, if but minimally, to assist my students in their desire to walk in God's light as well. The kingdom of heaven will be conquered, so to speak, when, hand in hand, all God's children enter the light on an equal footing.

Philip Smith, C.S.C.

December 15

The aspirations of a Christian soul should lead to the further imitation of Him who never turns His eyes from even the forgetful heart.

—Edward Sorin

WE LIVE IN forgetful times. It is not so much that we have forgotten God, but rather that we have forgotten our longing for God, or at least we have misplaced it. Somehow we have separated from God our longing for God. We direct it now toward lesser things, getting by on lesser joys, which prove passing, fading, and finally worthless. We need to redirect our spirit of longing, which sits at the center of our hearts, back toward its source. Longing is remembering, and remembering where our longing ultimately leads us is the way to retrain our forgetful hearts. For our hearts know longing, but no longer know what to do with it. They are hardened by fear of that very longing designed to give them abundant life.

Remembering our longings, though, is not about satisfying them. The deeper they run the less we are able to find any rest or satisfaction in them. The challenge, instead, is to learn to live in longing, in its open-ended nature, facing honestly its stark reminders of our incompleteness. As the mystics and saints of old have taught us, it is this incompleteness that returns us to the embrace of God. We can trust that if we live in our longing and follow it faithfully it will direct us back into the heart of God, a heart that never forgets.

Jeffrey Cooper, C.S.C.

December 16

What is true of a palace whose foundation has been laid and which is rising gradually to completion is verified, likewise, in a great work of charity. It is not one person alone who builds; nor is it one stone, or one single beam of wood which forms it. Each worker contributes something from his or her own trade; each stone is cut to fit into its one appointed place; and each piece of wood is arranged and placed so as to enhance the general effect of the entire building.

—Basil Moreau

FROM OUR FOUNDING, we as Holy Cross have gone forth together—to work together, to found institutions together, to pray together, to bring the message of the gospel in various corners of the world together. What we in Holy Cross have accomplished, we have accomplished together. This is the essence of our religious life.

As a Holy Cross priest, I have served at both the University of Notre Dame and the University of Portland. Whatever work I have done, whatever things I may have accomplished, I have done so as part of a community, a community of faith-filled, prayerful, talented, and diverse men who have come together as Holy Cross. In that community I find strength and hope and inspiration. In that community, I have been blessed.

Having served in leadership at these institutions, I have been privileged to witness the fruits of many Holy Cross men and lay colleagues who toil together as educators in the faith.

Alone, each one of us probably could have accomplished little, but together we have used the gifts God has given us—including our idiosyncrasies—and we have accomplished much. Most importantly, in accord with the vision of Fr. Moreau, we have worked together to educate both the minds and the hearts of our students. This is the character of any great work of charity; it is the outcome of individual talents brought together for the greater good.

E. William Beauchamp, C.S.C.

December 17

The aspirations of a Christian soul should lead to the further imitation of Him who never turns His eyes from even the forgetful heart.

—Edward Sorin

WHEN I SPEAK with others, I feel more at ease if we make eye contact. I get a better appreciation for the person and I feel more connected to him or her. Conversely, I feel on edge if a person looks away while we speak. For me, the eyes make all the difference.

Fr. Sorin reminds us to keep our eyes on Jesus Christ our Savior. Just as the Savior looks upon us with love, healing, and forgiveness, so we are encouraged to focus our eyes on him in order to imitate him. This is not always an easy task; it is much too easy to forget. After all, plenty of distractions in our material culture can take our eyes off of

Jesus—newer clothes, sportier cars, bigger houses, better cuisine, sleeker computers, and a more perfect physique. Even we priests aren't immune. There's the latest workshop on ministry in the sunniest resort, more luxurious vestments, and that ideal putter for the perfect golf game.

Yes, we are all human. Our eyes can go in all different directions at once, dragging our minds with them to everything but the Lord. On these occasions, we must renew our trust and belief that there's more to life than anything that this world alone can offer. We do this by looking once again into the eyes of Jesus. We turn our eyes to the One who never forgets us, the One to whom we've committed our lives, the Lord who comes to each of us in the Eucharist. And he draws us into closer union with himself.

Michael Belinsky, C.S.C.

December 18

Jesus was not content simply to become one of us in the Incarnation. To become one with us, He chose a life of poverty. His was the life of the most humble people. His life was obscure. He worked with His hands. He knew what it was to be poor and disowned by society.

—Basil Moreau

"I WANT TO thank God for all I have." One of our guests shared this as we gathered in prayer before we opened our hospitality center at our Holy Cross parish in downtown

Portland, Oregon. I know him. He carries all his possessions in a backpack and prays in thanks for God's generous gifts. He lives outside and prays in thanks for God's protective care. He knows the loneliness of days and nights and prays in thanks for God's loving presence. The grittiness of his poverty contrasts with the richness of his faith. His prayer of gratitude reveals his intimacy with God—simple and honest, face-to-face.

I have learned in my work at the parish that the poor cannot hide who they are. Poverty strips away money, possessions, intellect, and power and exposes the real person behind the pretense and false appearance. The poor cannot hide who they are from God. Nor can any of us. Jesus understood this. He wanted nothing so he could have what he most desired—loving, prayerful intimacy with the Father. He embraced a life of poverty, knowing that living anything more than that would raise walls that hide what is genuinely human, including fear, uncertainty, and suffering. Only in his poverty, could he see the Father and know the fullness of intimacy with him.

For many of us, the spiritual work we need to do is to strip away the false self. We need to acknowledge our poverty, to stop hiding, to confess our need for God. We seek to live faith from a place of grateful honesty, just like the guest at the parish.

Bob Loughery, C.S.C.

December 19

Let us say, from our innermost hearts, with the blind man: "O Lord, that I might see!" Once He found us on the road, He opened our eyes and showed us the true, the beautiful light; and we followed Him, blessing Him.

—Edward Sorin

"MY ONLY FRIEND is darkness." These haunting words of Psalm 88 capture the reality of darkness as both solitary pain and suffering and somehow companion. At one level, darkness frightens us; it seems cold, despairing, and hopeless. Yet at the same time, something about darkness attracts us like an old friend, consoling us, and allowing us to turn inward and away from the challenges of the world "out there." Indeed, at times we seek this darkness, this blindness.

But of course we are not blind. We tell ourselves that it is precisely because we see and know the world around us that we sometimes choose the darkness. Perhaps that is the very beginning of our "blindness." For we choose not to see our real selves and consequently do not see the world around us as it truly is—only as it seems to affect us. We try to live in a world of our own creation—our own darkness—and are thus reluctant to open our eyes to the glory of the Christ, the Light of the World.

The man born blind, after all, knows that he is blind. He knows that he cannot see and he longs to see; he longs for the light. We, too, must long for the same light, resisting temptation to retreat into the darkness of our own limitations. For if we admit to Jesus our blindness, he will open our eyes and hearts, showing to us himself, the true, the beautiful Light.

David Sherrer, C.S.C.

☩

December 20

There is one point on which there is a general need for reform. I refer once more to the rule on rising. On this point, listen to St. Vincent, the apostle of charity, who rose so promptly that the second stroke of the bell for rising never found him in the same position as the first.
—Basil Moreau

WHILE EVERYONE IN Holy Cross is introduced to the writings of Fr. Moreau early on in his formation, the selection of readings changes over the years. Today, for example, the Fr. Moreau presented to us inspires us to be zealous educators of the mind and heart. Years ago, we young religious heard instead a Fr. Moreau who earnestly exhorted us to heed the bells that woke us up or announced communal religious exercises. "Lie-a-beds," we constantly read, hardly made serious religious. When changes came, the bells were among the first things to go.

Perhaps only a few people would want to go back to that Fr. Moreau, but that might be a pity. Many religious traditions use bells not simply to announce a religious exercise but also to announce a spiritual presence. "Pay attention," they boom, clang, or jangle. "Stop what you are doing for a moment, and pay attention." Attention to what? It is attention to the voice of the Lord, to hear it, and to respond to it.

Sometimes the voice of the Lord cannot be missed as when Paul paid attention on his journey to Damascus. Sometimes the voice is very soft, as when Elijah the prophet paid attention when he heard the wind whisper. Sometimes the voice isn't immediately clear, as when the disciples on the road to Emmaus paid attention when the stranger revealed himself in the breaking of the bread. What are the sounds of our daily lives that urge us to this holy attentiveness? We pray with the Psalmist that if today we hear his voice, we will harden not our hearts.

Thomas P. Gariepy, C.S.C.

☩

December 21

I shall not attempt to describe for you my inmost feelings during these days of glorious and holy memory. Neither pen nor tongue could adequately express for you the thoughts of my mind and the emotions of my heart as I beheld the touching spectacle of the consecration of our Conventual Church.

—Basil Moreau

ON SUNDAY MORNING, December 21, 1997, thanks to a ride from a Good Samaritan, I arrived in Duchity, a village in the southern mountains of Haiti, after a seven-hour trip on a bad road that no words could describe. It was my first visit to that place. My eyes took in images of both natural beauty and extreme poverty. This was to be my new parish, and I was to be their first pastor. My heart was quickly beating, like that of an athlete on the field at the beginning of the game, anticipating simultaneously the joy of victory and the fear of defeat.

On that Sunday morning, inside the tiny chapel made of clay, the only visible sign of the Catholic community of Duchity was a group of people gathered for prayer. By the grace of God, I arrived just before the lay leader announced the opening song. Five years earlier the bishop had promised them a priest, and, after all the years they had patiently waited, he had finally arrived. The people's hearts were brimming over with joy, as they loudly exclaimed: "God is good! God never abandons his children! Blessed be the Lord!" These exclamations were clear expressions of gladness, hope, and faith. Suddenly, their joy invaded and overwhelmed me, and my fears disappeared. I quickly understood that my mission was, indeed, demanding and challenging, but I was not afraid. We concluded this extraordinarily joyful moment with the celebration of the Eucharist, that greatest of all thanksgivings in which God draws his people together and builds us into his Church—in Duchity, Haiti, and in every corner of the world.

Fritz Louis, C.S.C.

December 22

Our deliberations will include the pragmatic concerns of daily life, but they must also be a way for men of faith to explore the life of the spirit with one another, lest we should speak least about what means most to us.
—Holy Cross Constitutions

MY FATHER DIED in the opening minutes of Christmas 1987, but I did not receive word until New Year's Day. He was already buried. I was a Holy Cross religious ministering in Uganda and communication was difficult. The only reliable means of communicating was by letter, which took four weeks to reach the United States.

And so, I prayerfully sat at my desk and wrote three letters—one to my mom and one to each of my two brothers. Without pausing to think, I poured my thoughts onto the pages, writing straight from the heart. When I had finished the letters and later reread them, I was amazed at the depth of my communication with my family. I had written what I truly wanted to share with them, but what I never would have been able to say if I were sitting with them. A year later when I did get the opportunity to be with my family, each showed me the letter I had written.

Since that time I have suggested this method of writing from the heart to young East Africans who are preparing to become members of our congregation. Many have found it helpful when face-to-face communication is impossible because of distance, death, anger, or opportunities missed.

Writing from the heart has allowed my family to know me, and also my father, much more than I could have ever believed. When we speak or write truthfully from our hearts, we give voice to those things that matter the most to us. We are drawn closer to each other and to God. Communication itself, then, becomes an act of prayer.

James Nichols, C.S.C.

December 23

Our one ambition must be to bring forth children of Jesus Christ by means of Christian education or the apostolic ministry.

—Basil Moreau

I WENT TO visit a student from our school who had experienced a relapse in her leukemia. I was her principal at Saint George's College in Santiago, Chile, and I wanted to be with her and her family. It was the day before Christmas. I wondered how they would celebrate the birth of Jesus Christ when their every moment was a confrontation with pain and impending death. Yet young Javiera and her family received me with great joy. Javiera wanted me to sit by her side. We ate lunch together, and I stayed the afternoon. As I celebrated Christmas Mass that night with the Saint George's community and we prayed for Javiera, I knew that she already had told all her friends her great joy that I had been to visit her that day.

We in Holy Cross are frequently brought face-to-face with the pain and crosses of our students and their families. It is precisely in these moments, when we have neither an explanation nor a word of encouragement, that Christ makes us his voice, his hands, and above all his presence to transmit his great love to them. Even though we never know who might be listening to us or what it is they are really going to understand, it is above all our presence that illuminates and transforms the lives of others. For all educators—teachers, parents, and mentors alike—it is through our very presence that we make space for Christ to enter into the minds and hearts of others.

José Ahumada, C.S.C.

☧

December 24

What have we not learned around that mystical Crib? What did we know before we knelt and listened to the Word made Flesh? Who could say what we felt there at the feet of Jesus and Mary?

—Edward Sorin

KNEELING IS SOMETHING that we don't do very often; yet when we do, it is a powerful gesture. In Holy Cross we kneel before God and the community when we profess our vows, whether it be for the first time or for the last—forever. This powerful gesture signifies that we have found God in the life that we live and share in Holy Cross. Through it we also acknowledge that as we live the vowed life, we will follow and rely on the light and wisdom of our brothers in community.

And so our kneeling is a gesture of our commitment both to them and to the very Word made flesh.

Similarly, when we Christians kneel before the crib of our infant Savior, we are acknowledging that in this Child, God has provided us with what he promised long ago through the prophet Isaiah. Yes, a Son has been given us, a Son who will bring relief from burdens and abundant joy. He will be for us Wonder-Counselor, God-Hero, Father-Forever, Prince of Peace. Even though this Son is only an infant, our kneeling before him is a powerful gesture of faith that he is Emmanuel, God-with-us.

But our kneeling before Emmanuel is also significant because when we kneel, we acknowledge that we will follow him. Through this Child a light shines, and we, a people who walked in darkness, see its great light. No longer will we be lost by relying on ourselves, for we will follow this Light, this Child, wherever he may lead.

Ralph Haag, C.S.C.

December 25

Christmas and the Epiphany are, by excellence, the mystery of the humble. Alas, the proud will not enjoy the scene.

—Edward Sorin

TODAY IS THE day of realized anticipation and finished promises. Today our Savior has become one of us. Today we celebrate our life in the Trinity. On Christmas we rejoice in the Father's promise taking flesh and becoming hope for the humblest and the poorest. We rejoice in the redeeming mission of the Son made concrete in our world. We rejoice in the community realized in the fullness of the Holy Spirit. Hope, mission, and community—these form the threefold foundation on which Fr. Moreau built his religious family of Holy Cross.

It is from this threefold foundation that salvation spreads on epiphany to all times and places, all nations and cultures. For it is on epiphany that this hope is made manifest to the world by the light of a single bright star, that the mission extends to all nations through the faithful journeying of three wise men, and that the community of shepherds and parents gathers in praise of the God who has become incarnate in their midst.

Knowing that this hope, mission, and community will extend to the ends of the earth, we pause today to receive anew the grace of Christ's entry into our lives. For indeed it is only in welcoming Christ more fully into our own homes, it is only in sharing the wonder of his birth more generously with those in need in our neighborhoods, that we become people with a hope so strong in the Father's love that it carries us through the Cross, that we become disciples fully devoted to the mission of Christ in all the corners of the world, and that we truly live together as a community in the Spirit.

Marcelo Solar, C.S.C.

December 26

Who cares for the poor in this world of ease and comfort? Who feels for them? This, then, is our privileged lot, to see and attend to the needs of the suffering members of our beloved Savior.

—Edward Sorin

EVERY YEAR ON Christmas Day, the youth of La Luz, our Holy Cross parish in Guadalupe, Mexico, throw a party for the children from the poorest section of the parish. These are children who dwell in houses made of cardboard, tar paper, and perhaps a bit of tin for a roof. They live on dirt floors, walk dusty roads, and gather water from a common spigot. The celebration at the church is their only Christmas party. It is the only time that they receive any presents.

Our youth do a remarkable job with this event, from planning the puppet Christmas story to going door-to-door to round up all of the children in the neighborhood on Christmas morning. Time and time again I have been inspired by their example. They share their faith with great joy as they attend to the needs of their younger brothers and sisters in Christ.

But what touched me even more was one six year old girl. She left the party carrying many things in her arms. Just outside the church gate, however, she passed a four year old standing alone in the street. After walking about ten steps past him, the girl wheeled around and ran straight back to the little child. She then slowly took some of the candy that she was carrying and gave it to him, then one of her presents, a balloon, and some more candy. I couldn't believe it. She then simply turned around and literally skipped away down the street, back to her desperately poor neighborhood. That six-year-old girl models for all of us that the real gift in life, our true privilege, is to give abundantly as we have received.

Pete Logsdon, C.S.C.

December 27

Oh! Let the humble, candid and guileless souls of our Congregation gather around the poor, dear little Babe in His Crib, and present Him with the gold of their charity, the incense of their prayers, and the myrrh of their penitential life!

—Edward Sorin

WHEN I WAS studying in Japan, a group of sisters invited me to preside at Mass in their convent. After Mass, the nuns presented me, their visiting American priest, with a holy card featuring the Blessed Mother. The image of Mary was one with distinctly Japanese features and dress; she was wearing a kimono. At that point, I had just come from the main university church in downtown Tokyo, where the statue of Mary had distinctly Germanic features. It struck me that the historical Mary, a young Jewish girl in Palestine, probably had little physical resemblance to either image.

The little Babe in his crib, born of the young Jewish mother, is at once the Savior of all the world, the Deliverer of every people, and also a particular human being, fully present in time and space, with physical features and a cultural context determined by the circumstances of his birth. He belongs to every people and also to the Chosen People. Every nation wishes to claim him as its own, to depict him in familiar fashion, and yet he appears as a helpless baby at a specific place in a particular moment in history through the mystery of the Incarnation. We are all challenged to respond to this act of extraordinary generosity, to embrace both the universal mission and the very real humanity of our Savior through lives of charity and prayer—not only for our people, but for all the peoples of the world.

Art Wheeler, C.S.C.

December 28

Somewhat like the Magi, who came to adore the newborn Babe at Bethlehem, we, too, came from afar, guided by the star of divine inspiration.

—Edward Sorin

EACH YEAR IN our parish faith formation program the second graders prepare to receive the sacraments of reconciliation and Holy Eucharist. It is an important moment in their young lives. One year, when I stopped to visit the class, the teacher had an apple cut in two horizontally for each child. At first I thought the children were eating a healthy snack. Then I realized the apple was part of the lesson; each apple contained a starburst filled with seeds. I was intrigued as the teacher explained to the children that the star is like the soul shining deeply from within each one of us. The few dark seeds, she went on to say, are like our sins since baptism that need to be forgiven and then used to grow new life in fertile soil. How true it is. Our souls are within and are the real life breath of our existence. Our inner star, our soul, is the compass of our earthly lives, but it may occasionally need to be refocused when we have gone astray because of sin.

Fr. Sorin knew what it meant as a religious of Holy Cross and missionary to America to follow the star like the wise men who arrived at Bethlehem. It required looking within himself for God's guiding light in the depths of his soul. We, too, have to be faithful to where God is leading us in our Christian lives, cleansing our souls from our sins so that the light of Christ might once again become the light of our souls—leading us straight to him.

Jim Preskenis, C.S.C.

December 29

At the last moment an angel awakens Joseph the Protector and says to him: "Arise, and take the Child and His Mother, and fly into Egypt; for it will come to pass that Herod will seek the Child to destroy Him." The order admits of no delay; the next moment, Mary and Jesus, under the protection and guidance of Joseph, are on their journey, directing their steps towards Egypt.
—Edward Sorin

OUR FAITH MAKES us aware of our weakness. In the course of a lifetime we learn that when we depend upon our own strength, we fail. Eventually, we realize that we can do nothing except by the grace of God. This is an essential spiritual insight. But the example of St. Joseph reminds us of a further spiritual truth upon which we may ordinarily reflect too little: in Christ we have strength beyond our imagining. The lives of the saints testify that however unimpressive we may look, and whatever our circumstances may be, we can be pillars of strength for the kingdom of God.

Like St. Joseph, we should use our strength to protect others. For the weak and fearful, we should be a refuge. The innocent and idealistic should find in us shelter from cynicism and exploitation. Wherever we find holiness we should guard and foster it. Imagine how safe you or I would feel in the physical presence of St. Joseph. In Christ we can, in all humility, give such comfort to one another. And this is possible for any of us. Who among us has not known, for example, an elderly, seemingly frail Christian woman before whom Satan's legions would quail? When an angel spoke a word of warning to him in a dream, Joseph the Protector acted immediately and decisively to defend those entrusted to him. In that way he preserved and sustained all that was most precious in the world. In Christ, we may do the same.

Charles B. Gordon, C.S.C.

December 30

There will not be a single member of our association who will not make his own personal contribution to the progress, according to his strength, intellectual ability and particular aptitudes. One will do intellectual work and another, manual labor; this one will teach, that one will administer the sacraments; and all the while this activity of the individual will help the community; and the activity of the community will, in turn, help each individual.

—Basil Moreau

SOMETIMES I WONDER what my life would be like if I'd chosen a different path. I'd like to think I could be a good husband and father and that I might even make some money, but something tells me I would be a lot poorer in other ways. I think so because I tend to be cautious in how I define my abilities, and it is entirely possible that, left to my own devices, my life might be defined as safe and predictable. No such life exists in Holy Cross.

Since joining the Congregation, I have been asked to do things I never thought myself capable of doing. For the sake of the mission, the community has time and time again called me beyond myself, helping develop gifts I'd never seen. In those times when I have fallen short, when tasks have been beyond my talents, the community was there to pick me up, dust me off, and fill that gap with hope and grace.

So it is with all of us. If we see our lives and work as being in and for Jesus, then what we do is not what ultimately matters. God will use us and call out from us what his people need in a given time and place. Sometimes we are most effective when we are doing what we least expected to do. It is not what we do that makes us who we are. Instead, who we are and how we allow others to call us forth makes a big difference in what we do.

Peter Jarret, C.S.C.

December 31

Christianity, and with still greater reason the religious life, is nothing else than the life of Jesus Christ reproduced in our conduct.

—Basil Moreau

OF ALL THE surprises that Jesus' Incarnation unleashed—the revelation of the Beatitudes, the awesome power of the miracles, the scandal of the Cross, and the ultimate triumph of the resurrection—there is one mystery, easy to miss, that, in a sense, startles me more than all the others. One day Jesus beheld the crowds "like sheep without a shepherd," and so asked his disciples to "pray that the master of the harvest might send laborers out into the harvest." Is it not at least puzzling, if not downright shocking, that the self-proclaimed Good Shepherd should suddenly see the crowd as "shepherd-less"? Though, just as he did so, Jesus cast a longing, inviting eye towards his disciples as if to ask, "Perhaps you will help me?"

Here lies a great mystery. God performs the miracle of miracles—allowing his own Son to take on human flesh so that we might be saved. Then his Son, in the midst of his public ministry, announces that his own mission must continue in us, his followers. In hearing this summons, do we realize the deep mystery of cooperation into which God calls us? Do we dare accept this invitation to become, as Fr. Moreau bids, "reproductions" of Christ in the world?

For religious, certainly for all the faithful, it is an invitation into joy, a life of the Beatitudes, miracles, and, yes, the Cross and the resurrection, too. And yet it is by reproducing the life of Jesus Christ that we draw not only ourselves, but also others into the same saving mystery of the God who came to share in our lives so that we might share in his.

Lou DelFra, C.S.C.

THEMATIC INDEX

Kingdom of God: April 27, May 26, June 27, July 17, July 23, Oct 19, Dec 5

Loss: April 1, July 1

Mary: Jan 7, March 22, Aug 26, Oct 1, Oct 20

Mission: Jan 8, Jan 11, Jan 30, Feb 2, Feb 9, March 9, May 7, May 28, June 3, June 12, June 16, July 9, Aug 30, Sept 3, Sept 10, Sept 19, Sept 29, Oct 25, Nov 30, Dec 2, Dec 25, Dec 27, Dec 31

Obedience: Jan 29, Feb 24, March 5, March 29, April 28, June 1, July 12, Dec 4

Our Lady of Sorrows: Feb 20, March 25, May 13, Aug 22, Sept 15, Oct 26, Nov 22

Perseverance: Jan 10, April 20, April 23, June 10, June 18, June 24, July 10, July 14, August 20, Sept 30, Nov 10

Poverty: Jan 27, Feb 19, July 5, July 29, Aug 3, Sept 17, Sept 26, Nov 13

Prayer: Jan 14, Jan 17, Feb 18, Feb 25, March 7, March 11, March 17, March 31, April 20, May 16, May 23, July 11, July 22, July 30, Aug 7, Aug 17, Aug 29, Sept 2, Sept 5, Sept 21, Sept 27, Oct 1, Oct 7, Oct 9, Oct 15, Oct 23, Oct 29, Nov 3, Nov 9, Nov 23, Dec 1

Reconciliation: Feb 21, March 4, March 18, April 12, April 26, July 3, July 28, Oct 11

Religious Vows: Feb 7, Feb 10, March 21, April 9, June 28, Sept 6, Nov 18, Nov 24

Resurrection: March 23, April 15

Rule: August 25, October 14, Nov 8

Sacraments: May 6, August 27, Sept 8

Sacred Heart: Feb 1, May 14, June 6, June 23, July 15, August 16, Nov 19

Sacrifice: March 10, May 3, June 29, Sept 2, Oct 8

Service: Feb 11, April 4, April 11, June 8, June 19, June 20, June 27, Aug 8, Sept 8, Oct 2, Nov 26

Solidarity: Feb 6, April 8, June 12, June 16, Aug 8, Aug 30, Nov 7, Dec 2

Solitude: May 16, Aug 6, Aug 23, Nov 11

St. Joseph: March 15, March 19, May 1, Dec 29

Stewardship: April 17, Dec 13

Study: Jan 18, Aug 26, Nov 6

Suffering: Feb 15, Feb 28, March 8, April 13, May 9, May 27, May 30, June 25, July 2, July 6, Aug 13, Sept 11, Oct 18, Oct 19, Oct 28, Nov 22

Teaching: Feb 17, March 13, May 8, June 11, June 26, July 7, Aug 11, Aug 21, Oct 27, Oct 30, Nov 16, Nov 25

Trials: March 3, June 7, July 10, Oct 6, Nov 4, Nov 16, Nov 25

Unity: Feb 3, Feb 29, March 1, March 26, July 19, Sept 3, Sept 20, Oct 31, Dec 16, Dec 27

Vocation: Feb 7, Feb 18, March 2, March 19, May 3, May 21, May 22, June 10, Sept 22, Oct 5, Oct 17, Oct 29

Word of God: Oct 9, Dec 7

Work: Feb 25, June 5, Aug 5, Sept 27, Oct 13

Zeal: Jan 5, Jan 20, Jan 21, March 14, March 28, April 30, June 22, Sept 13, Sept 16, Oct 8, Nov 5, Nov 11, Nov 20, Nov 26, Dec 12

Source Index

March:

1: MCL 1; 2: HCC 44; 3: MCL 179; 4: HCC 77; 5: MCL 186; 6: JTC 12; 7: SCL 127; 8: S 557; 9: HCC 10; 10: SCL 48; 11: HCC 30; 12: JTC 136; 13: HCC 16; 14: MCL 79; 15: SCL 17; 16: FD 140; 17: SCL 121; 18: SCL 106; 19: MCL 138; 20: MCL 79; 21: HCC 43; 22: JTC 128; 23: HCC 119; 24: SCL 81; 25: SCL 128; 26: MCL 26; 27: HCC 4; 28: JTC 85; 29: MCL 165; 30: JTC 12; 31: MCL 25

April:

1: MCL 35; 2: MCL 11; 3: SCL 106; 4: JTC 93; 5: HCC 58; 6: HCC 52; 7: SCL 68; 8: CE 24; 9: HCC 45; 10: SCL 5; 11: SCL 82; 12: SCL 102; 13: SCL 91; 14: SCL 6; 15: JTC 133; 16: MCL 47; 17: SCL 68; 18: HCC 118; 19: CE 10; 20: SCL 121; 21: HCC 40; 22: MCL 25; 23: MCL 179; 24: MCL 136; 25: SCL 94; 26: HCC 78; 27: MCL 165; 28: MCL 178; 29: HCC 116; 30: SCL 46

May:

1: MCL 138; 2: SCL 1; 3: CR 62; 4: JTC 136; 5: JTC 11; 6: MCL 8; 7: HCC 42; 8: CE 3; 9: JTC 133; 10: CD 221; 11: MCL 183; 12: SCL 81; 13: HCC 120; 14: RC 247; 15: SCL 84; 16: SCL 60; 17: SCL 125; 18: JTC 11; 19: HCC 57; 20: HCC 21; 21: JTC 68; 22: MCL 94; 23: HCC 24; 24: MCL 182; 25: HCC 47; 26: HCC 9; 27: JTC 136; 28: MCL 140; 29: HCC 18; 30: SCL 23; 31: SCL 122

June:

1: MCL 47; 2: SCL 102; 3: JTC 92; 4: HCC 56; 5: HCC 22; 6: SCL 38; 7: MCL 179; 8: HCC 44; 9: MCL 23; 10: MCL 184; 11: FD 129; 12: HCC 14; 13: HCC 79; 14: JTC 98; 15: CR 268; 16: HCC 115; 17: MCL 165; 18: HCC 121; 19: CD 222; 20: HCC 34; 21: HCC 118; 22: CR 264; 23: MCL 153; 24: SCL 82; 25: SCL 6; 26: MCL 153; 27: MCL 28; 28: HCC 46; 29: HCC 22; 30: SCL 105

July:

1: SCL 85; 2: MCL 179; 3: MCL 174; 4: RC 168; 5: SCL 44; 6: SCL 46; 7: SCL 62; 8: SCL 82; 9: HCC 81; 10: MCL 25; 11: CR 265; 12: HCC 50; 13: MCL 79; 14: SCL 67; 15: RC 247; 16: JTC 93; 17: SCL 5; 18: JTC 133; 19: MCL 170; 20: MCL 34; 21: JTC 135; 22: HCC 25; 23: HCC 11; 24: MCL 182; 25: SCL 24; 26: SCL 82; 27: SCL 106; 28: MCL 5; 29: MCL 145; 30: MCL 159; 31: SCL 61

August:

1: SCL 46; 2: MCL 143; 3: HCC 51; 4: MCL 17; 5: SCL 46; 6: HCC 32; 7: SCL 5; 8: HCC 40; 9 HCC 112; 10: SCL 9; 11: SCL 93; 12: SCL 40; 13: MCL 23; 14: MCL 47; 15: MCL 94; 16: S 555; 17: SCL 123; 18: MCL 20; 19: MCL 26; 20: MCL 45; 21: SCL 105; 22: SCL 125; 23: MCL 1; 24: MCL 11; 25: MCL 79; 26: SCL 125; 27: JTC 92; 28: SCL 1; 29: HCC 26; 30: HCC 13; 31: CR 258

September:

1: HCC 27; 2: MCL 104; 3: HCC 46; 4: SCL 72; 5: JTC 97; 6: MCL 47; 7: HCC 8; 8: JTC 80-81; 9: CL 106; 10: MCL 14; 11: MCL 5; 12: CL 67; 13: MCL 104; 14: HCC 114; 15: JTC 127; 16: SCL 2; 17: MCL 145; 18: MCL 136; 19: SCL 73; 20: MCL 14; 21: MCL 11; 22: SCL 6; 23: MCL 65; 24: MCL 37; 25: SCL 46; 26: SCL 84; 27: MCL 14; 28: MCL 23; 29: HCC 3; 30: MCL 96

October:

1: SCL 20; 2: SCL 93; 3: HCC 34; 4: MCL 14; 5: HCC 5; 6: SCL 12; 7: MCL 96; 8: JTC 104; 9: JTC 79; 10: SCL 105; 11: JTC 137; 12: MCL 36; 13: SCL 16; 14: SCL 91; 15: MCL 79; 16: CL 62; 17: HCC 60; 18: SCL 66; 19: MCL 179; 20: JTC 22; 21: JTC 92-3; 22: MCL 96; 23: JTC 97; 24: HCC 7; 25: SCL 78; 26: JTC 129; 27: SCL 1; 28: MCL 34; 29: SCL 94; 30: MCL 41; 31: SCL 60

November:

1: SCL 2; 2: HCC 122; 3: SCL 121; 4: MCL 34; 5: SCL 46; 6: MCL 132; 7: HCC 15; 8: MCL 132; 9: SCL 77; 10: CL 17; 11: MCL 96; 12: CE 10; 13: MCL 145; 14: SCL 1; 15: MCL 11; 16: HCC 117; 17: SCL 91; 18: SCL 44; 19: S 556; 20: JTC 93-4; 21: SCL 80; 22: MCL 174; 23: SCL 111; 24: SCL 82; 25: CE 5; 26: HCC 14; 27: MCL 36; 28: SCL 23; 29: SCL 68; 30: HCC 9

December:

1: SCL 121; 2: HCC 13; 3: HCC 16; 4: MCL 177; 5: HCC 114; 6: JTC 75; 7: JTC 79; 8: CL 6; 9: SCL 81; 10: HCC 12; 11: MCL 14; 12: SCL 106; 13: HCC 45; 14: MCL 36; 15: SCL 77; 16: MCL 14; 17: SCL 77; 18: JTC 135-6; 19: SCL 106; 20: MCL 178; 21: MCL 86; 22: HCC 38; 23: MCL 20; 24: SCL 82; 25: SCL 28; 26: SCL 44; 27: SCL 28; 28: SCL 28; 29: SCL 78; 30: MCL 65; 31: MCL 137

CONTRIBUTORS

Ahumada, J., Feb 6, Dec 23

Allison, J., June 6, Aug 27

Alonso, J., May 2, Sept 17

Amakyi, M., Aug 30, Dec 2

Andrews, D., June 24

Anjus, E., Feb 4

Armstrong, P., Nov 18

Ayo, N., April 29, May 23,
  Oct 4, Oct 13, Dec 1

Banas, L., July 14

Beauchamp, W., Dec 16

Beaupre, R., July 8

Bednarczyk, P., March 19,
  July 9, Oct 28

Beebe, J., June 28, Sept 5

Belinsky, M., Aug 22,
  Dec 17

Berg, R., Nov 7

Bertone, T., May 29

Blantz, T., Sept 22

Blum, B., Aug 1

Bracke, J., Jan 31

Branigan, J., June 26

Bullene, R., Oct 11

Burasa, J., Jan 16

Burrell, D., March 26,
  Dec 13

Carey, J., April 4

Cecil, B., May 12

Cerda, S., April 6, June 27

Chamberland, G., June 25,
  July 22, Dec 4

Chambers, T., March 31

Clementich, L., Feb 17

Clifford, W., May 16

Colgan, A., Feb 8, Nov 9

Collins, A., Dec 10

Collins, L., Aug 3

Conley, J., Aug 2, Nov 10

Connelly, J., April 12,
  June 14

Connor, J, Oct 16

Connors, M., Aug 31

Cooper, J., Jan 17, April 22,
  Dec 15

Corpora, J., April 2

Cox, C., May 3, Sept 13,
  Nov 13

Cregan, M., Sept 19

Critz, R., Aug 15, Sept 23

D'Alonzo, A., May 4

Dailey, W., July 11, Oct 14

DeLaney, M., July 26

DelFra, L., Jan 22, Dec 31

DeRiso, J., Jan 20, Sept 11

Dilg, D., Feb 15, May 19

Dionne, G., June 5

Donato, J., June 8, Aug 25

Donnelly, J., May 27, July 7

Donoso, F., July 5

Dorwart, W., March 3,
  Aug 4

Dowd, R., April 3, June 12,
  July 19

Doyle, T., April 24

Dziekan, T., March 16,
  Sept 10, Nov 12

Ebey, C., July 12

Eckert, T., April 16, Oct 3

Ehrman, T., Oct 9

Epping, B., Jan 25, June 23,
  July 6, Nov 21

Esparza, J., May 10

Faiella, B., April 13

Fenstermaker, J., May 9

Fetters, D., April 20,
  June 29

Fillmore, R, Oct 27

Foldenauer, R., Feb 2

Foster, J., Oct 18

Gaffney, P., Jan 13, Feb 28

Gallagher, J., April 10,
  Aug 16

Gariepy, T., May 28, Dec 20

Gaughan, T., May 22, Dec 7

Giallanza, J., Jan 12,
  June 7, Oct 26

Gibson, S., Jan 11

Gilman, R., Feb 26

Gleason, J., May 13

Gordon, C., July 20, Nov 30,
  Dec 29

Gorski, G., Jan 8

Grasso, A., March 23,
  July 18

Gribble, R., April 17, Nov 8

Groody, D., Aug 28, Dec 5

Guffey, D., Feb 3

Haag, R., Dec 24

Haake, G., Jan 3, March 8,
  Oct 22

Haders, K., June 11

Harrod, A., Feb 21, Feb 29

Herman, J., March 14

Hesburgh, T., Jan 7,
  May 11, June 15,
  Sept 2, Oct 20

Hosinski, T., Aug 11, Oct 21

Inés, P., Dec 9

Issing, D., Feb 10, Sept 21

Jarret, P., Jan 1, April 26,
  June 1, Nov 2, Dec 30

Jenkins, J., Nov 26

Jenkins, W., Jan 18, Sept 6

Jenky, D., Sept 15

Jones, T., May 18, Oct 2,
  Oct 17

Kaminski, E., July 1, Oct 29

Kane, J., Sept 4, Nov 16

Kawooya, R., July 2

Keefe, J., July 27

King, J., Jan 4, Feb 27,
  April 27, Aug 17,
  Sept 12

Klawitter, G., April 28,
  June 13